Int

Homework
Workbook

Grade 5

Scott Foresman · Addison Wesley

enVisionMATH™
California

Scott Foresman
is an imprint of

pearsonschool.com   Glenview, Illinois · Boston, Massachusetts · Chandler, Arizona · Shoreview, Minnesota · Upper Saddle River, New Jersey

ISBN-13: 978-0-328-38445-7

ISBN-10: 0-328-38445-3

17 18 19 20   V001   15 14

Contents

Place Value

Place-value chart:

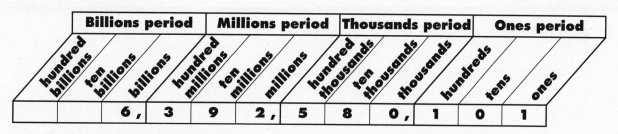

Billions period			Millions period			Thousands period			Ones period		
hundred billions	ten billions	billions	hundred millions	ten millions	millions	hundred thousands	ten thousands	thousands	hundreds	tens	ones
		6,	3	9	2,	5	8	0,	1	0	1

Expanded form: 6,000,000,000 + 300,000,000 + 90,000,000 + 2,000,000 + 500,000 + 80,000 + 100 + 1

Standard form: 6,392,580,101

Word form: six billion, three hundred ninety-two million, five hundred eighty thousand, one hundred one

---

Write the word name for each number and tell the value of the underlined digit.

1. 3,5<u>5</u>2,308,725

_____

_____

_____

2. <u>8</u>43,208,732,833

_____

_____

_____

3. Write 2,000,000,000 + 70,000,000 + 100,000 + 70,000 + 3,000 + 800 + 10 in standard form.

_____

4. **Number Sense** What number is 100,000,000 more than 5,438,724,022?

_____

Place Value

Write the word form for each number and tell the value of the underlined digit.

1. 34,23<u>5</u>,345

_____

_____

2. 1<u>9</u>,673,890,004

_____

_____

3. Write 2,430,090 in expanded form.

_____

Write each number in standard form.

4. 80,000,000 + 4,000,000 + 100 + 8   _____

5. twenty-nine billion, thirty-two million   _____

6. Number Sense What number is
10,000 less than 337,676?   _____

7. Which number is 164,502,423 decreased by 100,000?

A 164,402,423   **B** 164,501,423   **C** 164,512,423   **D** 264,502,423

8. Explain It Explain how you would write 423,090,709,000 in word form.

_____

_____

_____

_____

Comparing and Ordering Whole Numbers

Order these numbers from least to greatest: 4,752,213; 5,829,302; 4,234,295; 4,333,209.

Step 1: Write the numbers, lining up places. Begin at the left to find the greatest or least number.	**Step 2:** Write the remaining numbers, lining up places. Find the greatest and least of these.	**Step 3:** Write the numbers from least to greatest.
4,752,213 5,829,302 4,234,295 4,333,209 5,829,302 is the greatest.	4,752,213 4,234,295 4,234,295 4,333,209 4,333,209 4,752,213 is the 4,234,295 is the greatest of these. least.	4,234,295 4,333,209 4,752,213 5,829,302

Complete. Write >, <, or = in each ◯.

1. 7,642 ◯ 7,843

2. 2,858,534 ◯ 2,882,201

Order these numbers from least to greatest.

3. 768,265 769,205 739,802

_____

_____

4. Write the areas of each country in order from greatest to least.

_____

_____

_____

Country	Area in Square Miles
Albania	28,748
Burundi	27,830
Solomon Islands	28,450
Haiti	27,750

Comparing and Ordering Whole Numbers

Complete. Compare the numbers. Use < or > for each ◯.

1. 23,412 ◯ 23,098

2. 9,000,000 ◯ 9,421,090

Order these numbers from least to greatest.

3. 7,545,999   7,445,999   7,554,000

_____

4. Number Sense What digit could be in the ten millions place of a number that is less than 55,000,000 but greater than 25,000,000? _____

5. Put the trenches in order from the least depth to the greatest depth.

_____

_____

_____

_____

Depths of Major Ocean Trenches

Trench	Depth (in feet)
Philippine Trench	32,995
Mariana Trench	35,840
Kermadec Trench	32,963
Tonga Trench	35,433

6. These numbers are ordered from greatest to least. Which number could be placed in the second position?

2,643,022   1,764,322   927,322

A 2,743,022   **B** 1,927,304   **C** 1,443,322   **D** 964,322

7. Explain It Explain why 42,678 is greater than 42,067.

_____

_____

_____

Decimal Place Value

Here are different ways to represent 1.753.

Place-value chart:

Ones	.	Tenths	Hundredths	Thousandths
1	.	7	5	3

Expanded form: 1 + 0.7 + 0.05 + 0.003

Standard form: 1.753

Word form: one and seven hundred fifty-three thousandths

The following decimals are equivalent to 0.9.

0.9 = 0.90 and 0.9 = 0.900

Why? Because 9 tenths have 90 hundredths or 900 thousandths.

Write the word name for each number and tell the value of the underlined digit.

1. 6.0<u>2</u>

_____

_____

2. 5.<u>3</u>19

_____

_____

Write each number in standard form.

3. 7 + 0.7 + 0.04 + 0.005   _____

4. four and five hundred fifty-eight thousandths   _____

Write two decimals that are equivalent to each number.

5. 0.80   _____

6. 0.300   _____

Decimal Place Value

Write the word form for each number and tell the value of the underlined digit.

1. 4.34<u>5</u>

_____

2. 7.<u>8</u>80

_____

Write each number in standard form.

3. 6 + 0.3 + 0.02 + 0.001 _____

4. seven and five hundred thirty-three thousandths _____

Write two decimals that are equivalent to the given decimal.

5. 0.68 _____

6. 0.9 _____

7. Number Sense Explain why 0.2 and 0.020 are not equivalent.

_____

_____

_____

8. Cheri's time in the bobsled race was 1 min, 38.29 sec. Write the word form and the value of the 9 in Cheri's time.

_____

9. Which is the word form of the underlined digit in 46.<u>5</u>04?

   A 5 ones   **B** 5 tenths   **C** 5 hundredths   **D** 5 thousandths

10. Explain It Write the value for each digit in the number 1.639.

_____

Problem Solving: Look for a Pattern

Mr. Nagpi works in a machine shop. In the shop, the drill bits are kept in a cabinet with drawers. The drawers are marked with the diameter of the bits as shown on the right. Some of the labels are missing. Help Mr. Nagpi complete the drawer labels.

Drill Bits				
0.10 in.	0.12 in.	0.14 in.	0.16 in.	0.18 in.
0.20 in.	0.22 in.	0.24 in.	0.26 in.	0.28 in.
0.30 in.	0.32 in.	0.34 in.		

Read and Understand

What do you know?

Some drawers are labeled with decimals.

What are you trying to find?

A way to find the values of the missing labels

Plan and Solve

Find a pattern for the decimals.

1. Look for a pattern to the change in the tenth-values across a row or down a column.

2. Look for a pattern to the change in the hundredth-values across a row or down a column.

3. Use the patterns to complete the table.

1. The tenth-values are not increasing across a row. They are increasing by 1 down a column.

2. The hundredth-values are increasing by 2 across a row. They are not increasing down a column.

3. The missing labels in the third row are 0.36 in. and 0.38 in.

Find the pattern in the table. Then fill in the missing values in the table.

0.20	0.21	0.22	0.23	0.24
0.50	0.51	0.52	0.53	
0.80	0.81	0.82		

Problem Solving:
Look for a Pattern

Determine the pattern and then complete the grids.

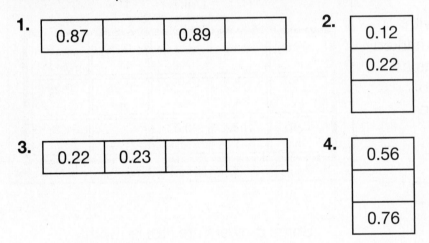

1.

| 0.87 | | 0.89 | |

2.

| 0.12 |
| 0.22 |
| |

3.

| 0.22 | 0.23 | | |

4.

| 0.56 |
| |
| 0.76 |

5. **Critical Thinking** In a list of numbers, the pattern increases by 0.001 as you move to the right. If the third number in the list is 0.064, what is the first number in the list? Explain how you know.

_____

_____

6. **Think About the Process** If 5 school buses arrive, each carrying exactly 42 passengers, which expression would you use to show how many total people arrived on the school buses?

   A 42 + 5   **B** 42 − 5   **C** 42 × 5   **D** 42 ÷ 5

7. **Explain It** Mishell arranged her coins in the following pattern: $0.27, $0.29, $0.31, $0.33. Explain what her pattern is, and then tell what the next amount of coins would be.

_____

_____

Mental Math

There are several ways that you can add and subtract numbers mentally to solve a problem.

Commutative Property of Addition

You can add two numbers in any order.

$15 + 27 = 27 + 15$

Compatible numbers are numbers that are easy to compute mentally.

$25 + 93 + 75$

25 and 75 are compatible because they are easy to add.

$25 + 93 + 75 = (25 + 75) + 93$
$= 100 + 93 = 193$

Associative Property of Addition

You can change the groupings of addends.

$17 + (13 + 10) = (17 + 13) + 10$

With **compensation**, you adjust one number to make computations easier and compensate by changing the other number.

$$\begin{array}{cc} 320 & -\ 190 \\ +\ 10 & +\ 10 \\ \Downarrow & \Downarrow \\ 330 & -\ 200 = 130 \end{array}$$

Add or subtract mentally.

1. $265 + 410 + 335 =$ _____

2. $885 - 155 =$ _____

3. $2,500 + 1,730 + 70 =$ _____

4. $1,467 - 397 =$ _____

5. **Number Sense** How many more strikeouts did Pitcher A have than Pitcher C?

_____

6. How many strikeouts did Pitcher B and Pitcher E have altogether?

_____

7. How many strikeouts were recorded by all five pitchers?

_____

Strikeout Data

Pitcher	Number of Strikeouts
A	372
B	293
C	220
D	175
E	205

Mental Math

Show how you can use mental math to add or subtract.

1. $70 + 90 + 30 =$ _____

2. $350 - 110 =$ _____

National Monuments

Name	State	Acres
George Washington Carver	Missouri	210
Navajo	Arizona	360
Fort Sumter	South Carolina	200
Russell Cave	Alabama	310

3. How many more acres are there at Navajo monument than at George Washington Carver monument?

_____

4. How many acres are there at Fort Sumter and Russell Cave combined?

_____

5. Fresh Market bought 56 lb of apples in August from a local orchard. In September, the market purchased an additional 52 lb of apples and 32 lb of strawberries. How many pounds of fruit did the market buy?

A 108 lb   **B** 140 lb   **C** 150 lb   **D** 240 lb

6. **Explain It** Write the definition and give an example of the Commutative Property of Addition.

_____

_____

_____

Rounding Whole Numbers and Decimals

Look at the numbers listed below. You can use the number line to help you round 8,237,650 to the nearest million. Is 8,237,650 closer to 8,000,000 or 9,000,000?

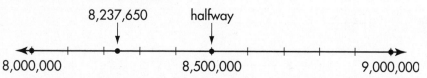

8,237,650 is less than halfway to 9,000,000. 8,237,650 is closer to 8,000,000.

The number line can also help you round 7.762 to the nearest tenth. Is 7.762 closer to 7.7 or 7.8?

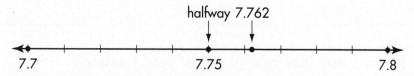

7.762 is more than halfway to 7.8. 7.762 is closer to 7.8.

Round each number to the place of the underlined digit.

1. 4,<u>7</u>25,806

2. <u>7</u>.049

_____

3. <u>1</u>65,023,912

4. 18.6<u>9</u>2

_____

5. Round the number of connected computers in Year 2 to the nearest ten million.

_____

Number of Computers Connected to the Internet	
Year 1	30,979,376
Year 2	42,199,279
Year 3	63,592,854

6. Number Sense Marc earned $9.37 per hour working at the library. Round his wage to the nearest ten cents.

_____

Rounding Whole Numbers and Decimals

Round each number to the place of the underlined digit.

1. 32.<u>6</u>0 _____

2. 48<u>9</u>,334,209 _____

3. 32<u>4</u>,650 _____

4. 32.<u>0</u>73 _____

5. **Reasoning** Name two different numbers that round to 30 when rounded to the nearest ten.

_____

In 2000, Italy produced 7,464,000 tons of wheat, and Pakistan produced 21,079,000 tons of wheat. Round each country's wheat production in metric tons to the nearest hundred thousand.

6. Italy _____

7. Pakistan _____

The price of wheat in 1997 was $3.38 per bushel. In 1998, the price was $2.65 per bushel. Round the price per bushel of wheat for each year to the nearest tenth of a dollar.

8. 1997 _____

9. 1998 _____

10. **Number Sense** Which number rounds to 15,700,000 when rounded to the nearest hundred thousand?

A 15,000,000   **B** 15,579,999   **C** 15,649,999   **D** 15,659,999

11. **Explain It** Write a definition of rounding in your own words.

_____

_____

Estimating Sums and Differences

During one week, Mr. Graham drove a truck to five different towns to make deliveries. Estimate how far he drove in all.

Mr. Graham's Mileage Log

Cities	Mileage
Mansley to Mt. Hazel	243
Mt. Hazel to Perkins	303
Perkins to Alerton	279
Alberton to Fort Maynard	277
Fort Maynard to Mansley	352

To estimate the sum, you can round each number to the nearest hundred miles.

$243 \Rightarrow 200$
$303 \Rightarrow 300$
$279 \Rightarrow 300$
$277 \Rightarrow 300$
$+352 \Rightarrow +400$
$1,500$ mi

Mr. Graham drove about 1,500 mi.

You can estimate differences in a similar way.

Estimate $7.25 - 4.98$.

You can round each number to the nearest whole number.

$7.25 \Rightarrow 7$
$-4.98 \Rightarrow -5$
2

The difference is about 2.

Estimate each sum or difference.

1. $19.7 - 6.9$

_____

2. $59 + 43 + 95$

_____

3. $582 + 169 + 23$

_____

4. $87.99 - 52.46$

_____

5. Estimation Brigid worked 16.75 hr. Kevin worked 12.50 hr. About how many more hours did Brigid work than Kevin?

_____

Estimating Sums and Differences

Estimate each sum or difference.

1. 5,602 − 2,344 _____

2. 7.4 + 3.1 + 9.8 _____

3. 2,314 + 671 _____

4. 54.23 − 2.39 _____

5. Number Sense Wesley estimated 5.82 − 4.21 to be about 2. Is this an overestimate or an underestimate? Explain.

_____

_____

6. Estimate the total precipitation in inches and in days for Asheville and Wichita.

_____

Average Yearly Precipitation of U.S. Cities

City	Inches	Days
Asheville, North Carolina	47.71	124
Wichita, Kansas	28.61	85

Reasonableness

7. Which numbers should you add to estimate the answer to this problem: 87,087 + 98,000?

A 88,000 + 98,000

B 87,000 + 98,000

C 85,000 + 95,000

D 80,000 + 90,000

8. Explain It Estimate the total weight of two boxes that weigh 9.4 lb and 62.6 lb using rounding and compatible numbers. Which estimate is closer to the actual total weight? Why?

_____

_____

Name _____

Adding and Subtracting

Find 35,996 + 49,801.

Step 1: Write the numbers, lining up places. Add the ones and then the tens.

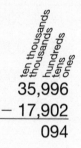

```
  ten thousands
   thousands
    hundreds
     tens
      ones
  3 5,9 9 6
+ 4 9,8 0 1
         9 7
```

Step 2: Continue adding hundreds, thousands and ten thousands. Regroup as needed.

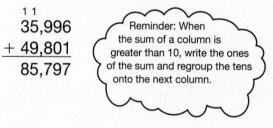

```
   1 1
  3 5,9 9 6
+ 4 9,8 0 1
  8 5,7 9 7
```

Reminder: When the sum of a column is greater than 10, write the ones of the sum and regroup the tens onto the next column.

So 35,996 + 49,801 = 85,797.

Find 35,996 − 17,902.

Step 1: Write the numbers, lining up places. Subtract the ones, tens, and hundreds.

```
  ten thousands
   thousands
    hundreds
     tens
      ones
  3 5,9 9 6
− 1 7,9 0 2
         0 9 4
```

Step 2: Continue by subtracting thousands. Regroup as needed.

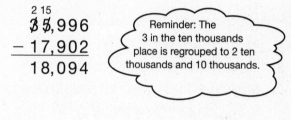

```
  2 15
  3̶ 5̶,9 9 6
− 1 7,9 0 2
  1 8,0 9 4
```

Reminder: The 3 in the ten thousands place is regrouped to 2 ten thousands and 10 thousands.

So 35,996 − 17,902 = 18,094.

Add or subtract

1.	2.	3.
7,502 + 9,909	64,782 − 33,925	835,029 − 26,332

Myronville School District has 23,081 students, and Saddleton School District has 45,035 students.

4. **Number Sense** How many more students are there in Saddleton than in Myronville?

_____

Adding and Subtracting

Add or subtract.

1.   29,543
   + 13,976

2.   93,210
   − 21,061

3.   369,021
   − 325,310

4.   893,887
   + 22,013

5. 971,234 + 55,423 = _____

6. **Number Sense** Is 4,000 a reasonable estimate for the difference of 9,215 − 5,022? Explain.

_____

For questions 7 and 8, use the table at right.

7. How many people were employed as public officials and natural scientists?

_____

8. How many more people were employed as university teachers than as lawyers and judges?

_____

People Employed in U.S. by Occupation in 2000

Occupation	Workers
Public officials	753,000
Natural scientists	566,000
University teachers	961,000
Lawyers and judges	926,000

9. Which is the difference between 403,951 and 135,211?

  A 200,000   **B** 221,365   **C** 268,740   **D** 539,162

10. **Explain It** Issac is adding 59,029 and 55,678. Should his answer be greater than or less than 100,000? Explain how you know.

_____

_____

Adding Decimals

In February, Chantell ran a 5K race in 0.6 hour. She ran another 5K race in May in 0.49 hour. What was her combined time for the two races?

Step 1: Write the numbers, lining up the decimal points. Include the zeros to show place value.

$$\begin{array}{r} 0.60 \\ + \ 0.49 \\ \hline \end{array}$$

You can use decimal squares to represent this addition problem.

Step 2: Add the hundredths.

$$\begin{array}{r} 0.60 \\ + \ 0.49 \\ \hline 9 \end{array}$$

Step 3: Add the tenths. Remember to write the decimal point in your answer.

$$\begin{array}{r} ^1 \ \ \ \\ 0.60 \\ + \ 0.49 \\ \hline 1.09 \end{array}$$

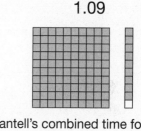

Chantell's combined time for the two races was 1.09 hours.

Add.

1. $2.97 + 0.35 =$ _____

2. $13.88 + 7.694 =$ _____

3. $39.488 + 26.7 =$ _____

4. $88.8 + 4.277 + 78.95 =$ _____

5. Number Sense Is 16.7 a reasonable sum for $7.5 + 9.2$? Explain.

_____

_____

6. How much combined snowfall was there in Milwaukee and Oklahoma City?

_____

City	Snowfall (inches) in 2000
Milwaukee, WI	87.8
Baltimore, MD	27.2
Oklahoma City, OK	17.3

Adding Decimals

Add.

1. 58.0
    + 3.6

2. 40.5
    + 22.3

3. 34.587
    + 21.098

4. 43.1000
    + 8.4388

5. 16.036 + 7.009 = _____

6. 92.30 + 0.32 = _____

7. **Number Sense** Reilly adds 45.3 and 3.21. Should his sum be greater than or less than 48? Tell how you know.

_____

_____

_____

In science class, students weighed different amounts of tin. Carmen weighed 4.361 g, Kim weighed 2.704 g, Simon weighed 5.295 g, and Angelica weighed 8.537 g.

8. How many grams of tin did Carmen and Angelica have combined?

_____

9. How many grams of tin did Kim and Simon have combined?

_____

10. In December the snowfall was 0.03 in. and in January it was 2.1 in. Which was the total snowfall?

    A 3.2 in.   **B** 2.40 in.   **C** 2.13 in.   **D** 0.03 in.

11. **Explain It** Explain why it is important to line up decimal numbers by their place value when you add or subtract them.

_____

_____

_____

Name _____

Subtracting Decimals

Mr. Montoya bought 3.5 lb of ground beef. He used 2.38 lb to make hamburgers. How much ground beef does he have left?

Step 1: Write the numbers, lining up the decimal points. Include the zeros to show place value.

$$\begin{array}{r} 3.50 \\ -2.38 \\ \hline \end{array}$$

You can use decimal squares to represent this subtraction problem.

Step 2: Subtract the hundredths. Regroup if you need to.

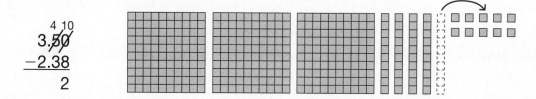

$$\begin{array}{r} \overset{4\;10}{3.\cancel{5}\cancel{0}} \\ -2.38 \\ \hline 2 \end{array}$$

Step 3: Subtract the tenths and the ones. Remember to write the decimal point in your answer.

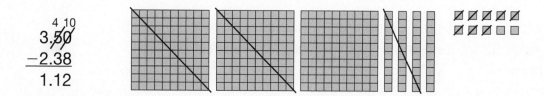

$$\begin{array}{r} \overset{4\;10}{3.\cancel{5}\cancel{0}} \\ -2.38 \\ \hline 1.12 \end{array}$$

Mr. Montoya has 1.12 lb of ground beef left over.

Subtract.

1.	82.7	2.	43.3	3.	7.28
	−5.59		−12.82		−4.928

Subtracting Decimals

Subtract.

1. 92.1
    − 32.6

2. 52.7
    − 36.9

3. 85.76
    − 12.986

4. 32.7
    − 2.328

5. 8.7 − 0.3 = _____

6. 23.3 − 1.32 = _____

7. **Number Sense** Kelly subtracted 2.3 from 20 and got 17.7. Explain why this answer is reasonable.

_____

_____

At a local swim meet, the second-place swimmer of the 100-m freestyle had a time of 9.33 sec. The first-place swimmer's time was 1.32 sec faster than the second-place swimmer. The third-place time was 13.65 sec.

8. What was the time for the first-place swimmer? _____

9. What was the difference in time between the second- and third-place swimmers? _____

10. Miami's annual precipitation in 2000 was 61.05 in. Albany's was 46.92 in. How much greater was Miami's rainfall than Albany's?

    A 107.97 in.   **B** 54.31 in.   **C** 14.93 in.   **D** 14.13 in.

11. **Explain It** Explain how to subtract 7.6 from 20.39.

_____

_____

_____

_____

Problem Solving:
Draw a Picture and Write
an Equation

A community center is raising funds to buy a computer. Here is a picture of the sign they put outside the center. How much more money must the center raise?

How to write an equation number sentence for a problem:

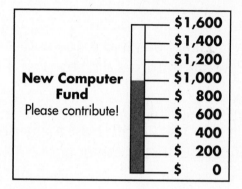

One Way

The goal is $1,600.

So far, $1,000 has been raised.

The amount yet to be raised is the unknown.

Think: The amount raised so far and the amount yet to be raised will reach the goal.

Write an equation.

$$1,000 + x = 1,600$$

Think: What number added to 1,000 will result in 1,600?

$$1,000 + \textbf{600} = 1,600$$

The amount yet to be raised is $600.

Another Way

The goal is $1,600.

So far, $1,000 has been raised.

The amount yet to be raised is the unknown.

Think: The difference between the goal and what has been raised so far is the amount yet to be raised.

Write an equation.

$$1,600 - 1,000 = x$$

Think: What number will result if 1,000 is subtracted from 1,600?

$$1,600 - 1,000 = \textbf{600}$$

The amount yet to be raised is $600.

A mason needs 22 bricks to make a stoop. So far he has carried 15 to the site. How many more bricks must he carry?

Draw a picture. Write an equation. Write a number sentence. Solve.

_____

Problem Solving: Draw a Picture and Write an Equation

For **1** and **2**, solve each problem by drawing a picture and writing an equation.

1. Dayana picked apples for 2 hours. She picked 28 apples in the first hour, and at the end of two hours, she had 49. How many apples did she pick during the second hour? _____

2. Dixon bought a pack of pencils and then gave 12 away. He now has 24 left. How many pencils were in the pack of pencils that Dixon bought? _____

Use the picture to help you write an equation and solve.

3. Rumina is baking 25 muffins for the bake sale. She has already baked 12. How many more does she need to bake?

25	
12	*n*

_____

4. **Estimation** Janet saved 22 dollars one month and 39 dollars the next month. She wants to buy a bicycle that costs $100. About how much more money does she need?

A about $40   **B** about $50   **C** about $60   **D** about $70

5. **Explain It** Stefany ran 2 miles each day for 14 days. How many miles did she run in 14 days? Explain two different ways to solve this problem, and then solve.

_____

_____

Multiplication Properties

You can use multiplication properties to help you multiply more easily.

Associative Property of Multiplication
You can change the grouping of the factors. The product stays the same.

$(3 \times 4) \times 4 = 48$ $3 \times (4 \times 4) = 48$

    Factors   Product   Factors   Product

$12 \times 4 = 48$ $3 \times 16 = 48$

Commutative Property of Multiplication
You can change the order of the factors. The product stays the same.

$7 \times 4 = 28$ $4 \times 7 = 28$

    Factors   Product   Factors   Product

Zero Property of Multiplication
When one of the factors is 0, the product is always 0.

$3 \times 0 = 0$ $0 \times 3 = 0$

    Factors   Product   Factors   Product

Identity Property of Multiplication
When one of the factors is 1, the product is always the other factor.

Identify the multiplication property or properties used in each equation.

1. $100 \times 0 = 0$ _____   **2.** $7 \times 2 = 2 \times 7$ _____

3. $1 \times 55 = 55$ _____   **4.** $(6 \times 7) \times 9 = 6 \times (7 \times 9)$ _____

Reasoning Use the multiplication properties to determine what number must be in the box.

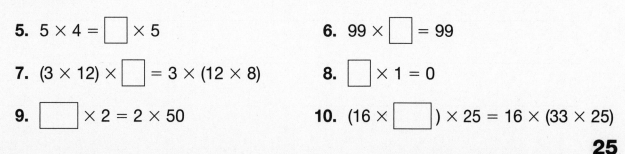

5. $5 \times 4 = \boxed{} \times 5$ **6.** $99 \times \boxed{} = 99$

7. $(3 \times 12) \times \boxed{} = 3 \times (12 \times 8)$ **8.** $\boxed{} \times 1 = 0$

9. $\boxed{} \times 2 = 2 \times 50$ **10.** $(16 \times \boxed{}) \times 25 = 16 \times (33 \times 25)$

Multiplication Properties

In **1** through **5**, write the multiplication property used in each equation.

1. $53 \times 6 = 6 \times 53$ _____

2. $0 \times 374{,}387 = 0$ _____

3. $5 \times (11 \times 4) = (5 \times 11) \times 4$ _____

4. $42 \times 1 = 42$ _____

5. $14 \times 5 = 5 \times 14$ _____

6. **Reasoning** Chan bought 2 large frozen yogurts at $1.50 each and 1 small bottle of water for $1.00. How much did she pay in total?

_____

_____

7. Dan has 4 shelves. He has exactly 10 books on each shelf. Judy has 10 shelves. She has exactly 4 books on each shelf. Who has more books? Explain.

_____

_____

8. **Algebra** If $3 \times 8 \times 12 = 8 \times 3 \times n$, what is the value of n?

A 3 **B** 8 **C** 12 **D** 18

9. **Explain It** Write a definition for the Associative Property of Multiplication in your own words and explain how you would use it to compute $4 \times 25 \times 27$ mentally.

_____

_____

_____

Estimating Products

A bus service drives passengers between Milwaukee and Chicago every day. They travel from city to city a total of 8 times each day. The distance between the two cities is 89 mi. In the month of February, there are 28 days. The company's budget allows for 28,000 total miles for February. Is 28,000 mi a reasonable budget mileage amount?

One Way to Estimate

Estimate 28 × 8 × 89.

Use rounding.

You can round 89 to 100 and 8 to 10. Then multiply.

28 × 10 × 100 = 280 × 100 = 28,000

Because this is an overestimate, there are enough miles.

Another Way to Estimate

Estimate 28 × 8 × 89.

Use compatible numbers.

Replace 28 with 30, 89 with 90, and 8 with 10. 30, 90, and 10 are compatible numbers because they are close to the actual numbers in the problem and they are easier to multiply. Now the problem becomes 30 × 90 × 10.

30 × 90 = 2,700	Multiply 3 × 9, then place two zeros after the product.
2,700 × 10 = 27,000	Multiply 27 × 1 using the Identity Property of Multiplication, then place three zeros after the product.

In the estimate, we used numbers greater than the original numbers, so the answer is an overestimate.

28,000 total miles is a reasonable budget amount.

Estimate each product. Use rounding or compatible numbers.

1. 42 × 5 × 90 = _____

2. 27 × 98 × 4 = _____

Mrs. Carter ordered new supplies for Memorial Hospital.

3. About how much will it cost to purchase 48 electronic thermometers?

_____

4. About how much will it cost to purchase 96 pillows?

_____

Supplies	
Electronic thermometers	$19 each
Pulse monitors	$189 each
Pillows	$17 each
Telephones	$19 each

Estimating Products

Estimate each product.

1. 68 × 21 = _____

2. 5 × 101 = _____

3. 151 × 21 = _____

4. 99 × 99 = _____

5. 87 × 403 = _____

6. 19 × 718 = _____

7. 39 × 51 = _____

8. 47 × 29 × 11 = _____

9. 70 × 27 = _____

10. 69 × 21 × 23 = _____

11. 7 × 616 = _____

12. 8,880 × 30 = _____

13. Number Sense Give three numbers whose product is about 9,000.

_____

14. About how much would it cost to buy 4 CD/MP3 players and 3 MP3 players?

_____

Electronics Prices	
CD player	$ 74.00
MP3 player	$ 99.00
CD/MP3 player	$199.00
AM/FM radio	$ 29.00

15. Which is the closest estimate for the product of 2 × 19 × 5?

A 1,150   **B** 200   **C** 125   **D** 50

16. Explain It Explain how you know whether an estimate of a product is an overestimate or an underestimate.

_____

_____

_____

Multiplying by 1-Digit Numbers

You can use your multiplication facts to multiply larger numbers by 1-digit numbers.

Nava and Cole each have 568 pennies in their coin banks. How many total pennies are there?

Step 1: Estimate your product so you can check for reasonableness.

$$\begin{array}{r} 568 \\ \times\ 2 \end{array} \rightarrow \begin{array}{r} 600 \\ \times\ 2 \\ \hline 1{,}200 \end{array}$$

Step 2: Multiply the ones. Place the ones digit in the ones place of the answer. The tens digit gets regrouped up above the tens column of the problem.

$$\begin{array}{r} 8 \\ \times\ 2 \\ \hline 16 \end{array} \quad \text{so} \quad \begin{array}{r} \overset{1}{5}68 \\ \times\ 2 \\ \hline 6 \end{array}$$

Step 3: Multiply the tens. Place the tens digit in the tens place of the answer. The hundreds digit gets regrouped up above the hundreds column of the problem. Be sure to add any extra tens to the product.

$$\begin{array}{r} 6 \\ \times\ 2 \\ \hline 12+1=13 \end{array} \quad \text{so} \quad \begin{array}{r} \overset{1}{5}68 \\ \times\ 2 \\ \hline 36 \end{array}$$

Step 4: Multiply the hundreds. Place the hundreds digit in the hundreds place of the answer. Be sure to add any extra hundreds to the product. Since this is your last place, write the thousands digit next to the hundreds digit in the product.

$$\begin{array}{r} 5 \\ \times\ 2 \\ \hline 10+1=11 \end{array} \quad \text{so} \quad \begin{array}{r} \overset{1}{5}68 \\ \times\ 2 \\ \hline 1{,}136 \end{array}$$

This answer is reasonable, since it is close to the estimate of 1,200.

For questions **1–6**, find each product.

1. $192 \times 4 =$ _____

2. $6 \times 51 =$ _____

3. $553 \times 8 =$ _____

4. $2 \times 917 =$ _____

5. $4{,}743 \times 5 =$ _____

6. $8{,}024 \times 3 =$ _____

Reasonableness

7. Shaylee multiplied 6,842 by 4 and gave the answer as 27,368. Without calculating, do you think this answer seems reasonable?

_____

_____

Multiplying by
1-Digit Numbers

Find each product. Estimate to check that your answer is reasonable.

1. 68 × 4 _____

2. 845 × 7 _____

3. 1,134 × 4 _____

4. 46 × 3 _____

5. 212 × 7 _____

6. 1,568 × 6 _____

7. 35 × 4 _____

8. 468 × 7 _____

9. 23 × 5 _____

10. 42 × 3 _____

11. 763 × 6 _____

12. 2,758 × 4 _____

13. The school auditorium has 8 rows of seats, divided into 3 sections. Each section has 15 seats. Which of the following would be the correct way to figure out the total number of seats?

A 8 × 15 **B** 8 × 3 × 15 **C** 3 × 3 × 8 **D** 8 × 3

14. Critical Thinking There are 4 fifth-grade classes in a school. Each class has 24 students. For each gym period, two fifth-grade classes take gym together. There are 10 gym periods in all during a school week. What information is NOT needed to figure out how many total students take a gym period together?

_____

_____

15. Explain It Why is it important to regroup correctly?

_____

_____

_____

Multiplying by 2-Digit Numbers

For the school pizza party, Principal Sanchez bought 72 pizzas. Each pizza cost $12. How much money did the principal spend on pizza?

You can use the distributive property to break the problem into parts you already know how to do.

Find 72×12.   Since, $12 = 2 + 10$

$72 \times 12 =$ $(72 \times 2) + (72 \times 10)$

$72 \times 12 =$ $144 + 720$

$72 \times 12 =$ 864

So, Principal Sanchez spent $864 on pizza for the school party.

In **1** through **6**, find the product. Estimate to check your answers for reasonableness.

1. $\begin{array}{r} 36 \\ \times\ 15 \\ \hline \end{array}$

2. $\begin{array}{r} 64 \\ \times\ 21 \\ \hline \end{array}$

3. $\begin{array}{r} 519 \\ \times\ 42 \\ \hline \end{array}$

4. $781 \times 19 =$

5. $2,691 \times 52 =$

6. $8,945 \times 28 =$

Number Sense

7. Kelsey delivers newspapers to 45 houses every day. In one year, how many newspapers will Kelsey have delivered?

Algebra   _____

8. $56 \times 23 = (56 \times 20) + (56 \times n)$. What is the value of n?

                                                            ____

Multiplying by 2-Digit Numbers

Find each product. Estimate to check that your answer is reasonable.

1. 88 × 41 _____

2. 45 × 17 _____

3. 134 × 62 _____

4. 4,662 × 13 _____

5. 221 × 72 _____

6. 3,568 × 16 _____

7. 356 × 32 _____

8. 4,568 × 27 _____

9. 52 × 23 _____

10. 332 × 13 _____

11. 7,443 × 26 _____

12. 445 × 275 _____

13. Han's class is decorating the school cafeteria with Back-to-School posters. On the walls, there are 12 rows that can fit 14 posters each. How many total posters will the class be able to hang up?

_____

14. The Hillside School has a total of 352 students. The PTA is planning a school trip. If each student contributes $12, how much will the PTA have to spend on the trip?

_____

15. **Reasonableness** In problem 14 above, how can you decide if your answer is reasonable?

_____

_____

16. **Explain It** How does adding partial products help you solve a multiplication problem?

_____

_____

Estimating and Multiplying with Greater Numbers

You can estimate the products of greater numbers by rounding the numbers you are multiplying. Then, use your estimate to check the reasonableness of the exact product.

Estimate the product of 421 × 3,715 and then solve.

Step 1. Round 421 to the hundreds place. Cover the digit in the hundreds place (4) with your hand. The number to the right of your hand tells you whether you round up or down. You round down because 2 is less than 5. So, 421 rounds to 400.

Step 2. Round 3,715 to the thousands place. Cover the digit in the thousands place (3) with your hand. The number to the right of your hand tells you whether you round up or down. You round up because 7 is greater than or equal to 5. So, 3,715 rounds to 4,000.

Step 3. Multiply 400 × 4,000. Since you have rounded your numbers, you can multiply 4 × 4 and add the total number of zeros to the end of your product. The product of 4 × 4 = 16 and there are five zeros in the problem. This is your estimated answer.

Step 4. Multiply 421 × 3,715.

```
      3,715
  ×     421
      3,715
     74,300
  1,486,000
  1,564,015
```

Because 1,564,015 is close to 1,600,000, you know that your answer is reasonable.

Estimate each product by rounding.

1.   131
       × 862

2.   592
       × 783

3.   1,849
       × 319

Estimate first. Then find the product.

4.   792
       × 184

5.   1,913
       × 465

6.   3,214
       × 569

Estimating and Multiplying with Greater Numbers

Estimate the products by rounding.

1. 573×653 _____

2. $7{,}321 \times 975$ _____

3. $4{,}684 \times 118$ _____

4. 774×823 _____

5. $4{,}873 \times 749$ _____

6. $9{,}555 \times 448$ _____

Estimate the products by rounding; then find the products.

7. $5{,}792 \times 987$ _____

8. 158×733 _____

9. 678×783 _____

10. $3{,}979 \times 235$ _____

11. The school bought new laptop computers for the computer lab. Each computer cost $998 dollars. The school bought 23 computers. Estimate the total cost of the computers.

_____

12. A popular singer has sold out the city theater for an 18-day run of concerts. The concert hall holds 4,752 seats. About how many people in all will attend the concerts?

_____

13. **Algebra** If $23 \times 81 \times 12 = 12 \times 23 \times n$, what is the value of n?

A 12

B 23

C 81

D 123

14. **Explain It** Explain how you would estimate the product of greater numbers in the operation $6{,}893 \times 556$.

_____

_____

_____

Exponents

You can use exponential notation to write a number that is being multiplied by itself.

There are two parts in exponential notation. The **base** tells you what factor is being multiplied. The **exponent** tells you how many of that factor should be multiplied together. The exponent is *not* a factor.

exponent

↓

$8^2 = 8 \times 8$ The base is 8, so 8 is the factor to be multiplied.
↑   The exponent is 2, so 2 factors of 8 should be
base   multiplied together.

You can write 8^2 in two other forms.

In **expanded** form, you write out your factors. Since 8^2 means you multiply two factors of 8, 8^2 in expanded form is 8×8.

In **standard** form, you write down the product of the factors. Since $8 \times 8 = 64$, 64 is the standard form of 8^2.

Write in exponential notation.

1. $2 \times 2 \times 2$ _____

2. $6 \times 6 \times 6 \times 6 \times 6$ _____

Write in expanded form.

3. 1^4 _____

4. 5^3 _____

Write in standard form.

5. $2 \times 2 \times 2 \times 2$ _____

6. 8^3 _____

7. A used car lot has 9 lanes for cars and 9 rows for cars in each lane. What is the exponential notation for the number of spaces on the lot? Can the owner fit 79 cars on the lot?

_____

Exponents

For questions **1–4**, write in exponential notation.

1. $13 \times 13 \times 13$ _____

2. $8 \times 8 \times 8 \times 8 \times 8 \times 8$ _____

3. 64×64 _____

4. $4 \times 4 \times 4 \times 4$
$\times 4 \times 4 \times 4 \times 4$ _____

For questions **5–8**, write in expanded form.

5. 2^5 _____

6. 20 squared _____

7. 11^4 _____

8. 9 cubed _____

For questions **9–12**, write in standard form.

9. $4 \times 4 \times 4$ _____

10. 14 squared _____

11. 6^5 _____

12. $9 \times 9 \times 9 \times 9$ _____

13. Number Sense Which of these numbers, written in expanded form, is equal to 625?

A $5 \times 5 \times 5 \times 5$

B 5×5

C $5 \times 5 \times 5$

D $5 \times 5 \times 5 \times 5 \times 5$

14. Number Sense Find the number equal to 6 raised to the second power.

A 18

B 36

C 6

D 12

15. Explain It Explain what 4 raised to the fourth power means.

_____

_____

Name _____

Problem Solving: Multiple-Step Problems

Kim has a $10 bill, a $20 bill, and 2 $5 gift certificates. He uses the gift certificates toward the purchase of a CD for $14.00. How much money does Kim have left after buying the CD?

Read and Understand

What do you know?

Kim has a ten-dollar bill, a twenty-dollar bill, and two five-dollar gift certificates.

He uses the 2 certificates toward the purchase of a CD that costs $14.00.

What are you trying to find?

How much money does Kim have left after he buys the CD?

Plan and Solve

Answer these hidden questions.

How much money does Kim have? $20.00 + $10.00 = $30.00

How much are the two certificates worth? $5.00 + $5.00 = $10.00

How much cash will Kim need to buy the CD? $14.00 − $10.00 = $4.00

Solve the problem. Money − cash paid for CD = Money left
$30.00 − $4.00 = $26.00

Write the answer in a complete sentence. Kim has $26 left after buying the CD.

Look Back and Check

Is your answer correct? Yes, $4.00 + $26.00 = $30.00

1. You can also find how much money Kim has left by completing the following expression.

   $10.00 + $20.00 + $5.00 + $5.00 − _____

Problem Solving:
Multiple-Step Problems

Solve.

1. Theater tickets for children cost $5. Adult tickets cost $3 more.
   If 2 adults and 2 children buy theater tickets, what is the total cost?

   _____

2. Luis has a $10 bill and three $5 bills. He spends $12.75 on the
   entrance fee to an amusement park and $8.50 on snacks.
   How much money does he have left?

   _____

3. **Number Sense** Alexandra earns $125 from her paper route
   each month, but she spends about $20 each month on personal
   expenses. To pay for a school trip that costs $800, about how
   many months does she need to save money for? Explain.

   _____

   _____

4. **Think About the Process** Patty is a member of the environmental
   club. Each weekday, she volunteers for 2 hours. On Saturday and
   Sunday, she volunteers 3 hours more each day. Which expression
   shows how to find the number of hours she volunteers in one week?

   A $2 + 5$

   B $2 + 2 + 2 + 2 + 2 + 5 + 5$

   C $2 + 2 + 2 + 3 + 3$

   D $2 + 3 + 3$

5. **Explain It** Marco's goal is to eat only 2,000 calories each day. One day
   for breakfast he consumed 310 calories, for lunch he consumed 200 more
   calories than breakfast, and for dinner he consumed 800. Did he make his
   goal? Explain.

   _____

Estimating Quotients

You can estimate quotients by using compatible numbers.

Carly picked 738 peaches off her peach tree. She filled 9 baskets with peaches. If each basket holds the same amount, about how many peaches are in each basket?

Estimate $738 \div 9$.

Find a compatible number for 738, and then divide.

$738 \div 9 =$
↓
$720 \div 9 = 80$

So there are about 80 peaches in each basket.

Another compatible number set you could use is:

$700 \div 10 = 70$

So there are about 70 peaches in each basket.

In both cases the estimate is less than the actual answer because the compatible numbers are less than 738. You know that the actual number of peaches in each basket will be greater than 70 or 80.

For questions **1–6,** estimate the quotients using compatible numbers.

1. $372 \div 5 \approx$ _____

2. $614 \div 2 \approx$ _____

3. $8,435 \div 8 \approx$ _____

4. $536 \div 23 \approx$ _____

5. $4,522 \div 61 \approx$ _____

6. $9,863 \div 26 \approx$ _____

Number Sense

7. If you estimate $342 \div 7$ by using $350 \div 7 = 50$, is 50 greater than or less than the exact answer? How did you decide? Is 50 an overestimate or an underestimate?

_____

_____

8. Weston's book has 427 pages. He reads 17 pages each night. About how long will it take Weston to finish his book?

_____

Name _____

Practice
4-2

Estimating Quotients

In **1** through **12**, estimate the quotients using compatible numbers.

1. 812 ÷ 9 _____

2. 366 ÷ 6 _____

3. 542 ÷ 6 _____

4. 19,008 ÷ 64 _____

5. 5,172 ÷ 74 _____

6. 2,622 ÷ 67 _____

7. 1,891 ÷ 32 _____

8. 461 ÷ 91 _____

9. 6,301 ÷ 81 _____

10. 7,952 ÷ 42 _____

11. 5,232 ÷ 5 _____

12. 2,759 ÷ 30 _____

13. During the summers throughout high school and for a year after, Lewis worked as a lifeguard at the beach. In that 5-year period, he saw a total of 461 dolphins swimming in the distance. About how many did he spot per summer in the 5 summers he worked?

_____

14. Reasonableness Lucien has 365 cookies to sell. He wants to store them in plastic bags that hold 12 cookies each. He estimates he will need 30 bags. Is he right? Why or why not?

_____

_____

15. Estimate the product for the following expression. 706 × 52 _____

A about 42,000   **B** about 35,000   **C** about 3,500   **D** about 2,800

16. Explain It Carl needs to estimate the quotient 547 ÷ 92. Explain how Carl could use compatible numbers to make a reasonable estimate.

_____

_____

© Pearson Education, Inc. 5

42

Connecting Models and Symbols

Divide 138 equally into
3 groups.

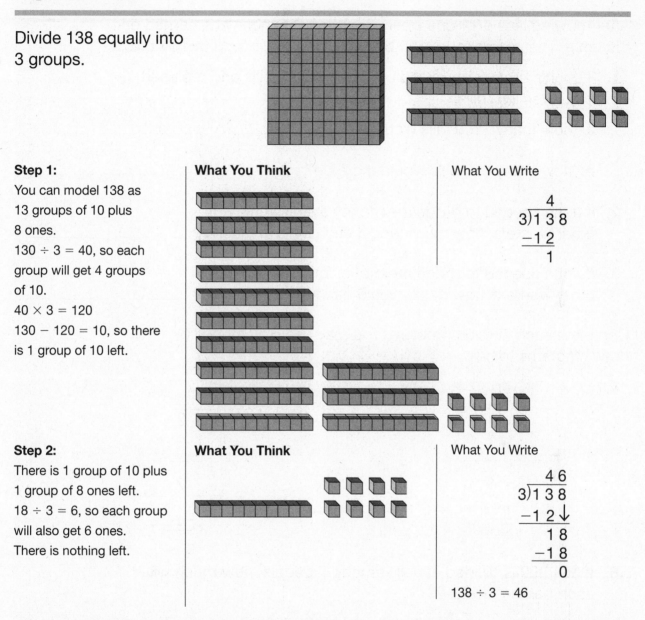

Step 1:

You can model 138 as
13 groups of 10 plus
8 ones.

$130 \div 3 = 40$, so each
group will get 4 groups
of 10.

$40 \times 3 = 120$

$130 - 120 = 10$, so there
is 1 group of 10 left.

What You Think

What You Write

$$\begin{array}{r} 4 \\ 3\overline{)1\ 3\ 8} \\ -1\ 2 \\ \hline 1 \end{array}$$

Step 2:

There is 1 group of 10 plus
1 group of 8 ones left.

$18 \div 3 = 6$, so each group
will also get 6 ones.
There is nothing left.

What You Think

What You Write

$$\begin{array}{r} 4\ 6 \\ 3\overline{)1\ 3\ 8} \\ -1\ 2\ \downarrow \\ \hline 1\ 8 \\ -1\ 8 \\ \hline 0 \end{array}$$

$138 \div 3 = 46$

Use models to help you divide.

1. $4\overline{)76}$ **2.** $2\overline{)94}$ **3.** $5\overline{)130}$

4. $7\overline{)238}$ **5.** $6\overline{)426}$ **6.** $3\overline{)264}$

7. Algebra If $n \div 3 = 57$, what is the value of n?

Connecting Models and Symbols

After mowing lawns for one week, John put the money he earned on the table. There were four $100 bills, three $10 bills, and five $1 bills.

1. If John's brother borrowed one of the $100 bills and replaced it with ten $10 bills,

    a. how many $100 bills would there be? _____

    b. how many $10 bills would there be? _____

2. If John needed to divide the money evenly with two other workers, how much would each person receive? _____

3. If John needed to divide the money evenly with four other workers, how much would each person receive? _____

Complete each division problem. You may use play money or draw diagrams to help.

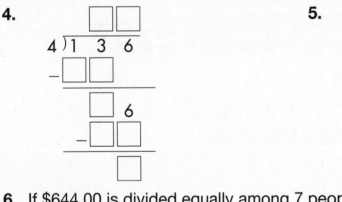

4.

5.

6. If $644.00 is divided equally among 7 people, how much will each person receive?

    A $82.00   **B** $92.00   **C** $93.00   **D** $103.00

7. **Explain It** Write a story problem using two $100 bills, nine $10 bills, and seven $1 bills.

    _____

    _____

    _____

Dividing by 1-Digit Divisors

You can use your basic division facts to divide greater numbers.

Find 64 ÷ 4.

Step 1: Estimate the quotient in order to find out how many digits the quotient will have.

$$64 ÷ 4$$

$$60 ÷ 6 = 10$$

So, the quotient will have 2 digits.

Step 2: Divide the tens by the divisor.

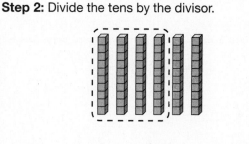

$$
\begin{array}{r}
1 \\
4\overline{)64} \\
-4 \\
\hline
2
\end{array}
$$
← 4 × 1 = 4
← subtract: 6 − 4 =
compare: 2 < 4

Step 3: Bring down the ones digit and continue dividing.

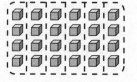

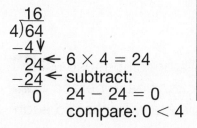

$$
\begin{array}{r}
16 \\
4\overline{)64} \\
-4↓ \\
\hline
24 \\
-24 \\
\hline
0
\end{array}
$$
← 6 × 4 = 24
← subtract:
   24 − 24 = 0
   compare: 0 < 4

Step 4: Check your answer by multiplying.

$$16 × 4 = 64$$

So, 64 ÷ 4 = 16.

In **1** through **6**, find the quotient. Check your answer by multiplying.

1. 4)592 _____

2. 5)335 _____

3. 6)708 _____

4. 3)282 _____

5. 9)828 _____

6. 2)976 _____

7. Jin has 774 pennies in his collection. He has his collection stored in 9 coin books. How many pennies are in each book?

_____

Dividing by 1-Digit Divisors

In **1** through **4**, use compatible numbers to decide where to place the first digit of the quotient.

1. 9)813   **2.** 4)600   **3.** 6)732   **4.** 5)464

_____ _____ _____ _____

In **5** through **12**, complete the calculation.

5. 9)279   **6.** 5)550   **7.** 8)659   **8.** 4)453

9. 6)684   **10.** 4)724   **11.** 5)7,295   **12.** 2)2,152

13. Mr. Perez collects fishing lures. He has 1,421 lures. If he stores them in 7 boxes and has the same number in each box, how many lures are in each box?

14. Estimation There are 14 days in 2 weeks. About how many 2-week periods are there in 1326 days?

15. George and 4 friends are building a 2-story clubhouse using bricks. In 6 days, they placed 905 bricks. If each person placed an equal number of bricks, how many bricks did each person place?

A 226   **B** 181   **C** 150   **D** 100

16. Explain It How can you tell before you divide 387 by 4 that the first digit of the quotient is in the tens place?

_____

_____

_____

Zeros in the Quotient

Sometimes when you divide you will need to use a zero in the quotient as a placeholder.

Find $1,842 \div 6$.

Step 1: Estimate your quotient to see where to place the first digit in the quotient.

$1,800 \div 6 = 300$

So, the first digit will be in the hundreds place.

Step 2: Divide the hundreds.

$$\begin{array}{r} 3 \\ 6\overline{)1842} \\ -18 \leftarrow \\ 0 \leftarrow \end{array}$$ $6 \times 3 = 18$
subtract:
$18 - 18 = 0$
compare: $0 < 6$

Step 3: Bring down the tens digit and divide.

$$\begin{array}{r} 30 \leftarrow \\ 6\overline{)1842} \\ -18\downarrow \\ 04 \leftarrow \end{array}$$

You cannot divide 6 into 4. To continue dividing, you need to bring down the ones digit.
But you need to use a zero as the placeholder for the tens place in the quotient.

Step 4: Bring down the ones digit and divide.

$$\begin{array}{r} 307 \\ 6\overline{)1842} \\ -18\downarrow \\ 042 \\ -42 \leftarrow \\ 0 \end{array}$$ $6 \times 7 = 42$
subtract:
$42 - 42 = 0$
compare: $0 < 6$

Step 5: Check by multiplying.

$307 \times 6 = 1,842$ So, $1,842 \div 6 = 307$.

Tip: Whenever you have a section you cannot divide because the digit is less than the divisor, use a zero as a placeholder in the quotient. Bring down the next digit and continue dividing.

In **1** through **3**, find each quotient.

1. $4\overline{)2,480}$ _____

2. $4\overline{)1,960}$ _____

3. $9\overline{)7,263}$ _____

4. **Estimation** Valley School District received 3,240 text books. An equal number of books must go to each of the 6 high schools in the district. About how many books will each high school receive?

_____

Zeros in the Quotient

Find each quotient. Check your answers by multiplying.

1. $490 \div 7 =$ _____

2. $326 \div 3 =$ _____

3. $916 \div 3 =$ _____

4. $720 \div 2 =$ _____

5. $2\overline{)9,410}$ **6.** $9\overline{)9,829}$ **7.** $6\overline{)12,027}$ **8.** $5\overline{)15,252}$

9. If there are 505 seats in an auditorium divided equally into 5 sections, how many seats are in each section? _____

10. A book company publishes 749 copies of a novel and distributes them to 7 bookstores. If each bookstore were to receive the same number of copies, how many copies would be sent to each store? _____

11. In one year, Dolores and Tom's four children saved $420 by recycling cans. When they divided the money equally, how much money did each child receive?

A $50   **B** $100   **C** $105   **D** $1,500

12. Explain It Explain why estimating before you divide $624 \div 6$ helps you place the first digit in the quotient.

_____

_____

_____

Dividing by 2-Digit Divisors

A roller coaster train holds 42 people. How many times must it run so that 354 people can ride?

Find 354 ÷ 42.

Step 1: Estimate your quotient to decide where the first digit the quotient should be placed.

350 ÷ 50 = 7

So, the quotient will start in the ones place.

Step 2: Divide the ones. Multiply and subtract.

```
        7  ← Try the number from the estimate.              8
  42)354        7 × 42 = 294                          42)354
   −294  ← 354 − 294 = 60                              −336  ← 8 × 42 = 336
     60  ← compare: 60 is NOT < 42                       18  ← 354 − 336 = 18
             so you need to increase                          compare: 18 < 42
             the number in the
             quotient.
```

Step 3: Since 18 < 42, you cannot divide anymore. This number is the remainder.

```
       8 R18
  42)354
   −336
     18
```

In order for everyone to ride the roller coaster, the train will have to go 9 times because after 8 times, there are still 18 people left in line.

In **1** through **3**, find the quotient. Check by multiplying.

1. 95)256 _____

2. 68)478 _____

3. 49)367 _____

4. On Thursday, an apple farmer produced 515 oz of apple juice. How many 64-oz cartons were filled? How many ounces of juice were left over?

_____

Name _____

Dividing by 2-Digit Divisors

Complete.

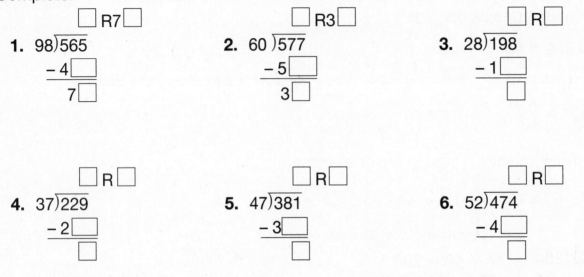

1. $98\overline{)565}$ ☐R7☐
   -4☐
   7☐

2. $60\overline{)577}$ ☐R3☐
   -5☐
   3☐

3. $28\overline{)198}$ ☐R☐
   -1☐
   ☐

4. $37\overline{)229}$ ☐R☐
   -2☐
   ☐

5. $47\overline{)381}$ ☐R☐
   -3☐
   ☐

6. $52\overline{)474}$ ☐R☐
   -4☐
   ☐

7. 89 student runners are warming up on the morning of Track and Field Day. The track has six lanes. The coach wants each lane to have as equal a number of runners as possible. How many runners are in each lane?

   _____

   _____

8. **Critical Thinking** Isaiah changes both his bike tires every 4 months. How many tires will he have changed after 2 years?

   _____

9. Robert and his sister Esther are going to make pancakes for their family reunion. They need 28 eggs. The store only sells eggs by the dozen, or 12 per box. They buy 3 dozen. How many more eggs will they have than the 28 they need?

   A 12 extra   **B** 8 extra   **C** 3 extra   **D** 0 extra

10. **Explain It** Explain why 0.5 and 0.05 are NOT equivalent.

    _____

    _____

Problem Solving:
Draw a Picture and
Write an Equation

Doug needs to paint 2,472 boards for his fence building company. Using a power spray, he can paint 206 boards in a day. How many days will it take to paint all the boards?

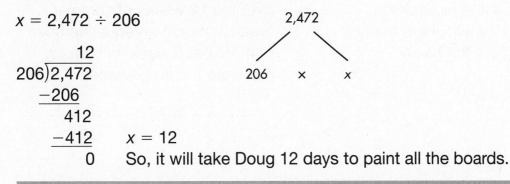

$x = 2,472 \div 206$

$$\begin{array}{r} 12 \\ 206\overline{)2,472} \\ -206 \\ \hline 412 \\ -412 \\ \hline 0 \end{array}$$

$x = 12$

So, it will take Doug 12 days to paint all the boards.

In **1** and **2**, draw a picture, write an equation, and solve.

1. Using the boards he painted, Doug can install 7 fences. How many boards are in each fence? Are they any boards left over?

_____

_____

2. Doug made $3,770 installing the 7 fences. He got paid a flat rate per fence plus $95 travel expenses for driving to the different locations. How much was the flat rate Doug was paid per fence?

_____

_____

Problem Solving: Draw a Picture and Write an Equation

Solve problems **1** and **2**. Draw a picture to show the main idea, and then write an equation and solve it.

1. Mandy has collected 4 times as many seashells as Jackson. Mandy has 36 shells. How many shells does Jackson have?

   _____

2. Jaime ran a total of 420 miles over the 12 weeks of summer break. If he ran an equal number of miles each week, how many miles did he run per week?

   _____

   _____

3. Erika saved $234 for presents for her three sisters, her parents, and her aunt. If she spends an equal amount on each present, how much can she spend on each person?

   _____

4. A box of seaweed crackers was divided among 7 children. Each child got 7 crackers. How many crackers were in the box?

   A 49   **B** 48   **C** 32   **D** 39

5. **Explain It** Why is it helpful to draw a picture when attempting to solve an equation?

   _____

   _____

   _____

Variables and Expressions

Translating words into algebraic expressions

A **variable** is a letter or symbol. It represents an unknown amount that can change.

You can do mathematical operations with variables and numbers.

You can state these operations in word expressions. You can also state them in algebraic expressions.

Operation	+	−	×	÷
Word expression	the sum of r and 3	the difference between r and 3	the product of r and 3	the quotient of r and 3
Algebraic expression	$r + 3$	$r − 3$	$3r$	$r \div 3$
Other ways of saying the word expression	3 added to r 3 more than r	3 subtracted from r 3 less than r	r multiplied by 3 3 times r	r divided by 3 3 equal parts of r

Complete the algebraic expression for each of the following word expressions.

1. the sum of b and 8

b ____ 8

2. the difference between m and 6

m ____ 6

3. the quotient of k and 16

k ____ 16

4. 7 less than z

z ____ 7

5. 2 more than d

d ____ 2

6. j divided by 4

j ____ 4

Circle the letter of the correct word expression for each algebraic expression.

7. $t − 13$ a. 13 subtracted from t b. t subtracted from 13

8. $4n$ a. 4 more than n b. 4 times n

9. $11 + s$ a. 11 more than s b. 11 less than s

10. $45a$ a. the product of a and 45   b. 45 more than a

11. $y \div 6$ a. y less 6   b. 6 equal parts of y

12. $v − 5$ a. 5 less than v b. v subtracted from 5

Variables and Expressions

For questions **1–4**, use a variable to write an algebraic expression
that represents the word phrase.

1. a number of apples divided into 12 baskets _____

2. 5 more than *s* _____

3. three times the cost for one hat _____

4. nine fewer than the total number of people _____

For **5–7**, translate each algebraic expression into words.

5. $3 + w$ _____

6. $8x$ _____

7. $40 - p$ _____

8. Write two different word phrases for the expression $\frac{t}{30}$.

_____

_____

9. **Number Sense** Do $5 + x$ and $x + 5$ represent the
same expression? Explain.

_____

_____

10. **Think About the Process** Dan is 12 in. taller than Jay.
Use *x* for Jay's height. Which expression shows Dan's height?

   A $x + 12$ **B** $x - 12$ **C** $12x$ **D** $\frac{x}{12}$

11. **Explain It** Explain what the expression $6x$ means.

_____

Using Patterns to Show Relationships

Chan makes beaded necklaces for gifts. To make a necklace, he strings beads onto thin ribbon. To tie the necklace, he cuts the ribbon 10 inches longer than the length he wants to bead. The chart shows the length of the ribbon for different beaded lengths.

Word Expression	Number Expression	Algebraic Expression
10 inches longer than 11-inch beaded section	$11 + 10$	
10 inches longer than 14-inch beaded section	$14 + 10$	
10 inches longer than z-inch beaded section		$z + 10$

Evaluating algebraic expressions

Zoe is going to use Chan's algebraic expression to make two necklaces. She wants to make one with a 10-inch beaded section. The other necklace will have a 12-inch beaded section. Here is how she evaluated the expression.

Algebraic Expression	Number Expression	Word Expression	Evaluated Expression
$z + 10$	$10 + 10$	10 inches longer than 10-inch beaded section	20
$z + 10$	$12 + 10$	10 inches longer than 12-inch beaded section	22

Chan also makes beaded bracelets. The chart shows the length of the beaded part of the bracelet. The second column shows the length of the ribbon he uses to make it.

Beaded Length (in.)	Ribbon Length (in.)
5	$5 + 7$
6	$6 + 7$
8	$8 + 7$

1. Write a word expression that describes the pattern of the relationship.

_____

_____

Patterns and Expressions

In **1–4**, evaluate each expression for $n = 3$ and $n = 8$.

1. $n + 10$

2. $\dfrac{24}{n}$

_____

_____

3. $n \times 5$

4. $36 - n$

_____

_____

Complete each table.

5.

n	0.5 + n
0.3	
0.1	
0.17	
0.12	

6.

n	48 ÷ n
1	
2	
3	
4	

7. Write a Problem Write a situation that can be represented by the algebraic expression $\$3.50t$.

_____

_____

8. Algebra If $a = 10$, which of the following is the correct solution for $a \times 0.1$?

A 0.01   **B** 0.1   **C** 1   **D** 10

9. Explain It Write one numerical expression and one algebraic expression. Then explain what the difference between a numerical and algebraic expression is.

_____

_____

Name _____

More Patterns and Expressions

You can use variables to write and evaluate expressions.

Sunny Rent-A-Car rents cars for $35 per day plus a $12 fee for cleaning the car when you return it. Write an algebraic expression for the total cost of a car rental. Evaluate the expression for a 2-day car rental; for a 3-day car rental; for a 5-day car rental.

Step 1. The total cost is the cleaning fee plus the cost per day times the number of days. Since the number of days can change, it is your variable. Use *d* for the number of days.

Step 2. To evaluate the expression, think about counting out the money to pay for the car rental. Each rental will have a stack of $12 for the cleaning fee. Then, each rental will have a stack of $35 for each day. A 2-day rental will have 2 stacks of $35. A 3-day rental will have 3 stacks of $35. A 5-day rental will have 5 stacks of $35.

Step 3. To solve for the total cost of the car rentals, multiply the number of stacks by $35. Then, add the $12 stack.

2-day rental
$(2 \times 35) + 12 = 82$
A 2-day rental will cost $82.
3-day rental
$(3 \times 35) + 12 = 117$
A 3-day rental will cost $117.
5-day rental
$(5 \times 35) + 12 = 187$
A 5-day rental will cost $187.

Cleaning fee	2-day rental	3-day rental	5-day rental
$12	$35	$35	$35 $35
	$35	$35 $35	$35 $35 $35

Write an algebraic expression for each phrase. Let *n* stand for the number. Evaluate each expression for $n = 4$.

1. 3 plus 4 times a number

2. 7 times a number, minus 2

3. 6 less than a number times 15

_____ _____ _____

More Patterns and Expressions

1. Write an algebraic expression to represent the cost of a concert ticket, *h*, with a service charge of $6.75.

_____

2. Write an algebraic expression to represent the cost of *m* gallons of gasoline if each gallon costs $1.45.

_____

Evaluate each expression for *n* = 3 and *n* = 6.

3. $0.2 \times n$ _____ _____

4. $n - 2.1$ _____ _____

5. $\frac{12}{n}$ _____ _____

6. $35 + n$ _____ _____

Complete each table.

7.

n	$0.9 + n$
0.5	
0.2	
0.15	
0.1	

8.

n	$96 \div n$
1	
2	
3	
4	

9. **Explain It** What is another way to write the expression 44*n*? What is another way to write the expression $44 \div n$?

_____

10. Which is the correct product of $n \times 7$ if *n* = $0.25?

   A $3.25   **B** $2.75   **C** $2.25   **D** $1.75

11. **Write a Problem** Write a situation that can be represented by the algebraic expression $3.25*d*.

_____

Distributive Property

Hector's rock collection is in 7 cases. Each case holds 28 rocks. How many rocks are in Hector's collection? You can use the Distributive Property to find the product of 7×28.

Step 1. Split 28 into $20 + 8$.
$7 \times 28 = 7 \times (20 + 8)$

Step 2. Multiply 7 times each part of the sum.
$(7 \times 20) + (7 \times 8)$

$140 + 56$

Step 3. Use addition to find the sum.
$140 + 56 = 196$

OR **Step 1.** Split 28 into $30 - 2$.
$7 \times 28 = 7 \times (30 - 2)$

Step 2. Multiply 7 times each part of the difference.
$(7 \times 30) - (7 \times 2)$

$210 - 14$

Step 3. Use subtraction to find the difference.
$210 - 14 = 196$

So, $7 \times 28 = 196$. Hector has 196 rocks in his collection.

Rewrite using the Distributive Property. Then find the product.

1. 3×42 _____   **2.** 39×5 _____   **3.** 6×147 _____   **4.** 19×70 _____

5. 54×67 _____   **6.** 90×83 _____   **7.** 364×26 _____   **8.** 45×678 _____

Algebra

For questions **9–12**, find the value of n.

9. $4 \times 62 = (4 \times n) + (4 \times 2)$ _____

10. $79 \times 20 = (80 \times 20) - (n \times 20)$ _____

11. $53 \times 118 = (53 \times 100) + (n \times 18)$ _____

12. $352 \times 75 = (n \times 75) + (50 \times 75) + (2 \times 75)$ _____

13. Joey's class is collecting food for the school canned food drive. There are 28 children in Joey's class. Each child brought in 15 cans of food. Use the Distributive Property to find out how many cans of food Joey's class collected.

Distributive Property

Use the Distributive Property to multiply mentally.

1. $5 \times 607 =$ _____

2. $16 \times 102 =$ _____

3. $7 \times 420 =$ _____

4. $265 \times 5 =$ _____

5. $44 \times 60 =$ _____

6. $220 \times 19 =$ _____

7. $45 \times 280 =$ _____

8. $341 \times 32 =$ _____

9. **Number Sense** Fill in the blanks to show how the Distributive Property can be used to find 10×147.

$10 \times (150 - 3) = (10 \times 150) - ($ _____ $\times 3) =$

$1,500 -$ _____ $=$ _____

10. In 1990, there were 1,133 tornadoes in the U.S. If there were the same number of tornadoes for 10 years in a row, what would be the 10-year total?

_____

11. There were 1,071 tornadoes in the U.S. in 2000. What is the number of tornadoes multiplied by 20?

_____

12. If $4 \times 312 = 4 \times 300 + n$, which is the value of n?

A 4 　　　 B 12 　　　 C 48 　　　 D 300

13. **Explain It** Margaret said that she used the Distributive Property to solve 4×444. Is her answer shown below correct? Explain.

$4 \times 444 = 4 \times (400 + 40 + 4) =$
$(4 \times 400) + (4 \times 40) + (4 \times 4) =$
$1,600 + 160 + 16 = 1,776$

_____

_____

Order of Operations

If you do not use the proper order of operations, you will not get the correct answer.

Evaluate $8 \div 2 + 3 \times 6 - (1 \times 5)$.

Step 1. Do the operations inside the parentheses.

$(1 \times 5) = 5$
$8 \div 2 + 3 \times 6 - 5$

Step 2. Multiply and divide in order from left to right.

$8 \div 2 = 4$ and $3 \times 6 = 18$
$4 + 18 - 5$

Step 3. Add and subtract in order from left to right.

$4 + 18 = 22$
$22 - 5 = 17$
So, $8 \div 2 + 3 \times 6 - (1 \times 5) = 17$

Write which operation should be done first.

1. $6 + 3 \times 2$ _____

2. $13 - 1 + 4 \div 2$ _____

3. $5 \times (7 - 2) + 1$ _____

4. $(19 + 23) - (4 \times 5)$ _____

For questions **5–8**, evaluate the expression for $x = 6$ and $y = 17$.

5. $4x + 5y$ _____

6. $2x + (20 - y)$ _____

7. $x \div 3 + y$ _____

8. $4y \div 2 + (8x + 10)$ _____

9. There are 22 students in Natalie's class. New reading books cost $7 each. Natalie's class raised $50 washing cars. If there are 2 teachers in Natalie's class, write and evaluate an expression to show how much more each teacher will have to pay to buy the new reading books.

_____

Number Sense

10. Carlos solved $20 - (2 \times 6) + 8 \div 4 = 29$. Is this the correct answer?

_____

_____

Order of Operations

Use the order of operations to evaluate each expression.

1. $4 \times 4 + 3 =$ _____

2. $3 + 6 \times 2 \div 3 =$ _____

3. $24 - (8 \div 2) + 6 =$ _____

4. $(15 - 11) \times (25 \div 5) =$ _____

5. $26 - 4 \times 5 + 2 =$ _____

6. $15 \times (7 - 7) + (5 \times 2) =$ _____

7. $(8 \div 4) \times (7 \times 0) =$ _____

8. $5 \times (6 - 3) + 10 \div (8 - 3) =$ _____

9. Explain It Which is a true statement, $5 \times 4 + 1 = 25$ or $3 + 7 \times 2 = 17$? Explain your answer.

_____

_____

Insert parentheses to make each statement true.

10. $25 \div 5 - 4 = 25$ _____

11. $7 \times 4 - 4 \div 2 = 26$ _____

12. $3 + 5 \times 2 - 10 = 6$ _____

13. Strategy Practice Insert parentheses in the expression $6 + 10 \times 2$ so that:

a. the expression equals 32. _____

b. the expression equals $(12 + 1) \times 2$. _____

14. Solve $(25 - 7) \times 2 \div 4 + 2$.

A 6 **B** 11 **C** 5 **D** 18

15. Write two order-of-operation problems. Then trade with a classmate and solve the problems.

_____

_____

Problem Solving:
Act It Out and Use Reasoning

In Mackenzie's class there are 23 students. 14 students have brown hair. 2 times as many students have blonde hair as have red hair. How many students have each color hair?

Draw a diagram to show what you know.

There are 9 students left. You know that two times as many have blonde hair as have red hair. Make a table to try different numbers and see which pair fits the problem.

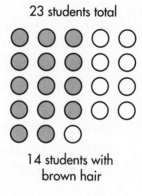

23 students total

14 students with brown hair

red		blonde	Do numbers add up to 9?
1	1 × 2 =	2	does not equal 9
2	2 × 2 =	4	does not equal 9
3	3 × 2 =	6	equals 9

Since 6 are two times 3 and 6 + 3 = 9, this is the correct answer.

So, in Mackenzie's class, there are 14 students with brown hair, 6 with blonde hair, and 3 with red hair.

In **1** and **2**, solve. Draw a picture and/or table to help find the answer.

1. Jacobson Animal Shelter has half as many cats as dogs. The shelter has 30 dogs. How many total animals does the shelter have?

   _____

2. Summer's mother gave Summer $20 to share with her 3 brothers equally. How much did each person get?

   _____

Problem Solving:
Act It Out and Reasoning

1. Christina collects stamps. She has 47 stamps in all. She has 20 stamps from Europe. The number of African stamps is 2 times the number of Asian stamps. How many stamps from each of these three continents does she have?

_____

2. **Write a Problem** Write a problem that can be solved by acting it out and using reasoning.

3. A public pool opened for the summer. A total of 246 people came swimming over the first 3 days it was open. On the first day, 79 came to swim. On the second day, 104 people swam. How many people swam on the third day?

_____   _____

4. Marissa earned $480 in the summer. If she earned $40 a week, how many weeks did she work?

   A 48   B 12   C 10   D 9

5. **Explain It** How could you use cubes to act out a problem?

_____

_____

_____

_____

Multiplying Decimals by 10, 100, or 1,000

You can use patterns to multiply decimals mentally by 10, 100, and 1,000.

Andrew starts selling his baseball cards for $0.10 each. After selling 10 cards, he has made $1.00. After selling 100 cards, he has made $10.00.

$.0.10 $.0.10 × 10 = $1.00 $0.10 × 100 = $10.00

When you multiply by	Move the decimal point
10	1 place to the right
100	2 places to the right
1,000	3 places to the right

If Andrew sold 1,000 cards, how much money would he make? _____

For questions **1–4**, find the product using mental math.

1. 6.1 × 10 _____

2. 100 × 37.98 _____

3. 92.3 × 1,000 _____

4. 0.418 × 100 _____

5. Myla has an antique flower vase that she bought for $15.75 many years ago. The vase's value is now 1,000 times as great. What is the value of the vase? _____

6. Raul can hit a golf ball 26.4 yards. A.J. can hit a golf ball 10 times as far. How far can A.J. hit the ball? _____

Reasonableness

7. Is 0.018 a reasonable answer for 1.8 × 100?

_____

_____

Name _____

Multiplying Decimals by 10, 100, or 1,000

Use mental math to find each product.

1. 53.7 × 10 _____

2. 74.3 × 100 _____

3. 66.37 × 1,000 _____

4. 1.03 × 10 _____

5. 92.5 × 10 _____

6. 0.8352 × 100 _____

7. 0.567 × 100 _____

8. 572.6 × 1,000 _____

9. 5.8 × 100 _____

10. 0.21 × 1,000 _____

11. 6.2 × 1,000 _____

12. 1.02 × 10 _____

13. 0.003 × 1,000 _____

14. 0.002 × 10 _____

15. 7.03 × 10 _____

16. 4.06 × 100 _____

17. Strategy Practice Kendra bought 10 gallons of gasoline at $3.26 per gallon. How much did she pay for the gasoline?

A $326.00   **B** $32.60   **C** $1.26   **D** $0.26

18. Strategy Practice Freddy is helping buy ingredients for salads for the school spaghetti dinner. He bought 10 pounds of onions at $0.69 per pound, 100 pounds of tomatoes at $0.99 pound, 1,000 pounds of bread crumbs at $0.09 per pound, and 100 pounds of lettuce at $0.69 per pound. Which of the things he bought cost the most?

A tomatoes   **B** lettuce   **C** bread crumbs   **D** onions

19. Explain It Marco and Suzi each multiplied 0.721 × 100. Marco got 7.21 for his product. Suzi got 72.1 for her product. Which student multiplied correctly? How do you know?

_____

_____

Estimating the Product of a Whole Number and a Decimal

You can estimate when you are multiplying a whole number by a decimal to check the reasonableness of your product.

Zane needs to buy 27 lb of roast beef for the company party. The roast beef costs $2.98 per pound. About how much will the roast beef cost?

There are two ways to estimate.

Round both numbers

$2.98 × 27
↓   ↓
$3 × 30 = $90

Adjust your factors to compatible numbers you can multiply mentally.

$2.98 × 27
↓   ↓
$3 × 25 = $75

The roast beef will cost about $90. The roast beef will cost about $75.

Estimate each product.

1. 0.8×22 _____ **2.** 19.3×6 _____ **3.** 345×5.79 _____

4. 966×0.46 _____

Use the chart to answer questions **5–7**.

Treatment	Cost
Shampoo	$7.95
Haircut	$12.95
Coloring	$18.25
Perm	$22.45

Number Sense

5. About how much would it cost for Angelina and her 4 sisters to get a shampoo and a haircut?

_____

6. Could 3 of the sisters get their hair colored for less than $100?

_____

7. Angelina gets 9 haircuts per year. About how much does she spend on haircuts for the year?

_____

Estimating the Product of a Whole Number and a Decimal

Estimate each product using rounding or compatible numbers.

1. 0.97×312

2. 8.02×70

3. 31.04×300

4. 0.56×48

_____

5. 0.33×104

6. 0.83×12

7. 0.89×51

8. 4.05×11

_____

9. 0.13×7

10. 45.1×5

11. 99.3×92

12. 47.2×93

_____

13. Critical Thinking José's father works 4 days a week at his office and 1 day a week at home. The distance to José's father's office is 23.7 miles. He takes a different route home, which is 21.8 miles. When José's father works at home, he drives to the post office once a day, which is 2.3 miles from his house. Which piece of information is not important in figuring out how many miles José's father drives per week to his office?

A the number of days at the office

B the distance to his office

C the distance to the post office

D the distance from his office

14. Strategy Practice Mrs. Smith took her three children to buy new snowsuits for the winter. Each snowsuit cost $25.99. How much did Mrs. Smith pay in total?

A $259.90   **B** $77.97   **C** $51.98   **D** $25.99

15. Explain It How can estimating be helpful before finding an actual product?

_____

_____

_____

Multiplying with Zeros in the Product

When you multiply decimals, sometimes your product does not have enough places for the decimal point. You will need to insert one or more zeros into your product to serve as placeholders.

Gabriella drove 0.3 miles yesterday. Sam drove 0.2 as far as Gabriella. How many miles did Sam drive?

A grid can help you visualize the product.

The squares that are shaded show 0.3. The squares with a dot show 0.2.

The squares that are both shaded and dotted show the product. $0.2 \times 0.3 = 6$ hundredths. To write this decimal correctly, you must add a zero in the tenths place as a placeholder.

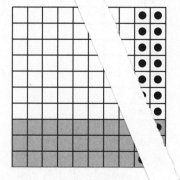

6 hundredths = 0.06

You can also count the number of decimal places in both factors. The total number of decimal places equals the number of decimal places in your product.

$$\begin{array}{r} 0.3 \\ \times\, 0.2 \\ \hline 6 \end{array}$$ 1 decimal place
1 decimal place

Since you need 2 decimal places in your product and you have only one digit in your product, you need to add a zero to the left of the 6 as a placeholder. The product then correctly becomes 0.06.

In questions **1–4**, find each product.

1. $\begin{array}{r} 0.03 \\ \times 0.42 \\ \hline \end{array}$

2. $\begin{array}{r} 4.01 \\ \times 0.02 \\ \hline \end{array}$

3. $\begin{array}{r} 0.16 \\ \times 0.05 \\ \hline \end{array}$

4. $\begin{array}{r} 7.06 \\ \times 0.01 \\ \hline \end{array}$

Algebra

If $0.4 \times 0.2 = 0.08$, what is the value of n in the following equations?

5. $0.4 \times n = 0.008$ _____

6. $0.4 \times n = 0.0008$ _____

7. $n \times 0.2 = 0.00008$ _____

Multiplying with Zeros in the Product

Find each product.

1.	0.3	2.	0.04	3.	5.04	4.	0.13
	$\times\,0.2$		$\times\,0.17$		$\times\,0.02$		$\times\,0.05$

5. 0.97×0.5

6. $8.02 \times .002$

7. $1.04 \times .03$

8. $1.06 \times .08$

_____

_____

_____

_____

9. 0.07×2.05

10. $0.80 \times .02$

11. 0.09×5.01

12. $4.05 \times .012$

_____

_____

_____

_____

13. The fifth-grade math textbook weighs 2.05 pounds. There are 88 students taking math at the Hillside School. What is the total weight of all the math textbooks?

_____

14. The Lopezes received a delivery of fuel oil totaling 53.00 gallons. The oil cost $3.05 per gallon. What did the Lopezes pay for the delivery?

_____

15. Maria spends 1.5 hours in the computer lab each afternoon. If the computer uses 0.09 kilowatts of electricity per hour, how many kilowatt hours does Maria use each afternoon?

A 13.50   B 1.35   C 0.135   D 0.0135

16. **Explain It** Is the product of 0.02×0.02 the same as the product of 0.2×0.002? Explain.

_____

_____

_____

_____

_____

Problem Solving:
Reasonableness

When solving a word problem, you want to make sure you answer the right question and that your answer is reasonable.

Sami earns $5.75 per hour babysitting. She babysat for 6 hours over last weekend. How much money did Sami make?

$5.75
$\times$ 6
─────
345.0   Sami made $345.00 over the weekend.

Step 1: Did you answer the right question?
The problem asked how much money Sami made, so you answered the right question.

Step 2: Is the answer reasonable? You can check for reasonableness by estimating.
$5.75 $\times$ 6 $\approx$
$6 $\times$ 6 $\approx$ $36
$345.00 is not close to $36, so the answer is not reasonable.

Step 3: Go back and find the mistake.
The decimal point was placed incorrectly in the product. The correct product is $34.50. This is close to the estimate of $36.

Sami made $34.50 over the weekend.

For questions **1** and **2**, look back and check. Tell if the right question was answered and if the answer is reasonable.

1. Abishek sold 13 paintings at the art show. Each painting sold for $25. How much money did Abishek make? Suggested answer: $325

_____

_____

2. Sara's mom gave her $12 to buy 2 tickets to the movie for Sara and her sister. Sara wants to buy popcorn, too. The tickets are $3.50 each and popcorn is $3.00. How much money will Sara have left? Suggested answer: $10.

_____

Problem Solving:
Reasonableness

In **1** and **2,** look back and check. Tell if the answer is reasonable. Explain why or why not.

1. Brendan bought 14 used records at a garage sale. He paid $0.75 for each record. How much did he pay?

_____

_____

2. Jesse bought 2.7 lb. of catfish for $5.50/lb. How much did he pay?

_____

_____

3. **Write a Problem** Write a real-world problem that you can solve by multiplying. Give an answer to be checked for reasonableness.

_____

4. Louis bought a T-shirt for $13.50 and a sweatshirt that cost $21.99. He paid with two twenty-dollar bills. How much change did he receive?

_____

5. Rachel needs to read 50 books to win her school library contest. She already has read 18 books but found out that 2 didn't count. Which equation below could she use to find out how many more books she needs to read?

A $y = 50 - 18$

C $50 = (y + 2) + 18$

B $50 = y + (18 - 2)$

D $y = (50 - 2) - 18$

6. **Explain It** If an estimate is close to the calculated answer, does that always mean the calculated answer is correct?

_____

Dividing Decimals
by 10, 100, or 1,000

You can use place-value patterns when you divide a decimal by 10, 100, or 1,000.

Sanjai has 27.5 lb of clay. If he uses the clay to make 10 bowls, how much clay will he use for each bowl? What if he makes 100 bowls from the clay? What if he makes 1,000 bowls?

Dividing a number by 10 moves the decimal point one place to the left.

$27.5 \div 10 = 2.75$

Dividing a number by 100 moves the decimal point two places to the left.

$27.5 \div 100 = 0.275$

Dividing a number by 1,000 moves the decimal point three places to the left.

$27.5 \div 1,000 = 0.0275$

Sanjai will use 2.75 lb for each of 10 bowls, 0.275 lb for each of 100 bowls, and 0.0275 lb for each of 1,000 bowls.

Remember: When you divide a number by 10, 100, or 1,000, your quotient will be smaller than that number.

For questions **1–6**, find the quotient. Use mental math.

1. $16.4 \div 10$ **2.** $38.92 \div 100$ **3.** $297.1 \div 100$

4. $540.9 \div 10$ **5.** $41.628 \div 1,000$ **6.** $0.33 \div 10$

7. The city has a long stretch of land it wants to turn into gardens. The land is 3,694.7 ft long. The city wants to make 100 gardens. How many ft long will each garden be?

_____

8. Reasonableness Connor divided 143.89 by 100. He said his answer was 14.389. Is this a reasonable answer?

_____

_____

_____

Dividing Decimals
by 10, 100, or 1,000

Find each quotient. Use mental math.

1. $86.6 \div 10 =$ _____

2. $192.5 \div 100 =$ _____

3. $1.99 \div 100 =$ _____

4. $0.87 \div 10 =$ _____

5. $228.55 \div 1,000 =$ _____

6. $0.834 \div 100 =$ _____

7. $943.35 \div 1,000 =$ _____

8. $1.25 \div 10 =$ _____

Algebra Write 10, 100, or 1,000 for each n.

9. $78.34 \div n = 0.7834$ **10.** $0.32 \div n = 0.032$ **11.** $(75.34 - 25.34) \div n = 5$

_____   _____   _____

12. There are 145 children taking swimming
lessons at the pool. If 10 children will be
assigned to each instructor, how many
instructors need to be hired? _____

13. Ronald ran 534.3 mi in 100 days. If he ran an equal
distance each day, how many miles did he run per day?

A 5   **B** 5.13   **C** 5.343   **D** 6.201

14. **Explain It** Carlos says that $17.43 \div 100$ is the
same as 174.3×0.01. Is he correct? Explain.

_____

_____

Dividing a Decimal by a Whole Number

Jia needs to cut a board into 3 equal pieces to make bookshelves. The board is 1.5 yd long. How long will each bookshelf be?

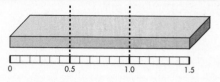

0   0.5   1.0   1.5

Laying a measuring tape next to the board, Jia sees that her board can be cut into 3 pieces that are each 0.5 yd long. Jia also writes out her problem to make sure her answer is correct.

Step 1. Write a decimal point in the quotient directly above the decimal point in the dividend.

Step 2. Divide as you would with whole numbers.

$$\begin{array}{r} 0.5 \\ 3\overline{)1.5} \\ \underline{15} \\ 0 \end{array}$$

Step 3. Check your quotient by multiplying.

$0.5 \times 3 = 1.5$

Since the quotient matches the measurement that Jia saw on her measuring tape, she knows that her answer is correct.

Sometimes you will need to add a zero to the right of the dividend so that you can continue dividing. Example: $8.1 \div 18$

$$\begin{array}{r} 0.45 \\ 18\overline{)8.10} \\ \underline{72} \\ 90 \\ \underline{90} \\ 0 \end{array}$$

For **1–6**, find each quotient. Check by multiplying.

1. $14\overline{)6.3}$

2. $77\overline{)2.31}$

3. $89\overline{)2.492}$

4. $123.08 \div 34$

5. $0.57 \div 30$

6. $562.86 \div 59$

7. A family of five people attends a theme park. They purchase 2 adult tickets for $27.50 each and 3 student tickets for $12.50 each. If the 5 tickets are purchased with a $100 bill, how much change do they receive? _____

Dividing a Decimal by a Whole Number

Find each quotient.

1. $13\overline{)68.9}$ **2.** $35\overline{)412.3}$ **3.** $90\overline{)14.4}$ **4.** $60\overline{)53.4}$

5. $123.08 \div 34 =$ _____   **6.** $0.57 \div 30 =$ _____

7. $562.86 \div 59 =$ _____   **8.** $24.4 \div 80 =$ _____

9. John paid $7.99 for 3 boxes of cereal. The tax was $1.69.
Excluding tax, how much did John pay for each box of cereal
if they all were the same price? _____

10. If a package of granola bars with 12 bars costs $3.48,
how much does each granola bar cost?

    A 44¢   **B** $1.00   **C** 29¢   **D** 31¢

11. Estimation $64.82 \div 11$ is

    A a little more than 6.   **B** a little less than 6.

    C a little more than 60.   **D** a little less than 60.

14. Explain It Explain how to divide 0.12 by 8.

_____

_____

_____

_____

Estimation: Decimals Divided by Whole Numbers

The merry-go-round in the Smithson Town Park took in $795.60 in the last six months. The ticket taker says that 442 people rode the merry-go-round during that time. About how much does it cost to ride?

You can estimate to find the quotient of $795.60 ÷ 442 either by rounding or using compatible numbers and mental math.

To round your numbers, cover the digit in the hundreds place with your hand. Look at the number next to your hand. Since 9 > 5, you round $795.60 up to $800. Since 4 < 5, you round 442 down to 400.

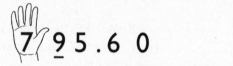

800 ÷ 400 = 2   It costs about $2 to ride.

Or you can use compatible numbers and mental math.

800 ÷ 400 = 2   It costs about $2 to ride.

Estimate each quotient.

1. 81.2 ÷ 19 _____   **2.** 376.44 ÷ 22 _____   **3.** 62.91 ÷ 16 _____

4. 763.85 ÷ 82 _____   **5.** 550.8 ÷ 9 _____   **6.** 486.5 ÷ 3 _____

Number Sense

7. Explain how you know an error was made when you find the quotient for 231.68 ÷ 16 is 144.8.

_____

_____

Reasonableness

8. Is 61.5 ÷ 15 a little less than 4, a little more than 4, a little less than 40, or a little more than 40?

_____

Estimation: Decimals Divided by Whole Numbers

Estimate each quotient.

1. $73.5 \div 10$ _____

2. $246.78 \div 83$ _____

3. $185.7 \div 3$ _____

4. $535.6 \div 35$ _____

5. $553.9 \div 90$ _____

6. $366.6 \div 12$ _____

7. $35.6 \div 7$ _____

8. $86.4 \div 4$ _____

9. $270.53 \div 3$ _____

10. $839.7 \div 90$ _____

11. $93.26 \div 3$ _____

12. $77.3 \div 11$ _____

13. Joseph is saving $23 a week to buy a graphing calculator that costs $275.53. About how many weeks will it take before he can buy the calculator?

_____

14. Juan works at a health food store two hours a day, three days a week. His weekly pay is $73.50. About how much does Juan make per hour?

_____

15. Reasonableness Which of the following is a reasonable estimate for the operation $566.3 \div 63$?

A about 16   **B** about 9   **C** about 4   **D** about 6

16. Explain It When would you estimate a quotient instead of finding the exact quotient?

_____

_____

_____

_____

Dividing a Decimal by a Decimal

Sebastian is shipping a box to his cousin. The box weighs 23.6 lb. The cost to ship the box is $88.50. How much does it cost per pound to ship the box?

To divide a decimal by a decimal, you need to change the problem into a simpler type of problem that you already know how to solve.

Step 1. To change this problem, you multiply the divisor by a power of 10 until it becomes a whole number.

$23.6 \times 10 = 236$

Step 2. You must also multiply the dividend by the same power of 10. Sometimes, you may have to add zeros as placeholders.

$88.50 \times 10 = 885.0$

Step 3. Place a decimal point in the quotient and divide as you would with whole numbers.

$$
\begin{array}{r}
3.75 \\
236\overline{)885.00} \\
\underline{708} \\
1770 \\
\underline{1652} \\
1180 \\
\underline{1180} \\
0
\end{array}
$$

The box costs $3.75 per pound to ship.

For questions **1–6**, find each quotient.

1. $0.104 \div 0.08$ _____

2. $5.49 \div 0.9$ _____

3. $50.4 \div 1.2$ _____

4. $0.427 \div 61$ _____

5. $0.8449 \div 0.71$ _____

6. $9.483 \div 8.7$ _____

7. Miriam needs to buy new notebooks for school. The notebooks cost $0.98 each including tax. Miriam's mother gave her $6.45 and told her to buy 8 notebooks. Did her mother give her enough money?

_____

8. Miriam finds a coupon in the store that reduces the price of notebooks to $0.75 each including tax. How many notebooks can Miriam buy now?

_____

Dividing a Decimal by a Decimal

Find each quotient.

1. $0.8\overline{)1.84}$ 2. $0.9\overline{)2.7}$ 3. $2.5\overline{)4.75}$ 4. $1.1\overline{)1.21}$

5. $7.1\overline{)6.39}$ 6. $0.8\overline{)0.648}$ 7. $1.3\overline{)10.725}$ 8. $0.2\overline{)0.51}$

9. $0.07\overline{)0.77}$ 10. $4.8\overline{)4.32}$ 11. $0.7\overline{)8.4}$ 12. $2.3\overline{)6.9}$

13. Chan paid $4.75 for trail mix that costs $2.50 a pound. How many pounds of trail mix did he buy?

_____

14. Max's family car has a gas tank that holds 12.5 gallons of gas. It cost $40.62 to completely fill the tank yesterday. What was the price of gas per gallon?

_____

15. **Strategy Practice** Strawberries cost $5.99 per pound, and bananas cost $0.59 per pound. How many pounds of bananas could you buy for the cost of one pound of strawberries?

   A 101.5 pounds   **B** 10.15 pounds   **C** 5.99 pounds   **D** .59 pounds

16. **Explain It** When dividing a decimal by a decimal, why is it sometimes necessary to add a zero to the right of the decimal point in the quotient?

_____

_____

_____

_____

Problem Solving: Multiple-Step Problems

A multiple-step problem is a problem where you may need more than one step to find your answer.

Marcie was in a 3-day charity walk. Her friend Gayle said she would give the charity $1.50 for each mile that Marcie walked. The first day, Marcie walked 26.42 miles. The second day, Marcie walked 32.37 miles. The third day, Marcie walked 28.93 miles. How much money did Gayle give?

Step 1.   Read through the problem again and write a list of what you already know.

Marcie walked 26.42, 32.37, and 28.93 miles.
Gayle gave $1.50 for each mile.

Step 2.   Write a list of what you *need* to know.

Total amount Gayle gave

Step 3.   Write a list of the steps to solve the problem.

Find the total number of miles Marcie walked.
Find the amount Gayle gave.

Step 4.   Solve the problem one step at a time.

$26.42 + 32.37 + 28.93 = 87.72$ total number of miles Marcie walked

$87.72 \times \$1.50 = \$131.58$ total amount Gayle gave

Use the information above to answer question 1.

1. Marcie's brother Tom was also in the charity walk. He only walked 0.8 as far as Marcie on the first day, 0.7 as far on the second day, and 0.9 as far on the third day. How many miles did Tom walk, rounded to the nearest hundredth of a mile?

_____

2. Diego is buying fruit at the store. Which costs less: 1 pound of each fruit or 4 pounds of peaches?

Fruit	Cost per pound
Apples	$0.89
Oranges	$1.29
Peaches	$0.99
Grapes	$1.09

_____

Problem Solving: Multiple-Step Problems

Write and answer the hidden question or questions in each problem and then solve the problem. Write your answer in a complete sentence.

Storewide Sale	
Jeans	$29.95 for 1 pair OR 2 pairs for $55.00
T-shirts	$9.95 for 1 OR 3 T-shirts for $25.00

1. Sue bought 2 pairs of jeans and a belt that cost $6.95. The tax on the items was $5.85. Sue paid the cashier $70.00. How much money did Sue receive in change?

   _____

2. A recreation department purchased 12 T-shirts for day camp. The department does not have to pay sales tax. It paid with a $100.00 bill. How much change did it receive?

   _____

   _____

3. When Mrs. Johnson saw the sale, she decided to get clothes for each child in her family. She bought each of her 6 children a pair of jeans and a T-shirt. She paid $14.35 in sales tax. How much was Mrs. Johnson's total bill?

   A $253.35   **B** $119.70   **C** $94.35   **D** $229.35

4. **Write a Problem** Write a two-step problem that contains a hidden question about buying something at the mall. Tell what the hidden question is and solve your problem. Use $8.95 somewhere in your equation. Write your answer in a complete sentence.

   _____

5. **Explain It** What are hidden questions and why are they important when solving multiple-step problems?

   _____

   _____

   _____

Basic Geometry Ideas

Points and lines are basic geometric ideas. Lines are sometimes described by relationships to other lines.

Draw	Write	Say	Description
•J	J	point J	J is a point. It shows an exact location in space.
← N O → / P Q	$\overleftrightarrow{NO}$ $\overrightarrow{PQ}$	line NO ray PQ	$\overleftrightarrow{NO}$ is a line. It is a straight path of points that goes on forever in two directions. $\overrightarrow{PQ}$ is a ray. It goes on forever in only one direction.
E F G H	$\overleftrightarrow{EF} \parallel \overleftrightarrow{GH}$	Line EF is parallel to line GH.	$\overleftrightarrow{EF}$ and $\overleftrightarrow{GH}$ are parallel lines. They are the same distance apart and will not cross each other.
S T V U	$\overleftrightarrow{SU}$ intersects $\overleftrightarrow{VT}$	Line SU intersects line VT.	$\overleftrightarrow{SU}$ and $\overleftrightarrow{VT}$ are intersecting lines. They pass through the same point.

Use the diagram on the right. Name the following.

1. two parallel lines

_____

2. two intersecting rays

_____

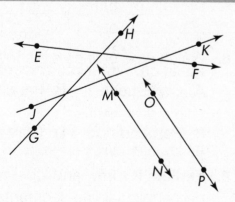

Basic Geometric Ideas

Use the diagram at the right. Name the following.

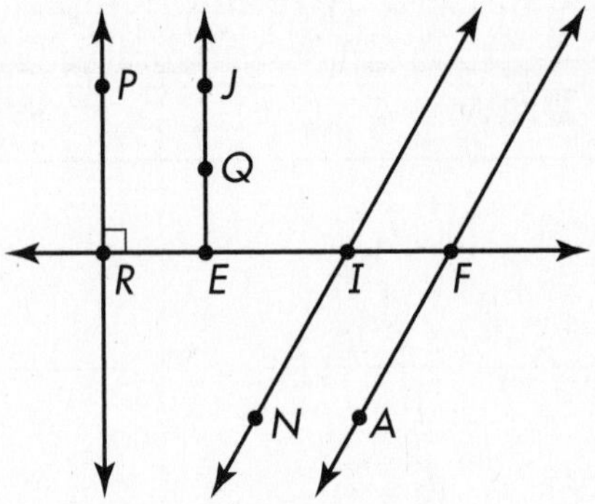

1. three points

_____

2. a ray

_____

3. two intersecting lines but not perpendicular

_____

4. two parallel lines   _____

5. a line segment   _____

6. two perpendicular lines   _____

7. Reasoning Can a line segment have two midpoints? Explain.

_____

_____

_____

8. Which type of lines are shown by the figure?

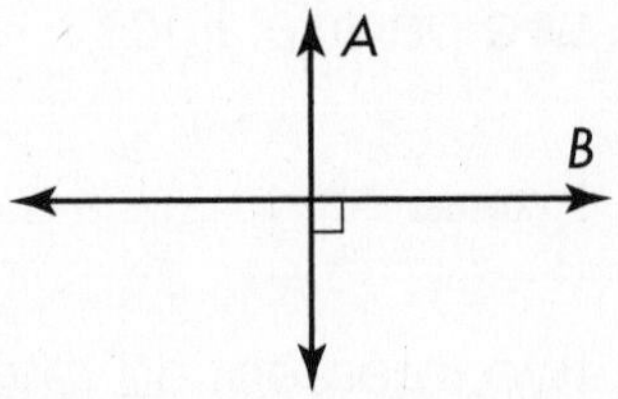

   A Congruent   **B** Parallel

   C Perpendicular   **D** Curved

9. Explain It Draw and label two
   perpendicular line segments $\overline{KL}$ and $\overline{MN}$.

Measuring and Classifying Angles

The chart below can help you describe and identify an angle.

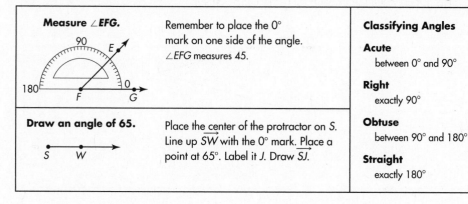

		Classifying Angles
Measure ∠EFG.	Remember to place the 0° mark on one side of the angle. ∠EFG measures 45.	**Acute** between 0° and 90°
		Right exactly 90°
Draw an angle of 65.	Place the center of the protractor on S. Line up SW with the 0° mark. Place a point at 65°. Label it J. Draw SJ.	**Obtuse** between 90° and 180°
		Straight exactly 180°

Classify each angle as acute, right, obtuse, or straight. Then measure each angle.

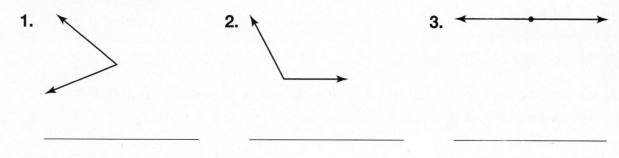

1. _____

2. _____

3. _____

Draw an angle with each measure.

4. 100°

5. 170°

6. Reasoning ∠ABC measures less than 180° but more than 90°. Is ∠ABC a right, an acute, an obtuse, or a straight angle?

_____

_____

Measuring and Classifying Angles

Classify each angle as *acute, right, obtuse,* or *straight.* Then measure each angle. (Hint: Draw longer sides if necessary.)

1.

_____

2.

_____

Draw an angle with each measure.

3. 120°

4. 180°

5. Draw an acute angle. Label it with the letters *A, B,* and *C.* What is the measure of the angle?

_____

6. Which kind of angle is shown in the figure below?

A Acute   **B** Obtuse

C Right   **D** Straight

7. Explain It Explain how to use a protractor to measure an angle.

_____

_____

_____

_____

Polygons

A polygon is a closed plane figure made up of line segments. Common polygons have names that tell the number of sides the polygon has.

A **regular polygon** has sides of equal length and angles of equal measure.

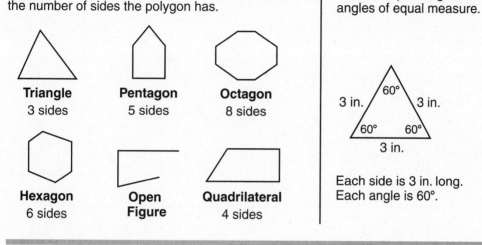

Triangle 3 sides	**Pentagon** 5 sides	**Octagon** 8 sides
Hexagon 6 sides	**Open Figure**	**Quadrilateral** 4 sides

Each side is 3 in. long.
Each angle is 60°.

Name each polygon. Then tell if it appears to be a regular polygon.

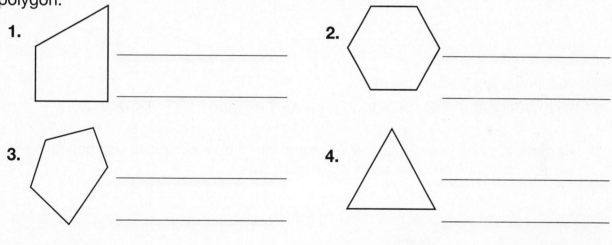

1. _____

_____

2. _____

_____

3. _____

_____

4. _____

_____

5. Reasoning Shakira sorted shapes into two different groups. Use geometric terms to describe how she sorted the shapes.

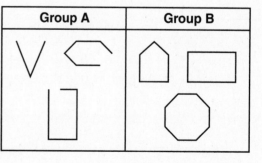

Group A	Group B

_____

_____

_____

Polygons

Name each polygon. Then tell if it appears to be a regular
polygon.

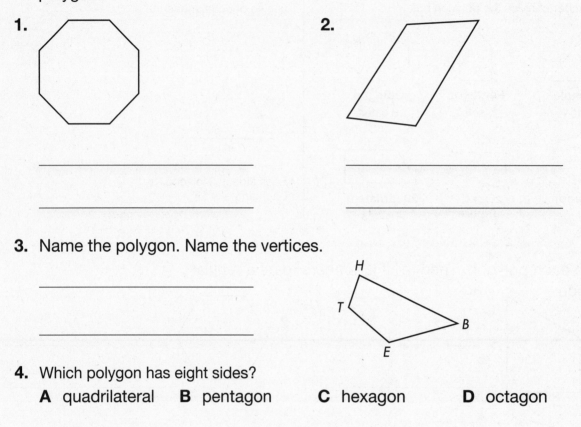

1.

_____

_____

2.

_____

_____

3. Name the polygon. Name the vertices.

_____

_____

4. Which polygon has eight sides?

A quadrilateral   **B** pentagon   **C** hexagon   **D** octagon

5. **Explain It** Draw two regular polygons and two that are irregular. Use geometric
terms to describe one characteristic of each type.

_____

_____

_____

Classifying Triangles

You can classify triangles by the lengths of their sides and the sizes of their angles.

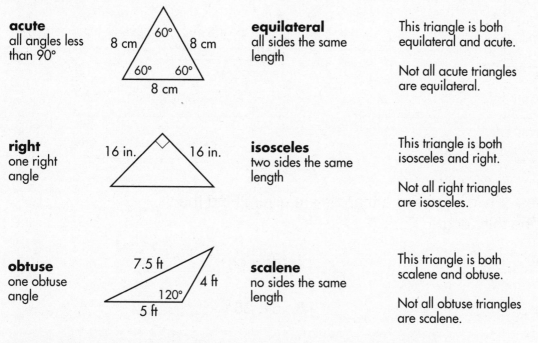

acute
all angles less than 90°

equilateral
all sides the same length

This triangle is both equilateral and acute.

Not all acute triangles are equilateral.

right
one right angle

isosceles
two sides the same length

This triangle is both isosceles and right.

Not all right triangles are isosceles.

obtuse
one obtuse angle

scalene
no sides the same length

This triangle is both scalene and obtuse.

Not all obtuse triangles are scalene.

Remember that the sum of the measures of the angles of a triangle is 180°.

Classify each triangle by its sides and then by its angles.

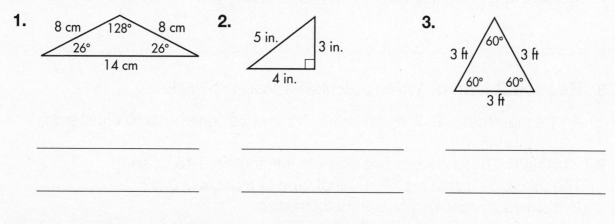

1.

2.

3.

_____   _____   _____

_____   _____   _____

The measures of two angles of a triangle are given. Find the measure of the third angle.

4. 40°, 100°, _____   **5.** 14°, 98°, _____   **6.** 38°, 38°, _____

Classifying Triangles

Classify each triangle by its sides and then by its angles.

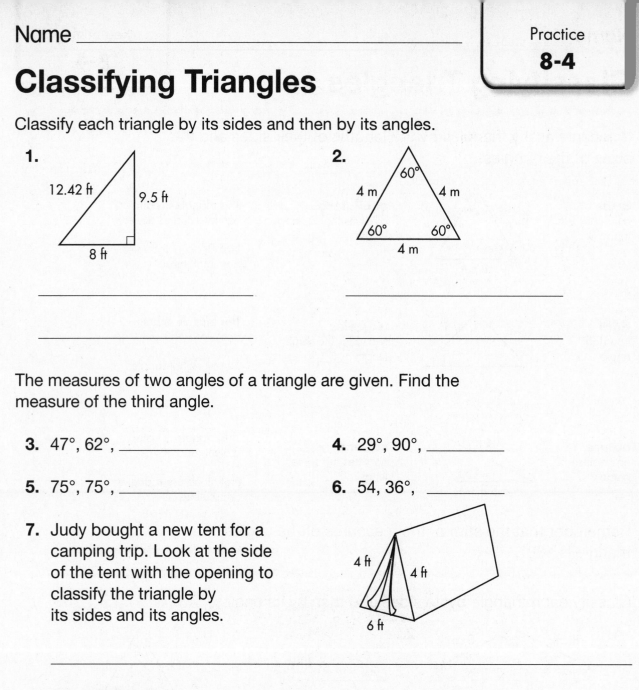

1.

12.42 ft   9.5 ft

8 ft

_____

_____

2.

60°

4 m   4 m

60°   60°

4 m

_____

_____

The measures of two angles of a triangle are given. Find the measure of the third angle.

3. 47°, 62°, _____

4. 29°, 90°, _____

5. 75°, 75°, _____

6. 54, 36°, _____

7. Judy bought a new tent for a camping trip. Look at the side of the tent with the opening to classify the triangle by its sides and its angles.

4 ft   4 ft

6 ft

_____

8. **Reasonableness** Which describes a scalene triangle?

A 4 equal sides   **B** 3 equal sides   **C** 2 equal sides   **D** 0 equal sides

9. **Explain It** The lengths of two sides of a triangle are 15 in. each. The third side measures 10 in. What type of triangle is this? Explain your answer using geometric terms.

_____

_____

Classifying Quadrilaterals

Quadrilateral	Definition	Example
Parallelogram	A quadrilateral with both pairs of opposite sides parallel and equal in length	5 in. / 2 in. / 2 in. / 5 in.
Rectangle	A parallelogram with four right angles	5 ft / 2 ft / 2 ft / 5 ft
Rhombus	A parallelogram with all sides the same length	4 in. / 4 in. / 4 in. / 4 in.
Square	A rectangle with all sides the same length	1 ft / 1 ft / 1 ft / 1 ft
Trapezoid	A quadrilateral with only one pair of parallel sides	2 in. / 2 in. / 3 in. / 6 in.

Remember that the sum of the measures of the angles
of a quadrilateral is 360°.

Classify each quadrilateral. Be as specific as possible.

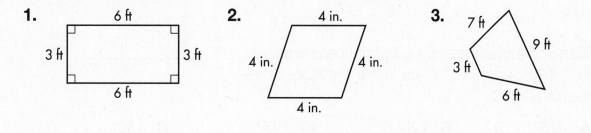

1. 6 ft / 3 ft / 3 ft / 6 ft

_____

2. 4 in. / 4 in. / 4 in. / 4 in.

_____

3. 7 ft / 9 ft / 3 ft / 6 ft

_____

The measures of three angles of a quadrilateral are given.
Find the measure of the fourth angle.

4. 65°, 150°, 89°, _____

5. 100°, 80°, 100°, _____

6. 82°, 78°, 90°, _____

Quadrilaterals

Classify each quadrilateral. Be as specific as possible.

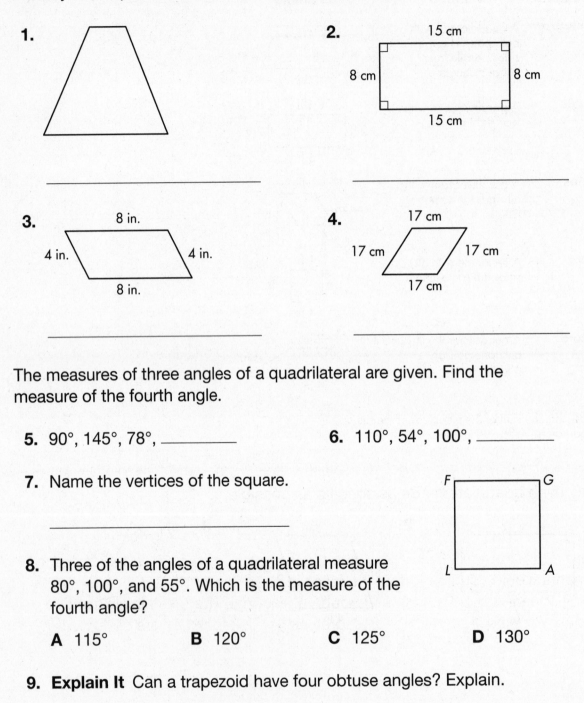

1.

_____

2. 15 cm

8 cm   8 cm

15 cm

_____

3. 8 in.

4 in.   4 in.

8 in.

_____

4. 17 cm

17 cm   17 cm

17 cm

_____

The measures of three angles of a quadrilateral are given. Find the measure of the fourth angle.

5. 90°, 145°, 78°, _____

6. 110°, 54°, 100°, _____

7. Name the vertices of the square.

_____

8. Three of the angles of a quadrilateral measure 80°, 100°, and 55°. Which is the measure of the fourth angle?

A 115°   **B** 120°   **C** 125°   **D** 130°

9. **Explain It** Can a trapezoid have four obtuse angles? Explain.

_____

_____

_____

Problem Solving:
Make and Test Generalizations

Carey made the following generalization: Any square can be cut in half through a diagonal. The result is always two isosceles triangles, each with a 90-degree angle. Test this generalization.

Test one example of the generalization.

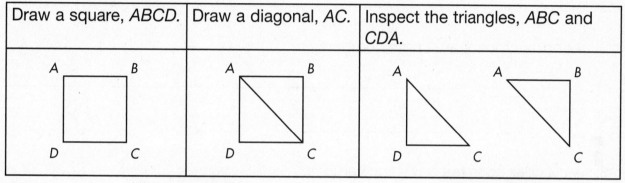

Draw a square, *ABCD*.	Draw a diagonal, *AC*.	Inspect the triangles, *ABC* and *CDA*.

Triangle *ABC*		**Triangle *CDA***	
1. $AB = BC$	All sides of a square are equal length.	1. $CD = DA$	All sides of a square are equal length.
2. Angle $B = 90°$	All angles of a square are 90°.	2. Angle $D = 90°$	All angles of a square are 90°.

Conclusion: Each triangle has two equal sides, only, and contains a right angle.

The generalization is true for the square, *ABCD*.

Looking at the square *ABCD* and at the triangles *ABC* and *CDA,* what additional statements would you use to test the following generalization?

Any square can be cut in half through a diagonal. The result is always two isosceles triangles, each with a 90-degree angle. The triangles are congruent.

_____

_____

_____

Problem Solving:
Make and Test Generalizations

For questions **1–4**, test the generalization and state whether it appears to be correct or incorrect. If incorrect, give an example to support why.

1. The sum of the angles in a square is 360 degrees.

   _____

2. All odd numbers are prime numbers.

   _____

   _____

3. A cylinder does not have any vertices.

   _____

4. If a figure has six faces, it must be a cube.

   _____

   _____

5. **Draw a Picture** Greg says that any two triangles can be put together to make a square or a rectangle. SungHee disagrees. Who is right? Draw a picture and explain your answer.

   _____

   _____

6. **Think About the Process** Which of the following is true about the statement: "Prime numbers can never be even numbers"?

   A Correct
   B Incorrect; all prime numbers are even.
   C Incorrect; 2 is an even prime number.
   D None of the above

Name _____

Understanding Factors

You can use the divisibility rules to find the factors of a number.

What are the factors of 92?

Possible Factor	Test of Divisibility	Result of Test	Factors Found
1	Is 92 a whole number?	Yes. Therefore it is divisible by 1.	$92 \div 1 = 92$ 1 and 92 are factors.
2	Is 92 an even number?	Yes. Therefore it is divisible by 2.	$92 \div 2 = 46$ 2 and 46 are factors.
3	Is the sum of the digits divisible by 3?	No. Therefore it is not divisible by 3.	3 is not a factor.
4	Are the last 2 digits divisible by 4?	Yes. Therefore it is divisible by 4.	$92 \div 4 = 23$ 4 and 23 are factors.
5	Is the last digit 5 or 0?	No. Therefore it is not divisible by 5.	5 is not a factor.
6	Is it divisible by both 2 and 3?	No. Therefore it is not divisible by 6.	6 is not a factor.
9	Is the sum of the digits divisible by 9?	No. Therefore it is not divisible by 9.	9 is not a factor.
10	Is the last digit 0?	No. Therefore it is not divisible by 10.	10 is not a factor.

The factors of 92 are 1, 2, 4, 23, 46, and 92.

Find all the factors of each number.

1. 12 _____

2. 35 _____

3. 45 _____

4. 49 _____

5. Number Sense Is 2,340 divisible by 90? How do you know?

_____

_____

_____

Understanding Factors

List all the factors of each number.

1. 36 _____

2. 90 _____

3. 84 _____

Number Sense A number is divisible by 4 if the last two digits
are divisible by 4. Write yes on the line if the number is divisible
by 4 and no if it is not.

4. 324 _____ **5.** 634 _____ **6.** 172 _____

7. A class of 80 students is graduating from elementary school.
The teachers need help figuring out how to line up the
students for the ceremony. One row of 80 students would be
too long. What other ways could the students be arranged
for the ceremony?

_____

_____

8. A number is divisible by another number when the _____
after division by that number is 0.

9. **Number Sense** What factor pair is missing for 45 if you
already know 1 and 45, 5 and 9?

A 7 and 6 **B** 8 and 6 **C** 3 and 15 **D** 4 and 12

10. **Explain It** Explain how to find all the factor pairs of 40.

_____

_____

_____

_____

Prime and Composite Numbers

Numbers such as 2, 3, 5, 7, and 11 are prime numbers. A prime number has *only two* factors, itself and 1. A whole number that has *more than two* factors is called a composite number.

3 is an example of a prime number. Its only factors are 1 and 3.

◯ ◯ ◯ $1 \times 3 = 3$

8 is a composite number. Its factors are 1, 2, 4, and 8.

◯ ◯ ◯ ◯ ◯ ◯ ◯ ◯ $1 \times 8 = 8$

◯ ◯ ◯ ◯
◯ ◯ ◯ ◯ $2 \times 4 = 8$

You can also use divisibility rules to tell whether a number is prime or composite. In the example above, 8 is an even number, so it is divisible by 2. Therefore, 8 is a composite number.

Write whether each number is prime or composite.

1. 17 _____

2. 47 _____

3. 80 _____

4. 13 _____

5. 65 _____

6. 22 _____

7. 59 _____

8. 33 _____

9. What are the first 10 composite numbers? Explain how you know.

_____

_____

_____

_____

Prime and Composite Numbers

Write whether each number is prime or composite.

1. 21 _____   **2.** 36 _____   **3.** 31 _____

4. 87 _____   **5.** 62 _____   **6.** 23 _____

7. 29 _____   **8.** 45 _____   **9.** 51 _____

For **10** and **11**, list all of the factors for each number. Then tell if the number is prime or composite.

10. 100 _____

11. 53 _____

12. **Number Sense** Audrey says that the prime factorization of 42 is 21 × 2. Is she correct? If not, tell why.

_____

_____

13. Is 4,564,282 prime or composite? Explain how you determined your answer.

_____

_____

14. Which of the following is a prime number?

A 105   **B** 27   **C** 19   **D** 9

15. **Explain It** Does it matter what two factors you select to complete a factor tree? Explain.

_____

_____

Finding Prime Factors of a Number

You can write a composite number as a product of prime numbers.

Find the prime factors of 27.

Think about a row of snap blocks that equals 27.

27

You can break these blocks into one 3-block piece and one 9-block piece because $3 \times 9 = 27$.

3 $\times$ **9**

3 is a prime number because you can't break it down farther. 9 is a composite number. You can break 9 down because $3 \times 3 = 9$.

3 $\times$ **3** $\times$ **3**

All of the block pieces are now prime numbers, so these are the prime factors of 27.

$3 \times 3 \times 3 = 27$

A factor tree is another way to show this.

```
              27          composite
             /  \
  prime   3  ×  9         composite
         /     /  \
        3  ×  3  ×  3     all prime numbers, so these
                          are the prime factors
```

Using exponents, you can write $3 \times 3 \times 3 = 3^3$ So, $27 = 3^3$

Find the prime factors of each number. If a number is prime, write prime.

1. 26 _____

2. 42 _____

3. 64 _____

4. 47 _____

5. 125 _____

6. 153 _____

Finding Prime Factors
of a Number

Find the prime factorization of each number. If a number is prime,
write prime.

1. 30 _____ 2. 16 _____ 3. 43 _____ 4. 35 _____

5. 42 _____ 6. 9 _____ 7. 50 _____ 8. 61 _____

9. 37 _____ 10. 125 _____ 11. 29 _____ 12. 49 _____

13. In the space to the right, create a
factor tree for the number 64.

14. **Strategy Practice** Field Day is in March on a day that is a
prime number. Which date could it be?

A March 4   **B** March 11   **C** March 18   **D** March 24

15. **Explain It** What is a factor tree, and how do you know when
a factor tree is completed?

_____

_____

_____

_____

Common Factors and Greatest Common Factors

The greatest common factor (GCF) of two numbers is the greatest number that is a factor of both.

Find the greatest common factor of 12 and 18.

You can use arrays to model the factors of 12.

$1 \times 12 = 12$ $2 \times 6 = 12$ $3 \times 4 = 12$

You can use arrays to model the factors of 18.

$1 \times 18 = 18$ $2 \times 9 = 18$ $3 \times 6 = 18$

Look at the arrays above. You can see that the common factors of 12 and 18 are 2, 3, and 6. The greatest common factor of 12 and 18 is 6.

Find the GCF of each pair of numbers.

1. 9, 27 _____

2. 25, 40 _____

3. 7, 36 _____

4. 40, 48 _____

5. Number Sense Can the GCF of 18 and 36 be greater than 18? Explain.

_____

_____

Common Factors and Greatest Common Factors

Find the GCF of each pair of numbers.

1. 15, 50 ————   **2.** 6, 27 ————   **3.** 10, 25 ————

4. 18, 32 ————   **5.** 7, 28 ————   **6.** 54, 108 ————

7. 25, 55 ————   **8.** 14, 48 ————   **9.** 81, 135 ————

10. Number Sense Can the GCF of 16 and 42 be less than 16? Explain.

_____

_____

_____

11. A restaurant received a shipment of 42 gal of
orange juice and 18 gal of cranberry juice. The
juice needs to be poured into equal-sized containers.
What is the largest amount of juice that each
container can hold of each kind of juice?   ————————

12. At a day camp, there are 56 girls and 42 boys.
The campers need to be split into equal groups.
Each has either all girls or all boys. What is the
greatest number of campers each group can have? ————————

13. Which is the GCF of 24 and 64?

A 4   **B** 8   **C** 14   **D** 12

14. Explain It Do all even numbers have 2 as a factor? Explain.

_____

_____

Problem Solving:
Try, Check, and Revise

Can you use similar square tiles to cover a floor without cutting the tiles?

Try

Look at the square tile and the floor.

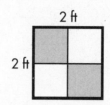 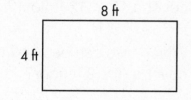

Ask yourself:

1. Can I divide the floor into a <u>whole number</u> of rectangles that are 2 feet wide?

   AND

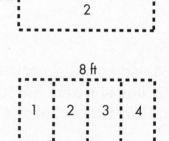

2. Can I divide the floor into a <u>whole number</u> of rectangles that are 2 feet long?

If the answers are both yes, you can use the tiles to cover the floor without cutting them.

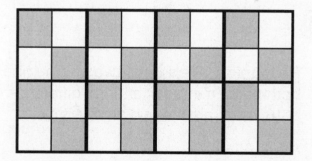

Check

Answer the following questions.
(Remember you cannot cut the tiles.)

1. Can you completely cover a 4 ft by 8 ft area with 3 ft by 3 ft tiles?   _____

2. Can you completely cover a 3 ft by 6 ft area with 3 ft by 3 ft tiles?   _____

3. Can you completely cover a 3 ft by 6 ft area with 2 ft by 2 ft tiles?   _____

Problem Solving:
Try, Check, and Revise

For questions **1** and **2**, suppose you have 2×2 ft, 3×3 ft, 4×4 ft, and 5×5 ft tiles.

1. Which tiles can be used to
cover a 12×12 ft floor?   _____

2. Which tiles can be used to
cover a 9×9 ft floor?   _____

3. What size rectangular floor can be completely covered by
using only 3×3 ft tiles OR 5×5 ft tiles? Remember, you
can't cut tiles or combine the two tile sizes.

_____

4. Adult tickets cost \$6 and children's tickets cost \$4.
Mrs. LeCompte says that she paid \$30 for tickets, for both
adults and children. How many of each ticket did she buy?

_____

_____

5. Reasoning The sum of two odd numbers is 42. They are
both prime numbers, and the difference of the two numbers
is 16. What are the two numbers?

A 20 and 22

B 17 and 25

C 9 and 33

D 13 and 29

6. Explain It Marcy wants to put tiles on a bathroom floor that
measures 10 ft $\times$ 12 ft. What kind of square tiles should she
buy to tile her floor? Explain.

_____

_____

Name _____

Meanings of Fractions

What fraction of the set of shapes are squares?

Step 1: Find the denominator.

How many shapes are there in the set?

There are 5 shapes in the set.

The denominator is the total number of shapes. So, the denominator is 5.

Step 2: Find the numerator.

How many squares are there in the set?

There are 3 squares in the set.

The numerator is the number of squares in the set. So, the numerator is 3.

Step 3: Write the fraction.

Write the numerator over the denominator.

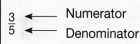
$\frac{3}{5}$ ← Numerator
← Denominator

$\frac{3}{5}$ of the set are squares.

Write the fraction that names the shaded part.

1.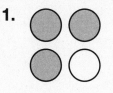

_____

2.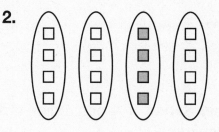

_____

3.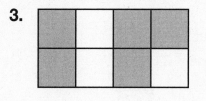

_____

4.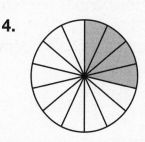

_____

5. **Number Sense** If $\frac{1}{5}$ of a region is not shaded, what part is shaded?

_____

6. Alex has 7 dimes and 3 nickels. What fraction of the coins are dimes?

_____

Meanings of Fractions

Write the fraction that names the shaded part.

1. L L L L L L _____

2. _____

In **3** and **4**, draw a model to show each fraction.

3. $\frac{4}{8}$ as part of a set

4. $\frac{5}{10}$ as part of a region

5. **Number Sense** If $\frac{5}{17}$ of a region is shaded, what part
   is not shaded? _____

6. Camp Big Trees has 3 red canoes and 4 blue canoes.
   What fraction of the canoes are red? _____

7. In a class of 24 students, 13 students are girls. What fraction
   of the students are boys?

   A $\frac{11}{13}$ B $\frac{11}{24}$ C $\frac{13}{24}$ D $\frac{24}{11}$

8. **Explain It** Trisha says that if $\frac{5}{7}$ of her pencils are yellow,
   then $\frac{2}{7}$ are not yellow. Is she correct? Explain.

   _____

   _____

   _____

Fractions and Division

Fractions can represent division. You can write a division expression as a fraction. For example:

Write a fraction for $5 \div 7$.

The first number in the division expression is the numerator of the fraction. The second number in the division expression is the denominator of the fraction.

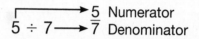

$$5 \div 7 \longrightarrow \frac{5}{7} \begin{array}{l} \text{Numerator} \\ \text{Denominator} \end{array}$$

So, $5 \div 7 = \frac{5}{7}$.

Give each answer as a fraction.

1. $3 \div 10$ **2.** $7 \div 12$ **3.** $2 \div 3$

_____   _____   _____

4. $8 \div 9$ **5.** $2 \div 5$ **6.** $1 \div 6$

_____   _____   _____

7. $6 \div 10$ **8.** $9 \div 13$ **9.** $14 \div 16$

_____   _____   _____

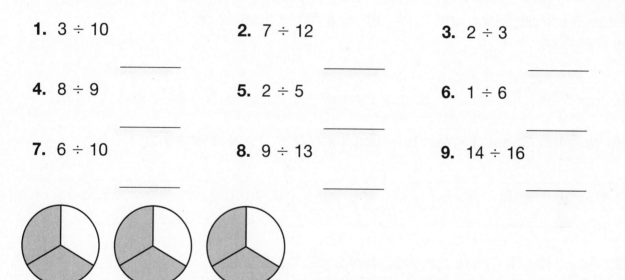

Reasoning Each of three congruent circles is divided into three equal parts. Use these three circles for **10–12**.

10. What part of a whole circle is shown by the white, or unshaded, area of one circle?

_____

11. What part of a whole circle is shown by the white, or unshaded, area of two circles?

_____

12. What part of a whole circle is shown by the white, or unshaded, area of three circles?

_____

Fractions and Division

Give each answer as a fraction. Then graph the answer on a number line.

1. $3 \div 7$

2. $4 \div 9$

3. $1 \div 5$

4. Use the number line to name the fraction.

_____

At a golf course, there are 18 holes. Of the 18 holes, 3 are par threes, 8 are par fours, and 7 are par fives. What fraction of the holes are

5. par fives? _____   **6.** par threes? _____   **7.** par fours? _____

8. Number Sense Explain how you know that $7 \div 9$ is less than 1.

_____

_____

9. After school, Chase spends 20 min reading, 30 min practicing the piano, 15 min cleaning his room, and 40 min doing his homework. Chase is busy for 105 min. What fraction of the time does he spend cleaning his room? _____

10. Venietta read 4 books in 7 weeks. How many books did she read each week?

A $\frac{6}{7}$ **B** $\frac{4}{7}$ **C** $\frac{3}{7}$ **D** $\frac{2}{7}$

11. Explain It In 5 min, Peter completed 2 math problems. Yvonne says he did $\frac{3}{5}$ of a problem each minute. Is she correct? Explain.

_____

_____

Name _____

Mixed Numbers and Improper Fractions

Write $\frac{13}{4}$ as a mixed number.

To write an improper fraction as a mixed number, draw a model.

Draw segments divided into 4 equal squares until you have
13 squares.

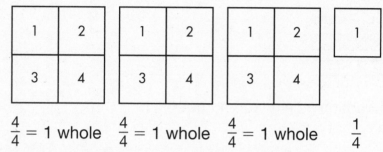

$\frac{4}{4}$ = 1 whole $\frac{4}{4}$ = 1 whole $\frac{4}{4}$ = 1 whole $\frac{1}{4}$

The 13 squares make up 3 wholes and $\frac{1}{4}$ of a whole.

$\frac{13}{4} = 3\frac{1}{4}$

Write $5\frac{1}{3}$ as an improper fraction.

To write a mixed number as an improper fraction, draw a model.

Draw equal parts to represent $5\frac{1}{3}$.

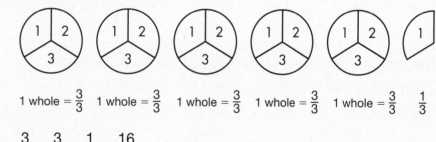

1 whole = $\frac{3}{3}$ 1 whole = $\frac{3}{3}$ 1 whole = $\frac{3}{3}$ 1 whole = $\frac{3}{3}$ 1 whole = $\frac{3}{3}$ $\frac{1}{3}$

$\frac{3}{3} + \frac{3}{3} + \frac{3}{3} + \frac{3}{3} + \frac{3}{3} + \frac{1}{3} = \frac{16}{3}$

Write each improper fraction as a mixed number.

1. $\frac{8}{3}$ _____   **2.** $\frac{10}{7}$ _____   **3.** $\frac{5}{2}$ _____

Write each mixed number as an improper fraction.

4. $1\frac{2}{5}$ _____   **5.** $4\frac{6}{7}$ _____   **6.** $2\frac{5}{8}$ _____

Mixed Numbers and Improper Fractions

Write an improper fraction and a mixed number for each model.

1.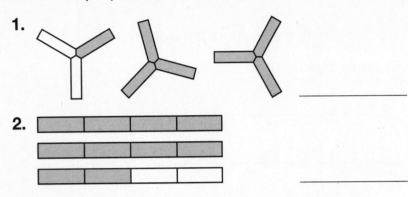

_____

2.

_____

Write each improper fraction as a mixed number.

3. $\frac{12}{7}$ _____

4. $\frac{7}{3}$ _____

5. $\frac{5}{2}$ _____

6. $\frac{9}{4}$ _____

7. $\frac{29}{13}$ _____

8. $\frac{34}{8}$ _____

Write each mixed number as an improper fraction.

9. $2\frac{4}{5}$ _____

10. $8\frac{7}{9}$ _____

11. $3\frac{6}{7}$ _____

12. $7\frac{1}{8}$ _____

13. $4\frac{3}{7}$ _____

14. $5\frac{1}{4}$ _____

15. Number Sense Jasmine has 41 lb of dog food to pour into 5 dishes. How many pounds of dog food should she pour in each dish?

A $4\frac{1}{5}$ lb
B $8\frac{1}{5}$ lb
C 10 lb
D $11\frac{1}{8}$ lb

16. Explain It Hank needs 3 quarters to play one video game each time. If he has 14 quarters, how many times can he play? Explain.

_____

_____

_____

_____

Equivalent Fractions

The fractions shown below are equivalent.
They all describe the same part of a whole.

To find equivalent fractions, multiply or divide the numerator and denominator by the same number.

$$\frac{3}{5} \times \frac{2}{2} = \frac{6}{10} \qquad \frac{6}{10} \times \frac{2}{2} = \frac{12}{20} \qquad \frac{12}{20} \div \frac{2}{2} = \frac{6}{10}$$

$$\frac{6}{10} \div \frac{2}{2} = \frac{3}{5} \qquad \frac{12}{20} \div \frac{4}{4} = \frac{3}{5}$$

Name two equivalent fractions for each fraction.

1. $\frac{1}{3}$ _____

2. $\frac{2}{12}$ _____

3. $\frac{4}{20}$ _____

4. $\frac{2}{16}$ _____

Find the missing number to make the fractions equivalent.

5. $\frac{4}{7} = \frac{8}{\square}$

6. $\frac{\square}{18} = \frac{4}{6}$

7. $\frac{3}{4} = \frac{\square}{12}$

8. $\frac{15}{\square} = \frac{3}{4}$

_____ _____ _____ _____

9. **Number Sense** Are $\frac{3}{4}$ and $\frac{12}{16}$ equivalent fractions? Explain.

_____

_____

Name _____

Equivalent Fractions

Name two equivalent fractions for each fraction.

1. $\frac{5}{15}$ **2.** $\frac{6}{36}$ **3.** $\frac{2}{12}$

_____   _____   _____

4. $\frac{4}{28}$ **5.** $\frac{3}{21}$ **6.** $\frac{2}{11}$

_____   _____   _____

Find the missing number to make the fractions equivalent.

7. $\frac{4}{13} = \frac{8}{x}$ _____   **8.** $\frac{12}{30} = \frac{n}{90}$ _____

9. $\frac{q}{54} = \frac{2}{9}$ _____   **10.** $\frac{14}{h} = \frac{7}{20}$ _____

11. Renie gave each of six people $\frac{1}{10}$ of a veggie pizza. Renie has $\frac{2}{5}$ of the pizza left. Explain how this is true.

_____

_____

12. Which fraction is equivalent to $\frac{3}{7}$?

A $\frac{3}{6}$ **B** $\frac{6}{14}$ **C** $\frac{3}{17}$ **D** $\frac{7}{7}$

13. **Explain It** Jacqueline had four $5 bills. She bought a shirt for $10. Explain what fraction of her money Jacqueline has left. Use equivalent fractions.

_____

_____

_____

Comparing and Ordering Fractions and Mixed Numbers

You can compare fractions by finding a common denominator.

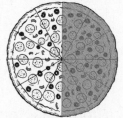 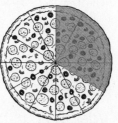

Samantha and her brother Jacob went out for pizza. Samantha ate $\frac{1}{2}$ of her pizza. Jacob ate $\frac{4}{12}$ of his pizza. Who ate more pizza?

Samantha's Pizza   Jacob's pizza

Because these fractions have different denominators, you need to find a common denominator. Then you can compare them.

Step1. Write out the multiples of the two denominators.

2: 2, 4, 6, 8, 10, ⑫
12: ⑫, 24, 36, 48, 60   Use 12 as the common denominator.

Step 2. Since you multiply 2×6 to get 12, you must multiply 1×6.
$$\frac{1}{2} = \frac{6}{12}$$

Step 3. Compare your equivalent fractions.
$$\frac{6}{12} > \frac{4}{12}$$ So, Samantha ate more pizza.

Remember: If you don't know the multiples of the denominators, you can multiply the denominators together to get a common denominator.

Compare. Write >, <, or = for each $\bigcirc$.

1. $\frac{2}{3} \bigcirc \frac{1}{6}$

2. $\frac{3}{4} \bigcirc \frac{1}{2}$

3. $\frac{5}{6} \bigcirc \frac{21}{24}$

Order the numbers from least to greatest.

4. $\frac{4}{5}, \frac{3}{5}, \frac{3}{4}$ _____, _____, _____

5. $1\frac{5}{6}, 1\frac{3}{6}, 1\frac{2}{12}$ _____, _____, _____

6. Geometry Sofia baked three kinds of pie. Sofia's Mom told her to bring $\frac{8}{16}$ of the apple pie, $\frac{4}{8}$ of the pecan pie, and $\frac{3}{6}$ of the pumpkin pie to school to share with her friends. Draw the pies and show which pie will have the greatest amount brought to school.

_____

Comparing and Ordering Fractions and Mixed Numbers

Compare the numbers. Write >, <, or = for each ◯.

1. $\frac{6}{7}$ ◯ $\frac{6}{8}$ **2.** $\frac{4}{9}$ ◯ $\frac{2}{3}$ **3.** $1\frac{1}{10}$ ◯ $1\frac{1}{12}$

4. $2\frac{4}{5}$ ◯ $2\frac{5}{6}$ **5.** $3\frac{6}{9}$ ◯ $3\frac{2}{3}$ **6.** $\frac{2}{5}$ ◯ $\frac{2}{8}$

Order the numbers from least to greatest.

7. $\frac{4}{6}, \frac{4}{8}, \frac{3}{4}, \frac{5}{8}$ _____

8. $4\frac{1}{4}, 4\frac{1}{8}, 4\frac{10}{11}, 4\frac{2}{15}$ _____

9. $1\frac{3}{7}, 1\frac{3}{4}, 1\frac{2}{4}, 1\frac{8}{13}$ _____

10. **Number Sense** How do you know that $5\frac{1}{4}$ is less than $5\frac{4}{10}$?

_____

_____

11. A mechanic uses four wrenches to fix Mrs. Aaron's car. The wrenches are different sizes: $\frac{5}{16}$ in., $\frac{1}{2}$ in., $\frac{1}{4}$ in., and $\frac{7}{16}$ in. Order the sizes of the wrenches from greatest to least.

_____

12. Which is greater than $6\frac{1}{3}$?

     A $6\frac{1}{6}$ **B** $6\frac{1}{5}$ **C** $6\frac{1}{4}$ **D** $6\frac{1}{2}$

13. **Explain It** Compare $3\frac{3}{22}$ and $3\frac{2}{33}$. Which is greater? How do you know?

_____

_____

Fractions in Simplest Form

There are two different ways to write a fraction in simplest form.

Write $\frac{20}{24}$ in simplest form.

Divide by Common Factors	**Divide by the GCF**

Divide by Common Factors

- Divide by common factors until the only common factor is 1.

- You can start by dividing by 2, since both numbers are even.

$$\frac{20 \div 2}{24 \div 2} = \frac{10}{12}$$

But both 10 and 12 are also even, so they can be divided by 2.

$$\frac{10 \div 2}{12 \div 2} = \frac{5}{6}$$

Divide by the GCF

- First find the GCF of 20 and 24.

  20: 1, 2, 4, 5, 10, 20

  24: 1, 2, 3, 4, 6, 8, 12, 24

- The GCF of 20 and 24 is 4. The common factors of 20 and 24 are 1, 2, and 4.

- Divide both numerator and denominator by 4.

$$\frac{20 \div 4}{24 \div 4} = \frac{5}{6}$$

$\frac{20}{24}$ written in simplest form is $\frac{5}{6}$.

Write each fraction in simplest form.

1. $\frac{16}{20}$ _____

2. $\frac{8}{16}$ _____

3. $\frac{5}{10}$ _____

4. $\frac{8}{32}$ _____

5. $\frac{18}{42}$ _____

6. $\frac{15}{100}$ _____

7. $\frac{18}{21}$ _____

8. $\frac{24}{40}$ _____

9. $\frac{55}{70}$ _____

10. **Number Sense** Explain how you can tell that $\frac{31}{33}$ is in simplest form.

_____

_____

_____

Fractions in Simplest Form

Write each fraction in simplest form.

1. $\frac{5}{10}$ _____

2. $\frac{6}{24}$ _____

3. $\frac{9}{27}$ _____

4. $\frac{3}{15}$ _____

5. $\frac{10}{12}$ _____

6. $\frac{9}{15}$ _____

7. $\frac{2}{18}$ _____

8. $\frac{25}{60}$ _____

9. $\frac{12}{72}$ _____

10. **Number Sense** Explain how you can tell $\frac{4}{5}$ is in simplest form.

_____

_____

_____

Write in simplest form.

11. What fraction of the problems on
the math test will be word problems?

Math Test
➡ 20 Multiple-choice problems
➡ 10 Fill in the blanks
➡ 5 Word problems

_____

12. What fraction of the problems on the math
test will be multiple-choice problems?   _____

13. Which is the simplest form of $\frac{10}{82}$?

A $\frac{1}{8}$ B $\frac{1}{22}$ C $\frac{10}{82}$ D $\frac{5}{41}$

14. **Explain It** Explain how you can find the simplest form of $\frac{100}{1,000}$.

_____

_____

_____

Tenths and Hundredths

Fractions can also be named using decimals.

8 out of 10 sections are shaded.

The fraction is $\frac{8}{10}$.

The word name is eight tenths.

The decimal is 0.8.

Remember: the first place to the right of the decimal is tenths.

Write $\frac{2}{5}$ as a decimal.

Sometimes a fraction can be rewritten as an equivalent fraction that has a denominator of 10 or 100.

$$\frac{2}{5} = \frac{2 \times 2}{5 \times 2} = \frac{4}{10}$$

$$\frac{4}{10} = 0.4$$

So, $\frac{2}{5} = 0.4$.

Write $3\frac{3}{5}$ as a decimal.

First write the whole number.

3

Write the fraction as an equivalent fraction with a denominator of 10.

Change the fraction to a decimal.

$$\frac{3}{5} = \frac{3 \times 2}{5 \times 2} = \frac{6}{10} = 0.6$$

Write the decimal next to the whole number.

3.6

So, $3\frac{3}{5} = 3.6$.

Write 0.07 as a fraction.

The word name for 0.07 is seven hundredths.

"Seven" is the numerator, and "hundredths" is the denominator.

So, $0.07 = \frac{7}{100}$.

Remember: the second place to the right of the decimal is hundredths.

Write each fraction or mixed number as a decimal.

1. $\frac{1}{5}$ _____

2. $\frac{6}{25}$ _____

3. $2\frac{3}{4}$ _____

4. $3\frac{9}{10}$ _____

Write each decimal as a fraction or mixed number.

5. 1.25 _____

6. 3.29 _____

7. 0.65 _____

8. 5.6 _____

9. Number Sense Dan says $\frac{3}{5}$ is the same as 3.5. Is he correct? Explain.

_____

_____

Tenths and Hundredths

Write a decimal and fraction for the shaded portion of each model.

1.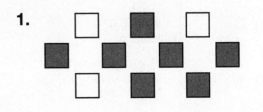

2.

_____ _____   _____ _____

Write each decimal as either a fraction or a mixed number.

3. 0.6 _____

4. 0.73 _____

5. 6.9 _____

6. 8.57 _____

Write each fraction or mixed number as a decimal.

7. $\frac{7}{10}$ _____

8. $\frac{33}{100}$ _____

9. $7\frac{2}{10}$ _____

10. $3\frac{9}{100}$ _____

Use division to change each fraction to a decimal.

11. $\frac{4}{5}$ _____

12. $\frac{12}{25}$ _____

13. $\frac{1}{50}$ _____

14. $\frac{11}{20}$ _____

15. **Think About the Process** When you convert 0.63 to a fraction, which of the following could be the first step of the process?

A Since there are 63 hundredths, multiply 0.63 and 100.

B Since there are 63 tenths, divide 0.63 by 10.

C Since there are 63 tenths, place 63 over 10.

D Since there are 63 hundredths, place 63 over 100.

Thousandths

Write 0.025 as a fraction.

Ones	Tenths	Hundredths	Thousandths
0	0	2	5

You can use a place-value chart to write a decimal as a fraction. Look at the place-value chart above. The place farthest to the right that contains a digit tells you the denominator of the fraction. In this case, it is thousandths. The number written in the place-value chart tells you the numerator of the fraction. Here, it is 25.

$0.025 = \frac{25}{1,000}$

Write $\frac{11}{1,000}$ as a decimal.

Ones	Tenths	Hundredths	Thousandths

You can also use a place-value chart to write a fraction as a decimal. The denominator tells you the last decimal place in your number. Here, it is thousandths. The numerator tells you the decimal itself. Write a 1 in the hundredths place and a 1 in the thousandths place. Fill in the other places with a 0.

$\frac{11}{1,000} = 0.011$

Write each decimal as a fraction.

1. 0.002   **2.** 0.037   **3.** 0.099

_____   _____   _____

Write each fraction as a decimal.

4. $\frac{5}{1,000}$ _____   **5.** $\frac{76}{1,000}$ _____   **6.** $\frac{40}{1,000}$ _____

7. Explain It Matt reasoned that he can write $\frac{9}{1,000}$ as 0.9. Is he correct? Explain your answer.

_____

_____

_____

Thousandths

Write each decimal as either a fraction or a mixed number.

1. 0.007 _____

2. 0.052 _____

3. 0.038 _____

4. 0.259 _____

5. 0.020 _____

6. 0.926 _____

Write each fraction as a decimal.

7. $\dfrac{73}{1,000}$ _____

8. $\dfrac{593}{1,000}$ _____

9. $\dfrac{854}{1,000}$ _____

10. $\dfrac{11}{1,000}$ _____

11. $\dfrac{5}{1,000}$ _____

12. $\dfrac{996}{1,000}$ _____

Write each of the numbers in order from least to greatest.

13. $\dfrac{5}{1,000}$, 0.003, $\dfrac{9}{1,000}$ _____

14. 0.021, 0.845, $\dfrac{99}{1,000}$ _____

15. Look at the model at the right. Write a fraction and a decimal that the model represents.

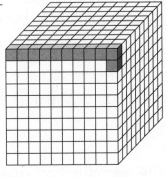

_____

16. Reasoning In Tasha's school, 0.600 of the students participate in a school sport. If there are one thousand students in Tasha's school, how many participate in a school sport?

A 6,000   **B** 600   **C** 60   **D** 6

17. Explain It Explain how knowing that $5 \div 8 = 0.625$ helps you find the decimal for $4\frac{5}{8}$.

_____

_____

Name _____

Fractions and Decimals on the Number Line

Show 0.8, $\frac{6}{20}$, and 0.519 on the same number line.

```
◄┼──┼──┼──◆──┼──◆┼──┼──◆──┼──┼►
  0      0.3  0.519   0.8    1
```

Step 1: Starting at 0, count 8 tenths to the right. This point is 0.8 or $\frac{8}{10}$.

Step 2: Change $\frac{6}{20}$ to a decimal. $\frac{6}{20}$ can be thought of as $6 \div 20$. $6 \div 20 = 0.3$

Starting at 0, count 3 tenths to the right. This point is $\frac{6}{20}$ or 0.3.

Step 3: Estimate the location of 0.519.

You know that 0.5 is the same as 0.500. You also know that 0.6 is the same as 0.600. So, 0.519 is between 0.5 and 0.6.

You know that $0.519 < 0.550$. So, 0.519 is between 0.500 and 0.550 and closer to 0.500 than to 0.550.

Show each set of numbers on the same number line.

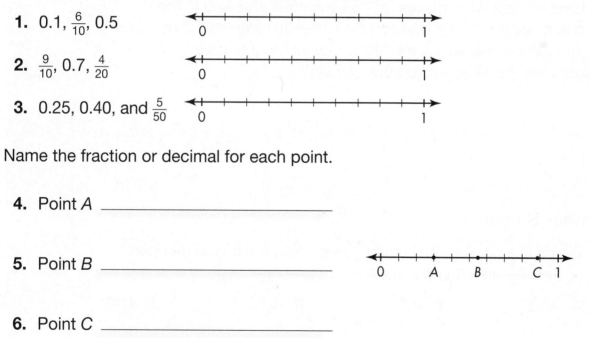

1. 0.1, $\frac{6}{10}$, 0.5

2. $\frac{9}{10}$, 0.7, $\frac{4}{20}$

3. 0.25, 0.40, and $\frac{5}{50}$

Name the fraction or decimal for each point.

4. Point *A* _____

5. Point *B* _____

6. Point *C* _____

Fractions and Decimals on the Number Line

Show the set of numbers on the same number line. Then order the numbers from least to greatest.

1. 0.75, $\frac{8}{10}$, 0.2, $\frac{2}{5}$ _____

Write a fraction or mixed number in simplest form and a decimal that name each point.

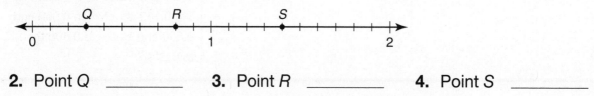

2. Point Q _____

3. Point R _____

4. Point S _____

5. Uma recorded the distances that volunteers walked in the charity event. Grace walked $1\frac{3}{5}$ mi, Wendell walked 1.3 mi, and Simon walked $1\frac{1}{10}$ mi. Show these amounts on a number line. Who walked the farthest?

_____

Number Sense

6. Which is a decimal that could go between the mixed numbers $4\frac{3}{5}$ and $4\frac{9}{10}$ on a number line?

A 4.45   **B** 4.5   **C** 4.75   **D** 4.92

7. Explain It Explain how you know that 5.5 is to the right of $5\frac{1}{4}$ on the number line.

_____

_____

Name _____

Problem Solving: Writing to Explain

An environmental scientist is studying an old apple orchard. The orchard is shown on the right. Some of the trees are infected with mold. Other trees are infested with beetles. Some trees are normal.

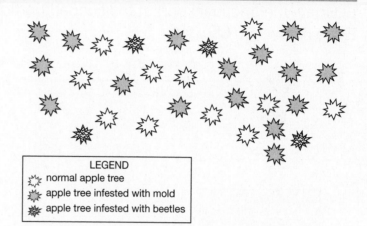

LEGEND
- normal apple tree
- apple tree infested with mold
- apple tree infested with beetles

The scientist knows that pictures and symbols can be used to write a good math explanation. So she decides to organize her findings in the chart on the right.

Use this chart to estimate the fractional part of the orchard that is infected with mold, using a benchmark fraction that is close to the actual amount.

A little more than half the grid is covered by trees that are infected with mold.

Use this chart to estimate the fractional part of the orchard that is infested with beetles. Explain how you decided.

_____

_____

_____

Problem Solving:
Writing to Explain

Estimate the fractional part of the shaded portions below.
Explain how you decided.

1. 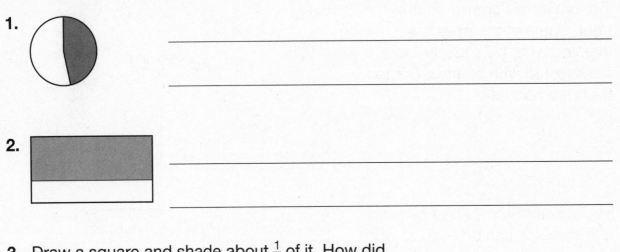 _____

_____

2. _____

_____

3. Draw a square and shade about $\frac{1}{8}$ of it. How did
you decide how much to shade?

_____

4. Draw two rectangles that are different sizes. Shade about $\frac{1}{2}$ of
each. Are the shaded parts the same amount? Explain.

_____

_____

_____

5. **Writing to Explain** Look at a picture of the American flag.
Approximately what part of the flag is blue? Explain.

_____

_____

Name _____

Adding and Subtracting Fractions with Like Denominators

Aisha cut her birthday cake into 10 slices. She and her friends ate 6 slices. Her parents ate 2 slices. What fraction of cake was eaten?

$\frac{6}{10}$ = amount of cake Aisha and her friends ate.

$\frac{2}{10}$ = amount of cake Aisha's parents ate.

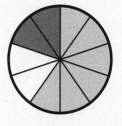

When two fractions have the same denominator, their sum or difference will also have the same denominator.

Step 1. Add the numerators.   **Step 2.** Write the sum over the denominator.

$$6 + 2 = 8$$ $$\frac{8}{10}$$

Step 3. Simplify the fraction if possible. $\frac{8}{10} = \frac{4}{5}$ So, $\frac{4}{5}$ of the cake was eaten.

You can do the same when subtracting fractions with like denominators.

How much more cake did Aisha and her friends eat than Aisha's parents?

$$\frac{6}{10} - \frac{2}{10} =$$

Step 1. Subtract the numerators.   **Step 2.** Place the difference over the denominator and simplify if possible.

$$6 - 2 = 4$$ $$\frac{4}{10} = \frac{2}{5}$$

Find the sum or difference. Simplify your answer.

1. $\frac{3}{8}$ **2.** $\frac{11}{12}$ **3.** $\frac{9}{10}$ **4.** $\frac{7}{9}$

$+\frac{3}{8}$ $-\frac{5}{12}$ $+\frac{4}{10}$ $-\frac{2}{9}$

5. Joachim has 15 medals he won at swim meets. Of the medals, 6 are first place, 4 are second place, 2 are third place, and 3 are fourth place. What fraction of Joachim's medals are first or second place?

_____

6. **Algebra** Mr. Lucero's cornbread recipe calls for 3 cups of cornmeal. He put in $1\frac{2}{3}$ cups from one open bag and $\frac{2}{3}$ cup from another open bag. How many cups of cornmeal does Mr. Lucero need to add when he opens a third bag?   _____

Adding and Subtracting Fractions with Like Denominators

Add or subtract. Simplify if possible.

1. $\dfrac{10}{12}$
  $+\dfrac{8}{12}$

2. $\dfrac{8}{9}$
  $-\dfrac{5}{9}$

3. $\dfrac{7}{10}$
  $+\dfrac{2}{10}$

4. $\dfrac{2}{3}$
  $-\dfrac{1}{3}$

5. $\dfrac{6}{8} + \dfrac{5}{8} + \dfrac{3}{8} =$ _____

6. $\dfrac{8}{10} - \dfrac{3}{10} =$ _____

7. $\dfrac{1}{4} + \dfrac{2}{4} + \dfrac{3}{4} =$ _____

8. $\dfrac{9}{11} - \dfrac{1}{11} =$ _____

9. $\dfrac{2}{5} + \dfrac{2}{5} + \dfrac{3}{5} =$ _____

10. $\dfrac{7}{8} - \dfrac{3}{8} =$ _____

11. What fraction could you add to $\dfrac{4}{7}$ to get a sum greater than 1?

_____

12. **Reasoning** Write three fractions, using 10 as the denominator, whose sum is 1.

_____

13. Which of the following represents the difference between two equal fractions?

A 1   **B** $\dfrac{1}{2}$ **C** $\dfrac{1}{4}$ **D** 0

14. **Explain It** In one night, George reads 3 chapters of a book with 27 chapters. After the second night, he has read a total of $\dfrac{8}{27}$ of the book. Explain how you would determine the number of chapters George read the second night. Solve the problem.

_____

_____

Common Multiples and LCM

Find the least common multiple (LCM) of 4 and 6.

One way: Show the multiples of 4 and 6.

4	6	
XXXX	XXXXXX	Are there the same number of X's in each column? Since the 1st column has fewer, add another set of 4 X's.

4	6	
XXXX	XXXXXX	Are there the same number of X's in each column? Since the 2nd column has fewer, add another set of 6 X's.
XXXX		

4	6	
XXXX	XXXXXX	Are there the same number of X's in each column? Since the 1st column has fewer, add another set of 4 X's.
XXXX	XXXXXX	

4	6	
XXXX	XXXXXX	Are there the same number of X's in each column? Yes. Since the columns are equal, the number of X's is the LCM. The LCM = 12.
XXXX	XXXXXX	
XXXX		

Another way: List the multiples of 4 and 6.

4: 4, 8, ⑫, 16, 20, ㉔, ...

6: 6, ⑫, 18, ㉔, 30, 36, ...

12 and 24 are common multiples.
The least common multiple is 12.

Find the least common multiple of each number pair.

1. 2 and 3 _____ **2.** 6 and 9 _____ **3.** 5 and 6 _____ **4.** 8 and 3 _____

5. Reasonableness Can the LCM of 9 and 17 be less than 17? Explain.

_____

_____

_____

_____

Common Multiples
and LCM

Find the LCM of each pair of numbers.

1. 3 and 6 _____   **2.** 7 and 10 _____

3. 8 and 12 _____   **4.** 2 and 5 _____

5. 4 and 6 _____   **6.** 3 and 4 _____

7. 5 and 8 _____   **8.** 2 and 9 _____

9. 6 and 7 _____   **10.** 4 and 7 _____

11. 5 and 20 _____   **12.** 6 and 12 _____

13. Rosario is buying pens for school. Blue pens are sold in
packages of 6. Black pens are sold in packages of 3, and
green pens are sold in packages of 2. What is the least
number of pens she can buy to have equal numbers of
pens in each color?

_____

14. Jason's birthday party punch calls for equal amounts of
pineapple juice and orange juice. Pineapple juice comes in
6-oz cans and orange juice comes in 10-oz cans. What is the
least amount he can mix of each kind of juice without having
any left over?

_____

15. **Reasonableness** Dawn ordered 4 pizzas each costing
between 8 and 12 dollars. What is a reasonable total cost
of all 4 pizzas?

A less than $24 **B** between $12 and $24 **C** between $32 and $48 **D** about $70

16. **Explain It** Why is 35 the LCM of 7 and 5?

_____

_____

Name _____

Adding Fractions with Unlike Denominators

Danisha ate $\frac{2}{3}$ cup of yogurt at breakfast. She ate $\frac{1}{4}$ cup of yogurt at lunch. How much yogurt did she eat today?

You can add fractions with unlike denominators.

Step 1. Find the least common denominator of the two fractions.	**Step 2.** Once you have equivalent fractions with the same denominator, add the numerators.	**Step 3.** Place the sum over the common denominator and simplify your fraction if possible.
multiples of 3: 3, 6, 9, ⑫, 15 $\quad \frac{8}{12}$ multiples of 4: 4, 8, ⑫, 16, 20 $\quad \frac{3}{12}$	$8 + 3 = 11$	Danisha ate $\frac{11}{12}$ cup of yogurt today.

For questions **1–5**, find the sum. Simplify if possible.

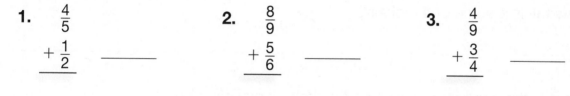

1. $\begin{array}{r} \frac{4}{5} \\ + \frac{1}{2} \\ \hline \end{array}$ _____

2. $\begin{array}{r} \frac{8}{9} \\ + \frac{5}{6} \\ \hline \end{array}$ _____

3. $\begin{array}{r} \frac{4}{9} \\ + \frac{3}{4} \\ \hline \end{array}$ _____

4. $\frac{1}{2} + \frac{1}{6} + \frac{3}{4} =$ _____

5. $\frac{2}{3} + \frac{1}{9} + \frac{5}{6} =$ _____

6. Kevin and some friends ordered several pizzas and cut them into different numbers of slices. Kevin ate $\frac{1}{6}$ of one pizza, $\frac{1}{4}$ of another, $\frac{5}{12}$ of another, and $\frac{1}{3}$ of another. Did Kevin eat the equivalent of a whole pizza? _____

7. Cathy spent $\frac{3}{10}$ of an hour on her math homework, $\frac{2}{5}$ of an hour on her science homework, and $\frac{3}{4}$ of an hour on her reading homework. How long did Cathy work on homework? _____

Name _____

Adding Fractions with Unlike Denominators

Find each sum. Simplify if necessary.

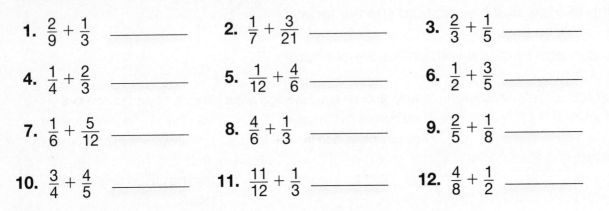

1. $\frac{2}{9} + \frac{1}{3}$ _____

2. $\frac{1}{7} + \frac{3}{21}$ _____

3. $\frac{2}{3} + \frac{1}{5}$ _____

4. $\frac{1}{4} + \frac{2}{3}$ _____

5. $\frac{1}{12} + \frac{4}{6}$ _____

6. $\frac{1}{2} + \frac{3}{5}$ _____

7. $\frac{1}{6} + \frac{5}{12}$ _____

8. $\frac{4}{6} + \frac{1}{3}$ _____

9. $\frac{2}{5} + \frac{1}{8}$ _____

10. $\frac{3}{4} + \frac{4}{5}$ _____

11. $\frac{11}{12} + \frac{1}{3}$ _____

12. $\frac{4}{8} + \frac{1}{2}$ _____

Jeremy collected nickels for one week. He is making stacks of his nickels to determine how many he has. The thickness of one nickel is $\frac{1}{4}$ in.

13. How tall is a stack of 4 nickels?

_____

14. What is the combined height of 3 nickels, 2 nickels, and 1 nickel?

_____

15. **Number Sense** Which fraction is greatest?

A $\frac{5}{6}$ B $\frac{7}{9}$ C $\frac{2}{3}$ D $\frac{9}{12}$

16. **Explain It** Which equivalent fraction would you have to use in order to add $\frac{3}{5}$ to $\frac{21}{25}$?

_____

Name _____

Subtracting Fractions with Unlike Denominators

You can subtract fractions with unlike denominators by using the least common multiple (LCM) and the least common denominator (LCD).

Beth wants to exercise for $\frac{4}{5}$ hour. So far she has exercised for $\frac{2}{3}$ hour. What fraction of an hour does she have left to go?

Step 1. Find the LCM of 5 and 3.

$\frac{12}{15}$ → $\frac{2}{15}$ → $\frac{10}{15}$ →

multiples of 5: 5, 10, (15,) 20

multiples of 3: 3, 6, 9, 12, (15)

Since 15 is the LCM, it is also your LCD.

Step 2. Using your LCD, write the equivalent fractions.

$$\frac{4}{5} \xrightarrow{\times 3} \frac{12}{15} \qquad \frac{2}{3} \xrightarrow{\times 5} \frac{10}{15}$$

Step 3. Subtract the numerators. Place the difference over the LCD. Simplify if possible.

$\frac{12}{15}$ → $\frac{2}{15}$ → $\frac{10}{15}$ →

$12 - 10 = 2$ $\frac{2}{15}$ hour left

In **1** through **5**, find each difference. Simplify if possible.

1. $\begin{array}{r} \frac{3}{4} \\ -\frac{2}{5} \\ \hline \end{array}$ _____

2. $\begin{array}{r} \frac{7}{10} \\ -\frac{1}{5} \\ \hline \end{array}$ _____

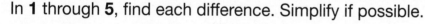

3. $\frac{7}{12} - \frac{1}{4} =$ _____

4. $\frac{5}{6} - \frac{3}{8} =$ _____

5. $\frac{23}{24} - \frac{7}{8} =$ _____

6. Natasha had $\frac{7}{8}$ gallon of paint. Her brother Ivan took $\frac{1}{4}$ gallon to paint his model boat. Natasha needs at least $\frac{1}{2}$ gallon to paint her bookshelf. Did Ivan leave her enough paint?

_____

Name _____

Subtracting Fractions with Unlike Denominators

Find the difference. Simplify if necessary.

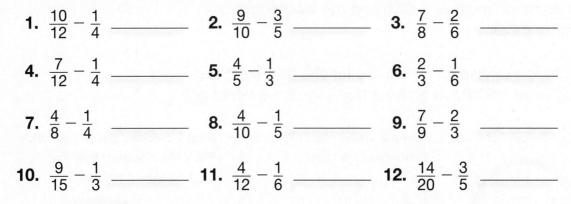

1. $\frac{10}{12} - \frac{1}{4}$ _____

2. $\frac{9}{10} - \frac{3}{5}$ _____

3. $\frac{7}{8} - \frac{2}{6}$ _____

4. $\frac{7}{12} - \frac{1}{4}$ _____

5. $\frac{4}{5} - \frac{1}{3}$ _____

6. $\frac{2}{3} - \frac{1}{6}$ _____

7. $\frac{4}{8} - \frac{1}{4}$ _____

8. $\frac{4}{10} - \frac{1}{5}$ _____

9. $\frac{7}{9} - \frac{2}{3}$ _____

10. $\frac{9}{15} - \frac{1}{3}$ _____

11. $\frac{4}{12} - \frac{1}{6}$ _____

12. $\frac{14}{20} - \frac{3}{5}$ _____

13. The pet shop owner told Jean to fill her new fish tank $\frac{3}{4}$ full with water. Jean filled it $\frac{9}{12}$ full. What fraction of the tank does Jean still need to fill?

_____

14. Paul's dad made a turkey pot pie for dinner on Wednesday. The family ate $\frac{4}{8}$ of the pie. On Thursday after school, Paul ate $\frac{2}{16}$ of the pie for a snack. What fraction of the pie remained?

_____

15. **Algebra** Gracie read 150 pages of a book she got for her birthday. The book is 227 pages long. Which equation shows how to find the amount she still needs to read to finish the story?

   A $150 - n = 227$ **B** $227 + 150 = n$ **C** $n - 150 = 227$ **D** $n + 150 = 227$

16. **Explain It** Why do fractions need to have a common denominator before you add or subtract them?

_____

_____

_____

Adding Mixed Numbers

Randy talks on the telephone for $2\frac{5}{6}$ hours, and then surfs the Internet for $3\frac{3}{4}$ hours. How many hours did he spend on the two activities?

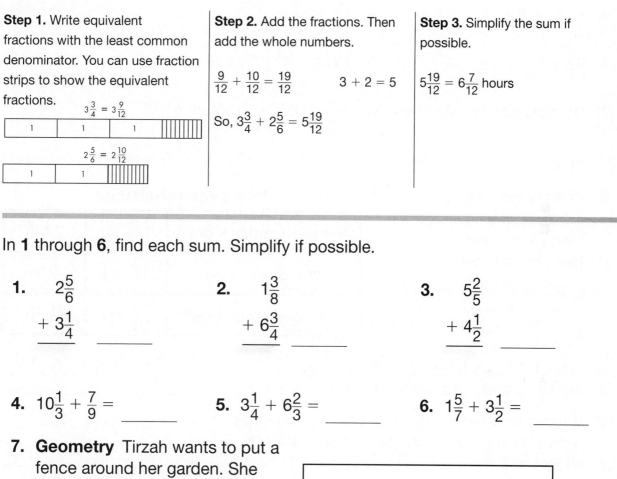

Step 1. Write equivalent fractions with the least common denominator. You can use fraction strips to show the equivalent fractions.

$3\frac{3}{4} = 3\frac{9}{12}$

$2\frac{5}{6} = 2\frac{10}{12}$

Step 2. Add the fractions. Then add the whole numbers.

$\frac{9}{12} + \frac{10}{12} = \frac{19}{12}$ $3 + 2 = 5$

So, $3\frac{3}{4} + 2\frac{5}{6} = 5\frac{19}{12}$

Step 3. Simplify the sum if possible.

$5\frac{19}{12} = 6\frac{7}{12}$ hours

In **1** through **6**, find each sum. Simplify if possible.

1. $2\frac{5}{6}$
   $+ 3\frac{1}{4}$ _____

2. $1\frac{3}{8}$
   $+ 6\frac{3}{4}$ _____

3. $5\frac{2}{5}$
   $+ 4\frac{1}{2}$ _____

4. $10\frac{1}{3} + \frac{7}{9} =$ _____

5. $3\frac{1}{4} + 6\frac{2}{3} =$ _____

6. $1\frac{5}{7} + 3\frac{1}{2} =$ _____

7. **Geometry** Tirzah wants to put a fence around her garden. She has 22 yards of fence material. Does she have enough to go all the way around the garden?

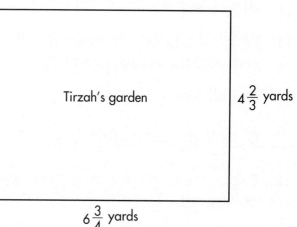

Tirzah's garden $4\frac{2}{3}$ yards

$6\frac{3}{4}$ yards

_____

_____

_____

_____

Adding Mixed Numbers

Estimate the sum first. Then add. Simplify if necessary.

1. $7\frac{2}{3} + 8\frac{5}{6}$ _____

2. $4\frac{3}{4} + 2\frac{2}{5}$ _____

3. $11\frac{9}{10} + 3\frac{1}{20}$ _____

4. $7\frac{6}{7} + 5\frac{2}{7}$ _____

5. $5\frac{8}{9} + 3\frac{1}{2}$ _____

6. $21\frac{11}{12} + 17\frac{2}{3}$ _____

7. Number Sense Write two mixed numbers with a sum of 3.

_____

8. What is the total measure of an average man's brain and heart in kilograms?

_____

Vital Organ Measures

Average woman's brain	$1\frac{3}{10}$ kg	$2\frac{4}{5}$ lb
Average man's brain	$1\frac{2}{5}$ kg	3 lb
Average human heart	$\frac{3}{10}$ kg	$\frac{7}{10}$ lb

9. What is the total weight of an average woman's brain and heart in pounds?

_____

10. What is the sum of the measures of an average man's brain and an average woman's brain in kilograms?

_____

11. Which is a good comparison of the estimated sum and the actual sum of $7\frac{7}{8} + 2\frac{11}{12}$?

A Estimated < actual

B Actual > estimated

C Actual = estimated

D Estimated > actual

12. Explain It Can the sum of two mixed numbers be equal to 2? Explain why or why not.

_____

_____

Subtracting Mixed Numbers

The Plainville Zoo has had elephants for $12\frac{2}{3}$ years. The zoo has had zebras for $5\frac{1}{2}$ years. How many years longer has the zoo had elephants?

Step 1: Write equivalent fractions with the least common denominator. You can use fraction strips.

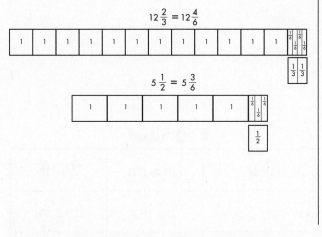

$12\frac{2}{3} = 12\frac{4}{6}$

$5\frac{1}{2} = 5\frac{3}{6}$

Step 2: Subtract the fractions. Then subtract the whole numbers. Simplify the difference if possible.

$\frac{4}{6} - \frac{3}{6} = \frac{1}{6}$ $12 - 5 = 7$

So, $12\frac{2}{3} - 5\frac{1}{2} = 7\frac{1}{6}$ years.

Tip: Sometimes you may have to rename a fraction so you can subtract.

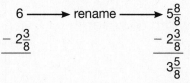

$$\begin{array}{r} 6 \\ -\ 2\frac{3}{8} \end{array} \longrightarrow \text{rename} \longrightarrow \begin{array}{r} 5\frac{8}{8} \\ -\ 2\frac{3}{8} \\ \hline 3\frac{5}{8} \end{array}$$

For questions **1–4**, find the difference. Simplify if possible.
Remember: You may have to rename a fraction in order to subtract.

1. $\begin{array}{r} 4\frac{3}{5} \\ -\ 2\frac{1}{3} \\ \hline \end{array}$ _____

2. $\begin{array}{r} 5\frac{6}{7} \\ -\ 1\frac{1}{2} \\ \hline \end{array}$ _____

3. $\begin{array}{r} 3 \\ -\ 1\frac{3}{4} \\ \hline \end{array}$ _____

4. $\begin{array}{r} 6\frac{5}{6} \\ -\ 5\frac{1}{2} \\ \hline \end{array}$ _____

Number Sense

5. Rename the number 7 so you can find the difference of $7 - 3\frac{5}{12}$.

_____

6. Robyn ran $5\frac{3}{4}$ miles last week. She ran $4\frac{1}{10}$ miles this week. How many more miles did she run last week?

_____

Name _____

Subtracting Mixed Numbers

Estimate the difference first. Then subtract. Simplify if necessary.

1. $10\frac{3}{4}$
   $-\ 7\frac{1}{4}$ _____

2. $7\frac{3}{7}$
   $-\ 2\frac{8}{21}$ _____

3. 3
   $-\ 2\frac{2}{3}$ _____

4. $17\frac{7}{8}$
   $-\ 12\frac{3}{12}$ _____

5. $9\frac{5}{9} - 6\frac{5}{6}$ _____

6. $4\frac{3}{4} - 2\frac{2}{3}$ _____

7. $6\frac{1}{4} - 3\frac{1}{3}$ _____

8. $5\frac{1}{5} - 3\frac{7}{8}$ _____

9. $8\frac{2}{7} - 7\frac{1}{3}$ _____

10. $2\frac{9}{10} - 2\frac{1}{3}$ _____

Strategy Practice The table shows the length and width of several kinds of bird eggs.

11. How much longer is the Canada goose egg than the raven egg?

_____

12. How much wider is the turtledove egg than the robin egg?

_____

Egg Sizes

Bird	Length	Width
Canada goose	$3\frac{2}{5}$ in.	$2\frac{3}{10}$ in.
Robin	$\frac{3}{4}$ in.	$\frac{3}{5}$ in.
Turtledove	$1\frac{1}{5}$ in.	$\frac{9}{10}$ in.
Raven	$1\frac{9}{10}$ in.	$1\frac{3}{10}$ in.

13. Which is the difference of $21\frac{15}{16} - 18\frac{3}{4}$?

A $2\frac{7}{16}$ B $2\frac{9}{16}$ C $3\frac{3}{16}$ D $3\frac{9}{16}$

14. **Explain It** Explain why it is necessary to rename $4\frac{1}{4}$ if you subtract $\frac{3}{4}$ from it.

_____

_____

Problem Solving:
Look for a Pattern

A store gift-wraps customers' purchases at the counter. The store hires Hector to make bows. On his first day he is given this table. Look for a pattern to help Hector complete the table.

Bow size	Ribbon Needed
small	$1\frac{1}{3}$ yards
medium	2 yards
large	$2\frac{2}{3}$
jumbo	

How to find a pattern using addition or subtraction

Step 1

Identify the pattern and write the rule.

$1\frac{1}{3} + ? = 2$

or $1\frac{1}{3} - ? = 2$

$1\frac{1}{3} + \frac{2}{3} = 2$

The rule may be add $\frac{2}{3}$.

Step 2

Compare the next term to check your rule.

$2 + \frac{2}{3} = 2\frac{2}{3}$

$2\frac{2}{3} = 2\frac{2}{3}$

Step 3

Continue the pattern.

$2\frac{2}{3} + \frac{2}{3} = 2\frac{4}{3}$

$= 2 + 1\frac{1}{3}$

$= 3\frac{1}{3}$

Hector decided to make a chart of the bow sizes. Help him by completing the chart below.

Ribbon Needed   **Bow Size**

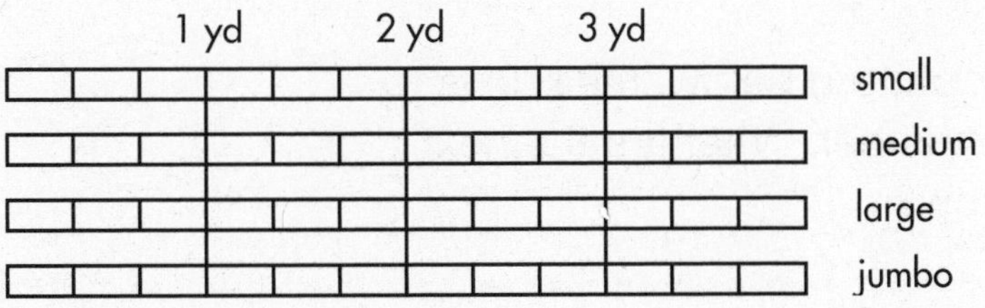

 1 yd   2 yd   3 yd

small

medium

large

jumbo

Problem Solving:
Look for a Pattern

Look for a pattern. Write the missing numbers or draw
the missing figures.

1. 3, 7, 11, _____, _____, _____, _____, 31, 35

2. $\frac{3}{4}$, $\frac{6}{4}$, $\frac{12}{4}$, _____, _____, _____, _____, $\frac{384}{4}$, $\frac{768}{4}$

3. $\frac{5}{6}$, $1\frac{1}{6}$, $1\frac{1}{2}$, $1\frac{5}{6}$, _____, _____, _____, _____, $3\frac{1}{2}$, $3\frac{5}{6}$

4. 12, 21, 30, _____, _____, _____, _____, 75, 84

5.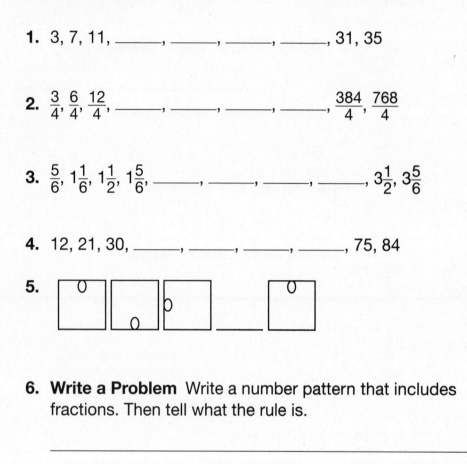

6. **Write a Problem** Write a number pattern that includes
fractions. Then tell what the rule is.

_____

_____

7. **Critical Thinking** In the number pattern below, the rule is to
add 6 and subtract 1 from each number. What are the next
three numbers in the pattern below?

3, 8, 13, _____, _____, _____ ...

A 19, 25, 31   **B** 18, 23, 28   **C** 15, 17, 19   **D** 15, 19, 26

8. **Explain It** In Exercise 5, what is the pattern? Describe the
pattern in words.

_____

_____

Multiplying Two Fractions

Musa and Karen are riding a bike path that is $\frac{4}{5}$ mile long. Karen's bike got a flat tire $\frac{3}{10}$ of the way down the path and she had to stop. How many miles did Karen ride?

You can find the product of two fractions by drawing a diagram.

Step 1. Draw a diagram using shading to represent $\frac{4}{5}$.

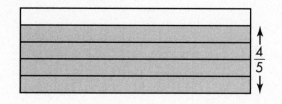

Step 2. Draw lines vertically using dots to represent $\frac{3}{10}$.

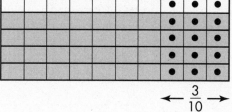

Step 3. Count the parts of the diagram that are shaded and dotted. This is the product numerator.

12

Step 4. Count the total number of parts of the diagram. This is the product denominator.

50

Step 5. Simplify if possible.

$$\frac{12}{50} = \frac{6}{25}$$

Another way to find the product:

Step 1. Multiply the numerators: $4 \times 3 = 12$.

Step 2. Multiply the denominators: $5 \times 10 = 50$.

Step 3. Simplify if possible: $\frac{12}{50} = \frac{6}{25}$.

In questions **1–6**, find the product. Simplify if possible.

1. $\frac{1}{3} \times \frac{2}{5} =$ _____

2. $\frac{5}{8} \times \frac{1}{4} =$ _____

3. $\frac{5}{6} \times \frac{3}{10} =$ _____

4. $\frac{1}{2} \times 6 =$ _____

5. $14 \times \frac{3}{7} =$ _____

6. $\frac{3}{5} \times \frac{1}{2} \times \frac{6}{7} =$ _____

7. Draw a picture Using a diagram, show $\frac{3}{7} \times \frac{1}{4}$.

Multiplying Two Fractions

Write the multiplication problem that each model represents then
solve. Put your answer in simplest form.

1.

2.

_____   _____

Find each product. Simplify if necessary.

3. $\frac{7}{8} \times \frac{4}{5} =$ _____

4. $\frac{3}{7} \times \frac{2}{3} =$ _____

5. $\frac{1}{6} \times \frac{2}{5} =$ _____

6. $\frac{2}{7} \times \frac{1}{4} =$ _____

7. $\frac{2}{9} \times \frac{1}{2} =$ _____

8. $\frac{3}{4} \times \frac{1}{3} =$ _____

9. $\frac{3}{8} \times \frac{4}{9} =$ _____

10. $\frac{1}{5} \times \frac{5}{6} =$ _____

11. $\frac{2}{3} \times \frac{5}{6} \times 14 =$ _____

12. $\frac{1}{2} \times \frac{1}{3} \times \frac{1}{4} =$ _____

13. Algebra If $\frac{4}{5} \times \blacksquare = \frac{2}{5}$, what is $\blacksquare$? _____

14. Ms. Shoemaker's classroom has 35 desks arranged in 5 by
7 rows. How many students does Ms. Shoemaker have in her
class if there are $\frac{6}{7} \times \frac{4}{5}$ desks occupied? _____

15. Which does the model represent?

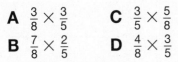

    A $\frac{3}{8} \times \frac{3}{5}$ **C** $\frac{3}{5} \times \frac{5}{8}$

    B $\frac{7}{8} \times \frac{2}{5}$ **D** $\frac{4}{8} \times \frac{3}{5}$

16. Explain It Describe a model that represents $\frac{3}{3} \times \frac{4}{4}$.

_____

_____

Dividing a Whole Number by a Fraction

The Highpoint Hockey team won 4 games this season. This is $\frac{2}{5}$ of the games they played. How many games did they play during this season?

Step 1. Draw four squares divided into fifths.

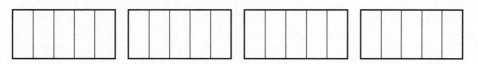

Step 2. Shade in each $\frac{2}{5}$ section of the squares.

$\frac{2}{5}$ $\frac{2}{5}$ $\frac{2}{5}$ $\frac{2}{5}$ $\frac{2}{5}$ $\frac{2}{5}$ $\frac{2}{5}$ $\frac{2}{5}$ $\frac{2}{5}$ $\frac{2}{5}$

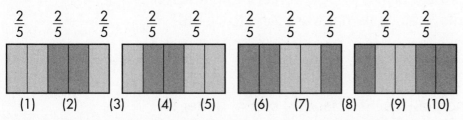

(1) (2) (3) (4) (5) (6) (7) (8) (9) (10)

Step 3. Count the total shaded sections. This is the quotient: 10 games

Another way to find the quotient:

Step 1. Write 4 as an equivalent fraction in fifths: $4 = \frac{20}{5}$.

Step 2. Divide the numerators and the denominators.
Simplify if possible: $\frac{20}{5} \div \frac{2}{5} = \frac{10}{1} = 10$.

For questions **1–3**, find the quotient.

1. $6 \div \frac{1}{3} =$ _____

2. $4 \div \frac{2}{7} =$ _____

3. $10 \div \frac{5}{8} =$ _____

4. The movie theater has 21 cups of popcorn. Each container they sell holds $\frac{3}{4}$ cup of popcorn. How many containers can the theater sell before they need to get more popcorn?

_____

Dividing a Whole Number by a Fraction

Find the quotient. You can draw pictures to help.

1. $8 \div \frac{2}{8}$ _____

2. $40 \div \frac{1}{5}$ _____

3. $8 \div \frac{8}{12}$ _____

4. $14 \div \frac{5}{6}$ _____

5. $12 \div \frac{1}{3}$ _____

6. $44 \div \frac{2}{4}$ _____

7. $66 \div \frac{5}{6}$ _____

8. $24 \div \frac{1}{3}$ _____

9. $9 \div \frac{2}{6}$ _____

10. $15 \div \frac{3}{4}$ _____

11. $5 \div \frac{1}{5}$ _____

12. $14 \div \frac{2}{7}$ _____

13. A sixth of the vegetable plants in a garden are tomatoes. If there are 192 plants in all, how many are tomato plants?

_____

14. Christina is making cookies. She needs $\frac{3}{4}$ cup of butter for each batch. How many complete batches can she make if she has 4 cups of butter?

_____

15. Strategy Practice John is traveling 30 miles on his bicycle. If he wants to ride $\frac{1}{5}$ of the way before stopping for water, how many miles will he need to ride before stopping?

A 5   **B** $8\frac{3}{4}$ **C** 6   **D** 15

16. Explain It When you divide a whole number by a fraction with a numerator of 1, explain how you can find the quotient.

_____

Dividing Two Fractions

You can divide two fractions using reciprocals.

You create a reciprocal when you flip a fraction upside down. The numerator becomes the denominator and the denominator becomes the numerator.

The reciprocal of $\frac{2}{3}$ is $\frac{3}{2}$.

Dividing by a fraction is the same as multiplying by the reciprocal.

Tamika had $\frac{7}{8}$ lb of cheese. She divided it into bags that each hold $\frac{2}{3}$ lb. How many bags did she have?

$$\frac{7}{8} \div \frac{2}{3} = \frac{7}{8} \times \frac{3}{2}$$

Solve for the product and simplify if possible.

$$\frac{7}{8} \times \frac{3}{2} = \frac{21}{16} = 1\frac{5}{16}$$

For questions 1–4, find the reciprocal.

1. $\frac{3}{8}$ _____

2. 6 _____

3. $\frac{2}{7}$ _____

4. $\frac{4}{11}$ _____

For questions 5–10, find the quotient. Simplify if possible.

5. $\frac{1}{4} \div \frac{3}{16} =$ _____

6. $\frac{2}{3} \div \frac{3}{5} =$ _____

7. $\frac{5}{6} \div \frac{1}{8} =$ _____

8. $\frac{9}{11} \div \frac{2}{5} =$ _____

9. $\frac{3}{7} \div \frac{1}{8} =$ _____

10. $\frac{7}{12} \div \frac{2}{9} =$ _____

11. Kyle had $\frac{5}{7}$ lb of birdseed. Each bird feeder holds $\frac{1}{5}$ lb of seed. Can Kyle fill 5 bird feeders?

_____

Name _____

Dividing Two Fractions

Write the reciprocal of each fraction or number.

1. $\frac{12}{13}$ _____   **2.** 32 _____   **3.** $\frac{3}{4}$ _____

Find each quotient. Simplify if possible.

4. $\frac{2}{3} \div \frac{4}{5}$ _____   **5.** $10 \div \frac{3}{5}$ _____   **6.** $12 \div \frac{2}{3}$ _____

7. $\frac{4}{8} \div \frac{1}{3}$ _____   **8.** $9 \div \frac{1}{2}$ _____   **9.** $\frac{3}{8} \div \frac{2}{3}$ _____

10. $8 \div \frac{3}{5}$ _____   **11.** $\left(\frac{1}{2} + \frac{2}{3}\right) \div 3$ _____   **12.** $\left(3 + \frac{2}{6}\right) \div 4$ _____

13. The price of a bowling ticket on Tuesday night is half the normal price of $2.75. How much will 4 tickets cost on Tuesday night?

_____

14. **Reasoning** Will $5 \div \frac{2}{7}$ have a whole number answer? Explain.

_____

_____

15. Gerald wants to buy paint for his room. Each can of paint is on sale for a third off the normal price of $12. What is the sale price of a can of paint?

A $6   **B** $4   **C** $10   **D** $8

16. **Explain It** How do you find the answer to $8 \div \frac{3}{4}$?

_____

_____

Problem Solving:
Missing or Extra Information

Missing information is information that was not given in the problem, but which you need to solve the problem.

Mrs. Chang is driving from Acton to Ayer. If she drives at 50 miles per hour, can she get there in 2 hours?

> To find the driving time required, you would divide the total distance by the speed. But the total distance is not given; without it, you cannot solve the problem.

Extra information is information given in the problem that has nothing to do with solving the question asked.

How many $\frac{3}{4}$-yd pieces can you cut from a 15-yd bolt of fabric if the fabric costs $22.50 per yard?

> To solve, you would divide the total length by the length of each piece. The price of the fabric makes no difference.

In **1** and **2**, decide if each problem has extra or missing information. Solve if possible.

1. Carly bought a new pair of jeans. The jeans were on sale for $\frac{1}{2}$ off the original price. How much did Carly spend?

    _____

    _____

2. Alexis runs $2\frac{1}{2}$ mi per day. She likes to run through the park near the river. Her friend Tony runs 4 mi per day. How far does Alexis run in 5 days?

    _____

    _____

Problem Solving:
Missing or Extra Information

Decide if each problem has extra or missing information. Solve if you have enough information.

1. Jared and Cody went on a backpacking trip for 3 days. They brought 2 boxes of spaghetti. Each box weighed 16 oz. They also brought 4 cans of sauce. Each can weighed 8 oz. How many ounces did each of them carry if each carried the same amount?

_____

2. Each backpack weighed 25 lb and each tent weighed 3 lb. If there are 30 backpackers, how much did their backpacks weigh altogether?

_____

For **3–5**, use the table at the right.

3. **Strategy Practice** The backpackers hiked the Black Hawk trail on Monday. They planned to hike on Tuesday. What is the total number of trails they hiked on Monday and Tuesday?

Trail Name	Length
Hiawatha	6 mi
Pontiac	2 mi
Black Hawk	10 mi
Keokuk	7 mi

_____

4. How much longer is twice around the Black Hawk trail than twice around the Hiawatha trail?

A 10 mi **B** 8 mi **C** 7 mi **D** 6 mi

5. **Explain It** Mariah hiked the Pontiac trail 5 days in 1 week. She did not hike on Wednesday and Friday. How many miles did she hike throughout 1 week? Explain your answer.

_____

_____

Multiplying Mixed Numbers

You can find the product of two mixed numbers.

Millwood City is constructing a new highway through town. The construction crew can complete $5\frac{3}{5}$ miles of road each month. How many miles will they complete in $6\frac{1}{2}$ months?

Step 1. Round the mixed numbers to whole numbers so you can make an estimate.

$$5\frac{3}{5} \times 6\frac{1}{2}$$

$$6 \times 7 = 42$$

So, they can complete about 42 miles.

Step 2. Write the mixed numbers as improper fractions.

$$5\frac{3}{5} \times 6\frac{1}{2} = \frac{28}{5} \times \frac{13}{2}$$

Step 3. Multiply the numerators and the denominators. Simplify the product if possible. Remember to look for common factors.

$$\frac{\overset{14}{\cancel{28}}}{5} \times \frac{13}{\underset{1}{\cancel{2}}} = \frac{182}{5} = 36\frac{2}{5}$$

Step 4. Compare your product to your estimate to check for reasonableness.

$36\frac{2}{5}$ is close to 42, so this answer is reasonable.

The construction crew will complete $36\frac{2}{5}$ miles of highway in $6\frac{1}{2}$ months.

For questions **1–6**, estimate a product. Then solve for each actual product. Simplify if possible.

1. $1\frac{3}{4} \times 2\frac{1}{2} =$ _____

2. $1\frac{1}{5} \times 1\frac{2}{3} =$ _____

3. $2 \times 2\frac{1}{4} =$ _____

4. $1\frac{2}{5} \times 2\frac{1}{4} =$ _____

5. $2\frac{1}{2} \times 10 =$ _____

6. $1\frac{2}{3} \times \frac{1}{5} =$ _____

7. Using the example above, the new highway will be a total of 54 miles long. Will the highway be finished in 8 months?

_____

8. Reasonableness Sayed gave an answer of $6\frac{6}{7}$ for the problem $4\frac{2}{7} \times 1\frac{3}{5}$. Using estimates, is this a reasonable answer?

_____

Multiplying Mixed Numbers

Estimate the product. Then complete the multiplication.

1. $5\frac{4}{5} \times 7 = \dfrac{\boxed{}}{5} \times \dfrac{7}{1} = \boxed{}$

2. $3\frac{2}{3} \times 5\frac{1}{7} = \dfrac{\boxed{}}{3} \times \dfrac{\boxed{}}{7} = \boxed{}$

Estimate. Then find each product. Simplify.

3. $4\frac{3}{5} \times \frac{2}{3}$ _____

4. $6 \times 2\frac{2}{7}$ _____

5. $7\frac{4}{5} \times 2\frac{1}{3}$ _____

6. $3\frac{3}{4} \times 2\frac{4}{5}$ _____

7. $2\frac{1}{5} \times \frac{7}{8}$ _____

8. $6\frac{1}{3} \times 1\frac{5}{6}$ _____

9. $1\frac{4}{5} \times 1\frac{1}{3} \times 1\frac{3}{4}$ _____

10. $\frac{3}{4} \times 2\frac{2}{3} \times 5\frac{1}{5}$ _____

11. **Algebra** Write a mixed number for p so that $3\frac{1}{4} \times p$ is more than $3\frac{1}{4}$.

_____

12. A model house is built on a base that measures $9\frac{1}{4}$ in. wide and $8\frac{4}{5}$ in. long. What is the total area of the model house's base?

_____

13. Which is $1\frac{3}{4}$ of $150\frac{1}{2}$?

   A 263 **B** $263\frac{1}{8}$ **C** $263\frac{3}{8}$ **D** $264\frac{3}{8}$

14. **Explain It** Megan's dog Sparky eats $4\frac{1}{4}$ c of food each day. Explain how Megan can determine how much food to give Sparky if she needs to feed him only $\frac{2}{3}$ as much. Solve the problem.

_____

_____

Dividing Mixed Numbers

You can find the quotient of two mixed numbers.

Blaine has $9\frac{3}{4}$ cups of strawberries. Each batch of strawberry jam uses $3\frac{1}{2}$ cups. How many batches of jam can Blaine make?

Step 1. Change the mixed numbers into improper fractions.

$$9\frac{3}{4} = \frac{39}{4} \quad 3\frac{1}{2} = \frac{7}{2} \quad \text{So, } 9\frac{3}{4} \div 3\frac{1}{2} = \frac{39}{4} \div \frac{7}{2}.$$

Step 2. Flip the divisor upside down to get the reciprocal.

The reciprocal of $\frac{7}{2}$ is $\frac{2}{7}$.

Step 3. Remember that dividing by a fraction is the same as multiplying by the fraction's reciprocal.

$$\text{So, } \frac{39}{4} \div \frac{7}{2} = \frac{39}{4} \times \frac{2}{7}$$

Step 4. Look for common factors and multiply. Simplify the product if possible.

$$\frac{39}{\overset{}{\underset{2}{4}}} \times \frac{\overset{1}{2}}{7} = \frac{39}{14} = 2\frac{11}{14} \text{ batches of jam}$$

For questions 1–6, find each quotient. Simplify if possible.

1. $2\frac{1}{2} \div 1\frac{1}{7} =$ _____

2. $5\frac{3}{5} \div 3\frac{1}{3} =$ _____

3. $8\frac{3}{4} \div 4\frac{1}{8} =$ _____

4. $7\frac{2}{3} \div 2\frac{4}{5} =$ _____

5. $6\frac{3}{8} \div 1\frac{2}{5} =$ _____

6. $4\frac{2}{9} \div 1\frac{5}{6} =$ _____

7. Larissa is painting boards for her mom's fence. Her mom gave her $6\frac{2}{3}$ gallons of paint. Each board takes $\frac{1}{5}$ gallon. Can Larissa paint all 30 boards?

_____

8. Algebra $4\frac{3}{8} \div 1\frac{2}{5} = \frac{35}{8} \times n$. Solve for n.

_____

Dividing Mixed Numbers

Find each quotient. Simplify if possible.

1. $1\frac{4}{5} \div 2\frac{1}{3}$ _____

2. $3\frac{1}{2} \div 1\frac{2}{3}$ _____

3. $3\frac{2}{3} \div 1\frac{5}{6}$ _____

4. $4\frac{2}{5} \div 3\frac{1}{3}$ _____

5. $1\frac{1}{6} \div 3$ _____

6. $4\frac{1}{5} \div 1\frac{7}{8}$ _____

7. $6\frac{1}{2} \div 7$ _____

8. $5\frac{1}{4} \div 1\frac{3}{4}$ _____

9. $2\frac{5}{8} \div 3\frac{1}{4}$ _____

10. $\frac{3}{5} \div 11$ _____

11. $3\frac{5}{6} \div 2$ _____

12. $\left(1\frac{2}{3} - \frac{1}{2}\right) \div 1\frac{2}{3}$ _____

13. How many spice racks can Marie make if she has $5\frac{2}{3}$ feet of lumber and the kind of spice rack she wants to make requires $1\frac{3}{4}$ feet of lumber?

_____

14. Roger is making and selling skateboards. He has $9\frac{1}{3}$ feet of lumber. He needs $3\frac{1}{2}$ feet to make one skateboard. How many can he make and sell?

A 2   **B** 3   **C** 5   **D** 6

15. Write a Problem Write your own word problem that involves dividing with mixed numbers.

_____

_____

_____

16. Explain It Explain how to estimate, and then find $6\frac{5}{6} \div 1\frac{1}{5}$.

_____

_____

_____

_____

Problem Solving: Draw a Picture and Write an Equation

Travis earned 3 stickers for each song he played in his piano lesson. He received a total of 24 stickers. How many songs did he play?

You can solve a problem like this by drawing a picture and writing an equation.

Step 1. Write out what you already know. Travis earned 3 stickers for each song he played. Travis had 24 stickers at the end of the lesson.

Step 2. Draw a picture to show what you know.

Travis's total stickers

Step 3. Write out what you are trying to find. How many songs did Travis play?

Step 4. Write an equation from your drawing. Since you are dividing Travis's total stickers into groups of 3 (stickers earned per song), this is a division problem.

$24 \div 3 = s$ s = number of songs Travis played

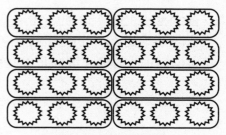

groups of 3 stickers Travis earned per song

Step 5. Solve the equation.

$24 \div 3 = 8$ $s = 8$
So, Travis played 8 songs during his lesson.

Step 6. Check your answer by working backward.
$8 \times 3 = 24$: your answer is correct.

Draw a picture, write an equation, and solve.

1. Sasha, Rudy, and Mario each have $1\frac{3}{4}$ cups of flour. Can they make a recipe for bread that needs 5 cups of flour?

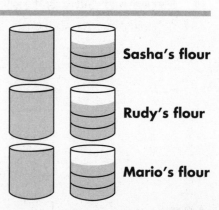

Sasha's flour

Rudy's flour

Mario's flour

_____

_____

Problem Solving: Draw a Picture and Write an Equation

Solve each problem. Draw a picture to show the main idea for each problem. Then write an equation and solve it. Write the answer in a complete sentence.

1. Bobby has 3 times as many model spaceships as his friend Sylvester does. Bobby has 21 spaceships. How many model spaceships does Sylvester have?

_____

_____

2. Dan saved $463 over the 12 weeks of summer break. He saved $297 of it during the last 4 weeks. How much did he save during the first 8 weeks?

_____

_____

3. A box of peanut-butter crackers was divided evenly among 6 children. Each child got 9 crackers. How many crackers were in the box?

   A 54   **B** 48   **C** 39   **D** 36

4. **Explain It** Why is it helpful to draw a picture when attempting to solve an equation?

_____

_____

Using Customary Units of Length

One customary unit of length is the inch. On most rulers it is divided into fractions to help you measure more precisely.

How to measure length

Measure the length of the pen to the nearest inch, nearest $\frac{1}{2}$ inch, $\frac{1}{4}$ inch, and $\frac{1}{8}$ inch.

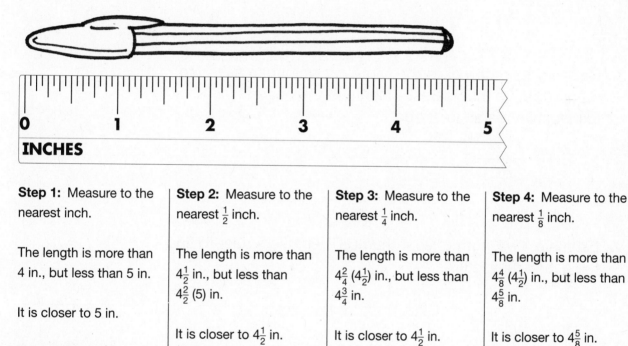

Step 1: Measure to the nearest inch.

The length is more than 4 in., but less than 5 in.

It is closer to 5 in.

The pen's length is closest to 5 in.

Step 2: Measure to the nearest $\frac{1}{2}$ inch.

The length is more than $4\frac{1}{2}$ in., but less than $4\frac{2}{2}$ (5) in.

It is closer to $4\frac{1}{2}$ in.

The pen's length is closest to $4\frac{1}{2}$ in.

Step 3: Measure to the nearest $\frac{1}{4}$ inch.

The length is more than $4\frac{2}{4}$ $(4\frac{1}{2})$ in., but less than $4\frac{3}{4}$ in.

It is closer to $4\frac{1}{2}$ in.

The pen's length is closest to $4\frac{1}{2}$ $(4\frac{2}{4})$ in.

Step 4: Measure to the nearest $\frac{1}{8}$ inch.

The length is more than $4\frac{4}{8}$ $(4\frac{1}{2})$ in., but less than $4\frac{5}{8}$ in.

It is closer to $4\frac{5}{8}$ in.

The pen's length is closest to $4\frac{5}{8}$ in.

Measure to the nearest inch, $\frac{1}{2}$ inch, $\frac{1}{4}$ inch, and $\frac{1}{8}$ inch.

1. ⬭⎯⎯

_____

Use your ruler to draw a line segment of each length.

2. $\frac{7}{8}$ inch

3. $2\frac{1}{4}$ inch

Using Customary
Units of Length

Measure each segment to the nearest inch, $\frac{1}{2}$ inch, $\frac{1}{4}$ inch, and
$\frac{1}{8}$ inch.

1. ├────────────────┤

2. ├──────────────────────┤

3. **Reasoning** Sarah gave the same answer when asked to
round $4\frac{7}{8}$ in. to the nearest $\frac{1}{2}$ inch and the nearest inch.
Explain why Sarah is correct

_____

_____

4. Estimate the length of your thumb. Then use a ruler to find
the actual measure.

_____

5. **Estimation** A real motorcycle is 18 times as large as a model
motorcycle. If the model motorcycle is $5\frac{1}{16}$ in. long, about
how long is the real motorcycle?

   A 23 in.   **B** 48 in.   **C** 90 in.   **D** 112 in.

6. **Explain It** If a line is measured as $1\frac{4}{8}$ in. long, explain how
you could simplify the measurement.

_____

_____

_____

Using Metric Units of Length

Measurements in the metric system are based on the meter.

Example A

Which metric unit of length would be most appropriate to measure the length of a bumblebee?

A bumblebee is very small, so the millimeter is the most appropriate unit of length.

Example B

Write mm, cm, m, or km to complete the following sentence.

A chair is about 1 _____ tall and a child's hand is about 8 _____ wide.

A chair is about 1 m tall, and a child's hand is about 8 cm wide.

Example C

What is the length of the branch to the nearest centimeter and to the nearest millimeter?

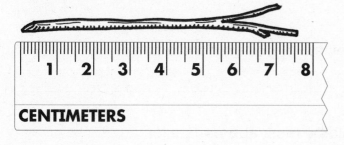

Step 1 Measure to the closest centimeter.

The length of the twig is more than 7 cm but less than 8 cm.

The twig's length is closest to 8 cm.

Step 2 Measure to the closest millimeter.

The length of the twig is more than 70 mm but less than 80 mm.

The length of the twig is more than 75 mm but less than 76 mm.

The twig's length is closest to 76 mm.

Which unit would be most appropriate for each measurement?
Write mm, cm, m, or km.

1. distance between two cities _____

2. width of a room _____

3. Measure the line segment below to the nearest centimeter and to the nearest millimeter. |————————————|

_____ ; _____

Name ______________________

Practice
13-2

Using Metric Units of Length

Measure each segment to the nearest centimeter or millimeter.

1. |———————————————| ______________

2. |——————————| ______________

Number Sense Some of the events at an upcoming track and field meet are shown at the right.

Track and Field Events

50-m dash
1,500-m dash
400-m dash
100-m dash

3. In which event or events do athletes travel more than a kilometer?

____

4. In which event or events do athletes travel less than a kilometer?

____

5. **Reasonableness** Which unit would be most appropriate for measuring the distance from Chicago to Miami?

A mm **B** cm **C** m **D** km

6. **Explain It** List one item in your classroom you would measure using centimeters and one item in the classroom you would measure using meters.

____

____

Perimeter

The perimeter is the distance around the outside of a polygon.
You can find the perimeter in two different ways.

Add the lengths of the sides:

Find the perimeter of the figure.

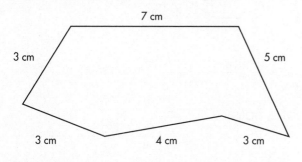

To find the perimeter, add up the sides.

3 + 3 + 7 + 5 + 3 + 4 = 25

So, the perimeter of the figure is 25 cm.

Use a formula:

Find the perimeter of the rectangle.

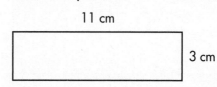

11 cm

3 cm

Perimeter = (2 × length) + (2 × width)
$P = (2 \times l) + (2 \times w)$
$P = (2 \times 11) + (2 \times 3)$
$P = 22 + 6 = 28$ cm

So, the perimeter of the rectangle is 28 cm.

Find the perimeter of each figure.

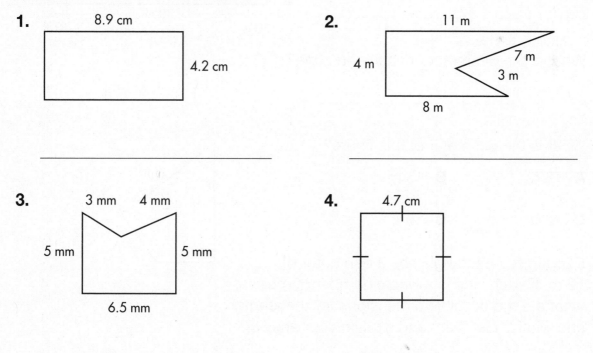

1. 8.9 cm

4.2 cm

_____

2. 11 m

4 m

7 m

3 m

8 m

_____

3. 3 mm   4 mm

5 mm   5 mm

6.5 mm

_____

4. 4.7 cm

_____

5. Number Sense The perimeter of a square is 24 in.
What is the length of each side?   _____

Perimeter

Find the perimeter of each figure.

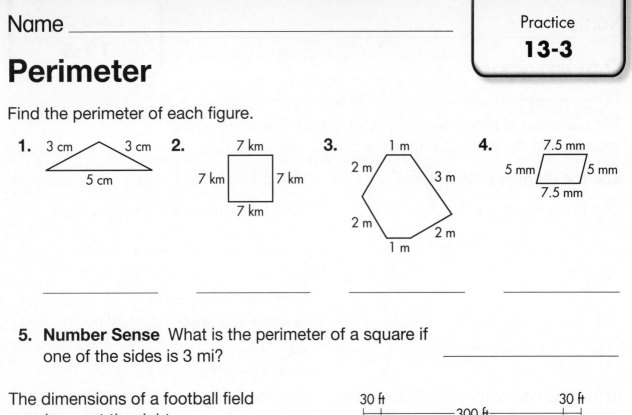

1. 3 cm   3 cm   **2.**   7 km   **3.**   1 m   **4.**   7.5 mm

       5 cm   7 km   7 km   2 m   3 m   5 mm   5 mm
                          7 km   7.5 mm
                                        2 m   2 m
                                           1 m

_____   _____   _____   _____

5. **Number Sense** What is the perimeter of a square if
    one of the sides is 3 mi?   _____

The dimensions of a football field
are shown at the right.

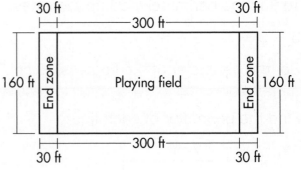

6. What is the perimeter of the entire
    football field including the end
    zones?

_____

7. What is the perimeter of each end zone?

_____

8. What is the perimeter of this figure?

    A 18 m   **B** 15 m

    C 12 ft   **D** 10 ft

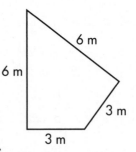

9. **Explain It** A rectangle has a perimeter of
    12 m. If each side is a whole number of meters,
    what are the possible dimensions for the length
    and width? List them and explain your answer.

_____

_____

_____

Areas of Squares and Rectangles

You can use formulas to find the areas of rectangles and squares.

Find the area of the rectangle.

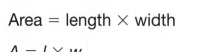

Use this formula for rectangles:

Area = length × width

$A = l \times w$

$A = 5\ m \times 4\ m$

$A = 20$ square meters $= 20\ m^2$

Find the area of the square.

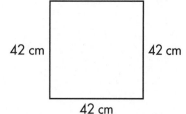

Use this formula for squares:

Area = side × side

$A = 42\ cm \times 42\ cm$

$A = 1,764$ square centimeters
$= 1,764\ cm^2$

Find the area of each figure.

1.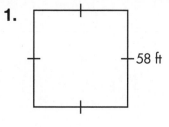

58 ft

_____

2. 5.5 in.

3.2 in.

_____

3. a square with a side of 12.4 m _____

4. a rectangle with a length of 9.7 cm
and a width of 7.3 cm _____

5. **Number Sense** If the area of a square
is 81 in^2, what is the length of one side? _____

6. What is the area of the tennis court?

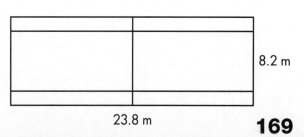

8.2 m

_____

23.8 m

Areas of Squares and Rectangles

Find the area of each figure.

1.

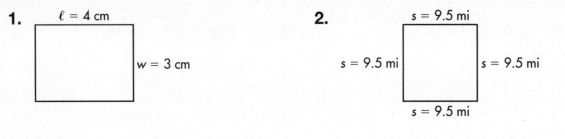

$\ell = 4$ cm

$w = 3$ cm

2.

$s = 9.5$ mi

$s = 9.5$ mi $s = 9.5$ mi

$s = 9.5$ mi

_____   _____

3. a rectangle with sides 6.5 km and 3.4 km   _____

4. a square with a side of 10.2 ft   _____

5. a rectangle with sides 9 m and 9.2 m   _____

6. Number Sense Which units would you use to measure the
area of a rectangle with $l = 1$ m and $w = 34$ cm? Explain.

_____

_____

7. Which of the following shapes has an area of 34 ft^2?

A a square with $s = 8.5$ m

B a rectangle with $l = 15$ ft, $w = 2$ ft

C a square with $s = 16$ ft

D a rectangle with $l = 17$ ft, $w = 2$ ft

8. Explain It The area of a square is 49 m^2. What is the length
of one of its sides? Explain how you solved this problem.

_____

_____

_____

Area of Parallelograms

The formula used to find the area of a parallelogram is similar to the one you used to find the area of a rectangle. Instead of using length × width, use base × height.

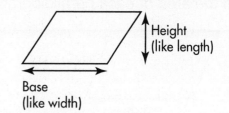

Height
(like length)

Base
(like width)

How to find the area of a parallelogram:

Find the area of the parallelogram.

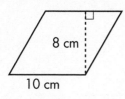

8 cm

10 cm

Area = base × height

$A = b \times h$

$A = 10 \text{ cm} \times 8 \text{ cm}$

$A = 80 \text{ cm}^2$

How to find the missing measurement of a parallelogram:

Area = 55 cm² base = 11 cm
height = ? cm

Remember, area = base × height.

$55 \text{ cm}^2 = 11 \text{ cm} \times ? \text{ cm}$

$55 \text{ cm}^2 = 11 \text{ cm} \times 5 \text{ cm}$

So, the height of the parallelogram is 5 cm.

Find the area of each parallelogram.

1.

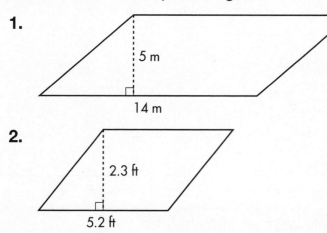

5 m

14 m

_____

2.

2.3 ft

5.2 ft

_____

Find the missing measurement for each parallelogram.

3. $A = 72 \text{ in.}^2$, $b = 9$ in, $h =$ _____

4. $A = 238 \text{ ft}^2$, $b =$ _____, $h = 14$ ft

Area of Parallelograms

Find the area of each parallelogram.

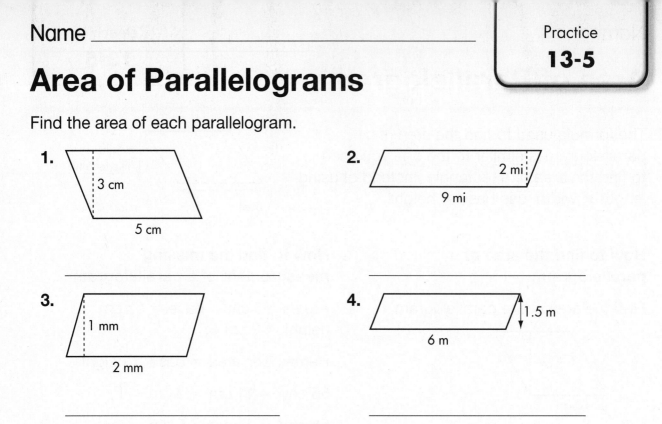

1.

3 cm

5 cm

2.

2 mi

9 mi

_____

_____

3.

1 mm

2 mm

4.

1.5 m

6 m

_____

_____

Algebra Find the missing measurement for the parallelogram.

5. $A = 34$ in^2, $b = 17$ in., $h =$ _____

6. List three sets of base and height measurements for parallelograms with areas of 40 square units.

_____

_____

7. Which is the height of the parallelogram?

A 55 m

B 55.5 m

C 5 m

D 5.5 m

$A = 44$ m^2

$h = ?$

$b = 8$ m

8. Writing in Math What are a possible base and height for a parallelogram with an area of 45 ft^2 if the base and height are a whole number of feet? Explain how you solved this problem.

_____

_____

Area of Triangles

Area of a triangle $= \frac{1}{2} \times$ base $\times$ height

How to find the area of a triangle:

4 ft

3 ft

$A = \frac{1}{2} \times b \times h$

$A = \frac{1}{2} \times 3 \text{ ft} \times 4 \text{ ft}$

$A = \frac{1}{2} \times 12 \text{ ft}^2$

$A = 6 \text{ ft}^2$

How to find the missing measurement of a triangle:

Area $= 100 \text{ cm}^2$ base $= 40$ cm
height $= ?$ cm

Remember, Area $= \frac{1}{2} \times$ base $\times$ height.

$100 \text{ cm}^2 = \frac{1}{2} \times 40 \text{ cm} \times ? \text{ cm}$

$100 \text{ cm}^2 = 20 \text{ cm} \times ? \text{ cm}$

$100 \text{ cm}^2 = 20 \text{ cm} \times 5 \text{ cm}$

So, the height of the triangle is 5 cm.

Find the area of each triangle.

1.   **2.**   **3.**

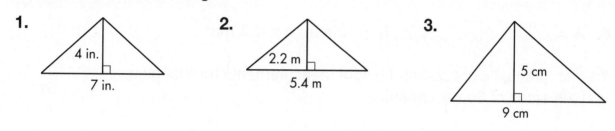

4 in.

7 in.

2.2 m

5.4 m

5 cm

9 cm

_____   _____   _____

Find the missing measurement for each triangle.

4. $A = 16 \text{ in}^2$, $b = 8$ in., $h =$ _____

5. $A = 20 \text{ m}^2$, $b =$ _____, $h = 4$ m

6. $A =$ _____, $b = 6.4$ ft, $h = 7.6$ ft

7. $A = 14 \text{ cm}^2$, $b = 2$ cm, $h =$ _____

Area of Triangles

Find the area of each triangle.

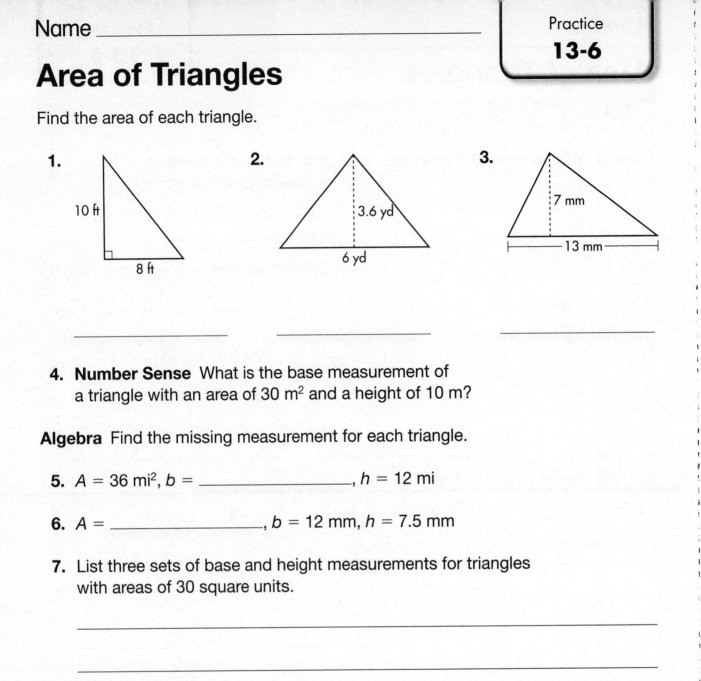

1.

10 ft

8 ft

_____

2.

3.6 yd

6 yd

_____

3.

7 mm

13 mm

_____

4. Number Sense What is the base measurement of
a triangle with an area of 30 m² and a height of 10 m?

Algebra Find the missing measurement for each triangle.

5. $A = 36$ mi², $b =$ _____, $h = 12$ mi

6. $A =$ _____, $b = 12$ mm, $h = 7.5$ mm

7. List three sets of base and height measurements for triangles
with areas of 30 square units.

_____

_____

8. Which is the height of the triangle?

    A 4.5 ft   **B** 6 ft

    C 8 ft   **D** 9 ft

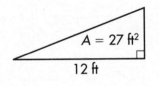

$A = 27$ ft²

12 ft

9. Explain It Can you find the base and height measurements
for a triangle if you know that the area is 22 square units?
Explain why or why not.

_____

_____

Problem Solving: Draw a Picture and Make an Organized List

In a garden, a landscaper has to make a small patio using twelve 1-foot-square tiles. The patio must have the smallest possible perimeter. What should be the dimensions of the patio?

Draw a picture.

1. Construct pictures of rectangles using the twelve tiles.

2. List the perimeter of each figure in a table.

3. Count tile edges or calculate to find the perimeter.

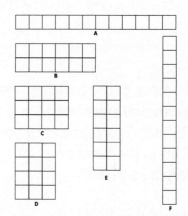

Solve.

Both the 3 × 4-tile and the 4 × 3-tile patios have the same perimeter, 14 feet. This value is the smallest perimeter in the table. The landscaper can use either design.

Rectangle	Length in feet	Width in feet	Perimeter in feet
A	12	1	26
B	6	2	16
C	4	3	14
D	3	4	14
E	2	6	16
F	1	12	26

The landscaper must build another patio with the smallest perimeter possible using nine 1-foot-square tiles. What should be the dimensions?

_____

Problem Solving:
Draw a Picture and Make an
Organized List

Draw a picture and make a list to solve.

1. Erica painted a picture of her dog. The picture has an area of 3,600 cm^2 and is square. She has placed the picture in a frame that is 5 cm wide. What is the perimeter of the picture frame?

_____

2. The new playground at Middledale School will be enclosed by a fence. The playground will be rectangular and will have an area of 225 yd^2. The number of yards on each side will be a whole number. What is the least amount of fencing that could be required to enclose the playground?

_____

3. Reasoning Evan is thinking of a 3-digit odd number that uses the digit 7 twice. The digit in the tens place is less than one. What is the number?

  A 770   **B** 707   **C** 777   **D** 717

4. Explain It Explain how you solved Exercise 3.

_____

_____

_____

Solids

The solid's vertices are: *A, B, C, D, E, F, G,* and *H.*

The solid's edges are: $\overline{AC}$, $\overline{AB}$, $\overline{CD}$, $\overline{DB}$, $\overline{AH}$, $\overline{BG}$, $\overline{HG}$, $\overline{HE}$, $\overline{GF}$, $\overline{EF}$, $\overline{CE}$, and $\overline{DF}$.

The solid's faces are: *ACEH, BDFG, ABCD, EFGH, CDEF,* and *ABHG.*

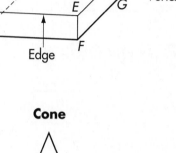

Here are some common solid figures:

Cube **Rectangular Prism** **Cylinder** **Cone**

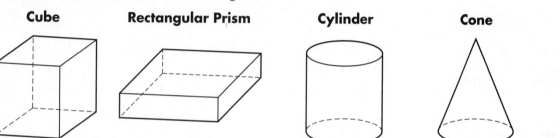

Use the solid at the right for **1–3.**

1. Name the edges.

_____

_____

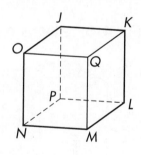

2. Name the faces.

_____

3. Name the vertices.

_____

What solid figure does each object resemble?

4.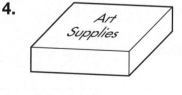

5.

6.

_____   _____   _____

Solids

For **1–3**, use the solid at the right.

1. Name the vertices.

    _____

2. Name the faces.

    _____

    _____

3. Name the edges.

    _____

    _____

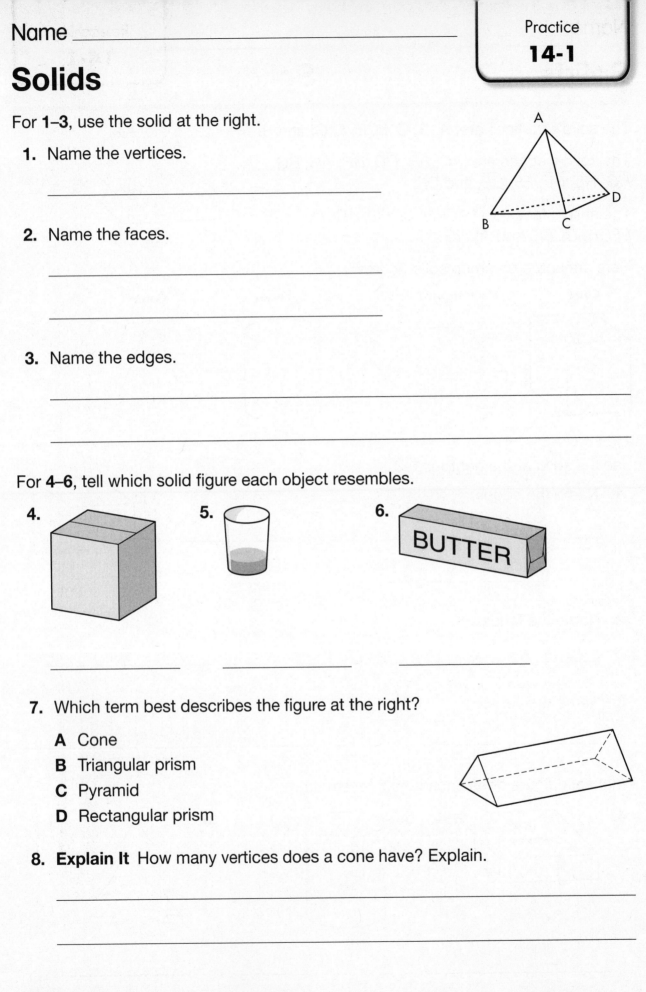

For **4–6**, tell which solid figure each object resembles.

4.

5.

6. BUTTER

    _____   _____   _____

7. Which term best describes the figure at the right?

    A Cone

    B Triangular prism

    C Pyramid

    D Rectangular prism

8. **Explain It** How many vertices does a cone have? Explain.

    _____

    _____

Relating Shapes and Solids

If each net on the left were folded, it would form the figure on the right.

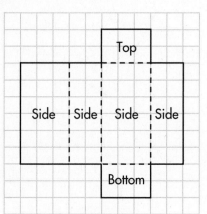

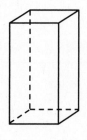

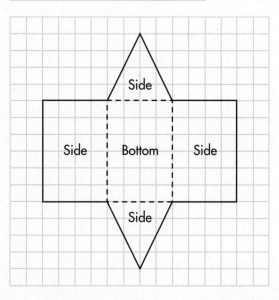

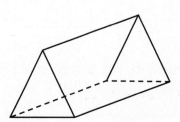

What does each net represent?

1.

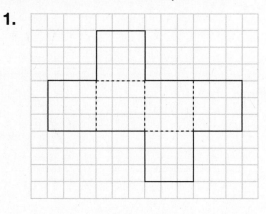

_____

2.

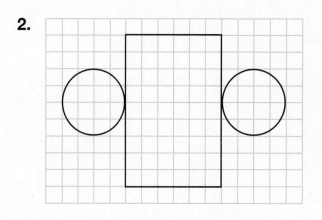

_____

Relating Shapes and Solids

For **1** and **2**, predict what shape each net will make.

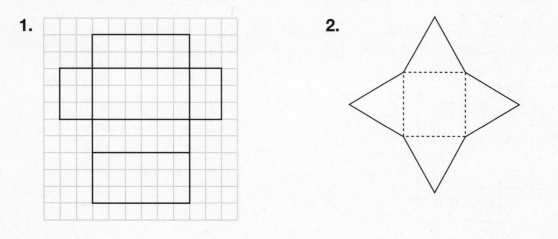

1.

2.

_____   _____

Reasoning For **3–5**, tell which solid figures could be made from the descriptions given.

3. A net that has 6 squares   _____

4. A net that has 4 triangles   _____

5. A net that has 2 circles and a rectangle   _____

6. Which solid can be made by a net that has exactly one circle in it?

A Cone   **B** Cylinder   **C** Sphere   **D** Pyramid

7. **Explain It** Draw a net for a triangular pyramid.
Explain how you know your diagram is correct.

_____

_____

_____

_____

Name _____

Surface Area

The **surface area** of a rectangular prism is the sum of the areas of all of its faces.

Danica has a wood block. She wants to paint it. In order to know how much paint to buy, Danica needs to find the surface area of the block.

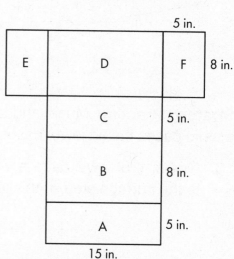

If you could "unfold" this block, it would look like this:

You can find the area of each face by multiplying the length times the width.

    area of A = 15 × 5 = 75
    area of B = 15 × 8 = 120
    area of C = 15 × 5 = 75
    area of D = 15 × 8 = 120
    area of E = 8 × 5 = 40
    area of F = 8 × 5 = 40

Adding all the areas together will give the total surface area.

75 + 120 + 75 + 120 + 40 + 40 = 470 in²

Another way to find the surface area of a rectangular prism is to use the following formula.

    surface area = 2(l × w) + 2(l × h) + 2(w × h)
    Remember: l = length, w = width, h = height
    surface area = 2(15 × 5) + 2(15 × 8) + 2(5 × 8)
    surface area = 150 + 240 + 80
    surface area = 470 in²

In **1** through **3**, find the surface area of each figure.

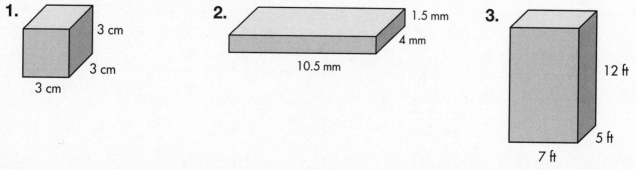

1.   3 cm   3 cm   3 cm

2.   1.5 mm   4 mm   10.5 mm

3.   12 ft   5 ft   7 ft

© Pearson Education, Inc. 5

Surface Area

Find the surface area of each rectangular prism.

1.

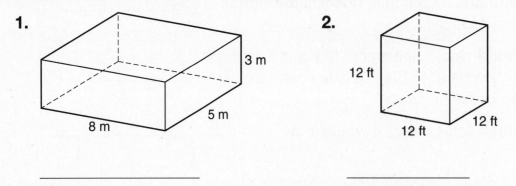

3 m

5 m

8 m

2.

12 ft

12 ft

12 ft

_____   _____

Strategy Practice Music and computer CDs are often stored in plastic cases called jewel cases.

3. One size of jewel case is 140 mm × 120 mm × 4 mm. What is the surface area of this jewel case?

_____

4. A jewel case that holds 2 CDs is 140 mm × 120 mm × 9 mm. What is the surface area of this jewel case?

_____

5. What is the surface area of a rectangular prism with the dimensions 3 in. by 4 in. by 8 in.?

A 96 in.^{2} **B** 112 in.^{2} **C** 136 in.^{2} **D** 152 in.^{2}

6. Explain It Explain why the formula for finding the surface area of a rectangular prism is helpful.

_____

_____

_____

Views of Solids

Here is how each figure on the left would look like from the front, side, and top. In each figure, the number of cubes hidden by the view is given beneath it.

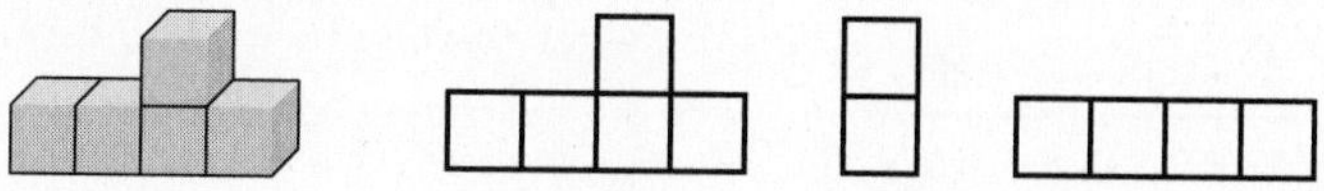

Front   Side   Top

There are no hidden cubes.

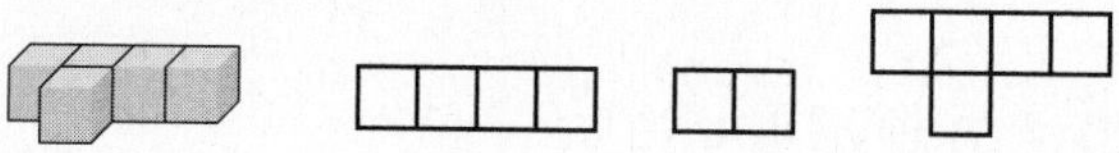

Front   Side   Top

There are no hidden cubes.

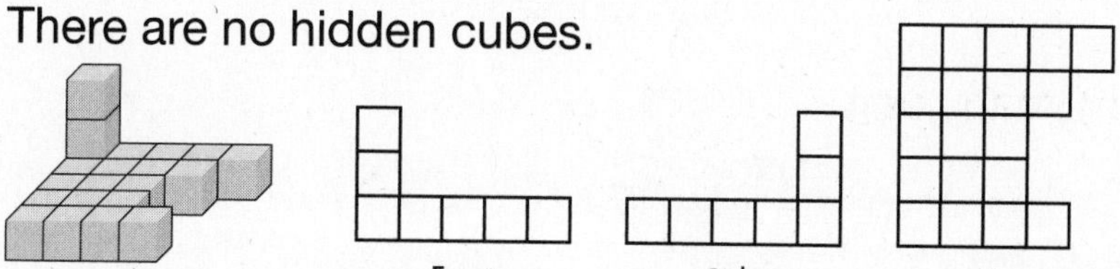

Front   Side   Top

There is one hidden cube.

Look at the figure. Label its front, side, and top views.

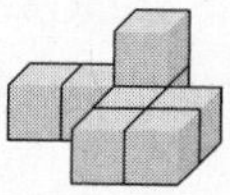

1. _____

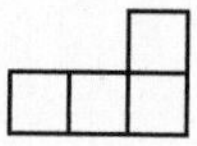

2. _____

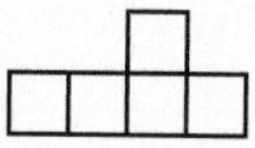

3. _____

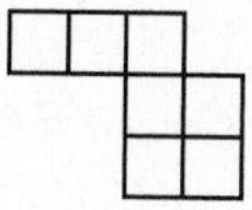

How many cubes are hidden in each figure?

4. _____

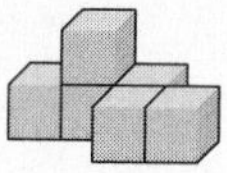

5. _____

6. _____

Views of Solids

For 1 and 2, draw front, side, and top views of each stack of unit blocks.

1.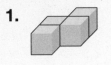

2.

3. **Reasoning** In the figure for Exercise 2, how many blocks are not visible?

_____

4. In the figure at the right, how many unit blocks are being used?

   A 8

   B 9

   C 10

   D 11

5. **Explain It** A figure is made from 8 unit blocks. It is 3 units tall. What is the maximum length the figure could be? Explain.

   _____

   _____

   _____

Models and Volume

Volume is the measure of space inside a solid figure. If you had a box, the number of cubic units it would take to fill the box would be the volume.

Find the volume of this box.

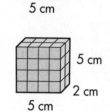

5 cm

2 cm

5 cm

You can fill this box with cubes that each measure 1 cm × 1 cm × 1 cm.

5 cm

2 cm

5 cm

It takes 50 cubes to fill the box.

So, the volume is 50 cm³.

You can also find the volume using the following formula.

$V = (l \times w) \times h$

Remember: l = length, w = width, h = height

$V = (5 \text{ cm} \times 2 \text{ cm}) \times 5 \text{ cm}$

$V = 50 \text{ cm}^3$

The volume is 50 cm³

In **1** through **3**, find the volume by counting unit cubes.

1.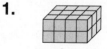

unit cube = 1m³ _____

2.

unit cube = 1in³ _____

3.

unit cube = 1mm³ _____

Models and Volume

Find the number of cubes needed to make each rectangular prism. You can use unit cubes or you can count the cubes by looking at the drawing.

1. _____

2. _____

3. _____

4. _____

5. _____

6. _____

7. Draw a Picture In the space below, draw a model of a rectangular prism 4 cubes long, 5 cubes wide, and 2 cubes high.

8. How many cubes would it take to make a model of a rectangular prism that is 3 units long by 2 units wide and is 4 units high?

A 48   **B** 24   **C** 12   **D** 6

9. Explain It How can you find the volume of a rectangular prism?

_____

_____

_____

_____

_____

Volume

Volume is a measure of the space inside a solid figure. It is measured in cubic units. A **cubic unit** is the volume of a cube which has edges that are 1 unit.

How to find the volume of a rectangular prism

Counting unit cubes:

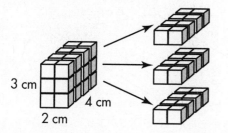

Count the cubes in each layer: 8 cubes.

Multiply by the number of layers.

8 cubes × 3 = 24 cubes

The volume of each cube is 1 cm³.

The volume of the prism is 24 cm³.

Using a formula:

You know the length, l, the width, w, and the height, h. Calculate the volume, V, using the formula $V = l \times w \times h$.

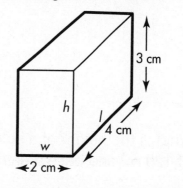

$V = 2 \text{ cm} \times 4 \text{ cm} \times 3 \text{ cm}$

$V = 24 \text{ cm}^3$

---

1. Find the volume of the rectangular prism using a formula.

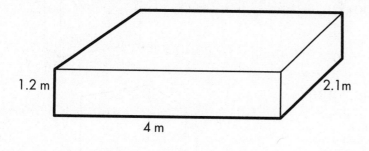

_____

Name _____

Volume

Find the volume of each rectangular prism.

1. base area 56 in.², height 6 in. _____

2. base area 32 cm², height 12 cm _____

3. base area 42 m², height 8 m _____

4.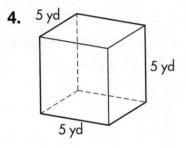

5 yd

5 yd

5 yd

_____

5.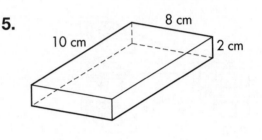

10 cm   8 cm   2 cm

_____

6. Algebra What is the height of a solid with
a volume of 120 m³ and base area of 30 m²? _____

Michael bought some cereal at the grocery store.

7. What is the base area of the box?

_____

8. What is the volume of the box?

_____

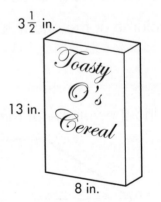

$3\frac{1}{2}$ in.

Toasty O's Cereal

13 in.

8 in.

9. What is the base area of this figure?

A 3.2 m²

B 32 m²

C 320 m²

D 3,200 m²

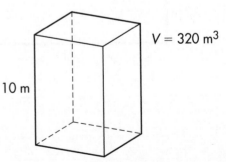

$V = 320$ m³

10 m

10. Explain It Explain how you would find
the base area of a rectangular prism if
you know the volume and the height.

_____

Problem Solving: Use Objects and Solve a Simpler Problem

At a math fair, Willie saw a puzzle about a giant cube made of identical white smaller cubes. The giant cube was 4 × 4 × 4. It contained 64 smaller cubes. Each of the six faces of the giant cube was painted red. The puzzle asked, "If the giant cube were taken apart, how many smaller cubes would have only one face painted red?" Here is how Willie tried to solve the puzzle.

1. Construct cubes using 8 and 27 smaller cubes. Imagine painting each of the larger cubes.

2. Classify the smaller cubes. *Think: Where are the cubes located in the larger cube? How are they painted differently from each other?*

3. Make a table.

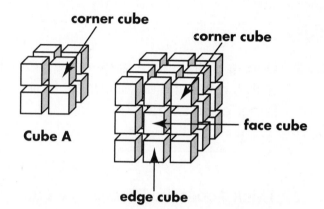

Cube A

Cube B

Location	Cube A		Cube B	
	Number	Painted Faces	Number	Painted Faces
Corner	8	3	8	
Edge	none		12	
Face	none		6	
Center	none		1	

Willie organized the data about the 64 smaller cubes in the giant cube. Use the table above to complete the table below. One set of data has already been completed.

Small cubes		
Painted Surfaces	Location in giant cube	Number
3	corner (*Think: Same as a 3 × 3 × 3.*)	8
2	edge (*Think: One more than a 3 × 3 × 3 on each edge.*)	
1	face (*Think: Three more than a 3 × 3 × 3 on each face.*)	
0	center (*Think: The center is now 2 × 2 × 2.*)	

Problem Solving: Use Objects and Solve a Simpler Problem

Use objects to help you solve a simpler problem. Use the solution to help you solve the original problem.

1. **Number Sense** Six people can be seated at a table. If two tables are put together, 10 people can be seated. How many tables are needed to make a long table that will seat 22 people?

_____

2. Donna is building a large cube that will have 5 layers, each with 5 rows of 5 small cubes. How many small cubes will the larger cube contain?

_____

3. **Think About the Process** Jerome's job duties include feeding the fish. There are 5 kinds of fish that he feeds: guppies, zebra danios, betas, platys, and neon tetras. Use the following clues to find the order in which Jerome feeds them.

   - Jerome feeds the guppies third.
   - Jerome does not feed the betas right before or right after the guppies.
   - Jerome feeds the zebra danios last.
   - Jerome feeds the platys after the betas.

   A Guppies, zebra danios, betas, platys, and neon tetras

   B Betas, platys, guppies, neon tetras, zebra danios

   C Neon tetras, zebra danios, guppies, platys, betas

   D Betas, guppies, platys, neon tetras, zebra danios

4. **Explain It** Suppose Ann is placing bowling pins in the following manner: 1 pin in the first row, 2 pins in the second row, 3 pins in the third row, and so on. How many pins will she use if she has 5 rows in her placement? Explain.

_____

Understanding Integers

You can use integers to represent word descriptions.

Remember: An integer is a whole number or its opposite ($+7$ and -7 are integers). 0 is its own opposite.

Use a positive integer to represent word descriptions that show an increase.

up 3 floors	$+3$
45 degrees above zero	$+45$
5 steps forward	$+5$

Use a negative integer to represent word descriptions that show a decrease.

300 feet below sea level	-300
cut off 10 inches	-10
2 steps backward	-2

In **1** through **8**, write an integer for each word description.

1. win 5 games _____

2. earned $3 _____

3. lose 100 points _____

4. grew 20 inches _____

5. spent $14 _____

6. 2,200 feet above sea level _____

7. go down 8 floors _____

8. 15 minutes before test time _____

Draw a Picture

Draw a number line to show the following:

9. $+11$

10. -2

Understanding Integers

Write an integer for each word description.

1. a withdrawal of $50 **2.** a temperature rise of 14° **3.** 10° below zero

_____   _____   _____

Use the number line for 4–7. Write the integer for each point.

4. A _____ **5.** B _____ **6.** C _____ **7.** D _____

Compare. Use >, <, or = for each ◯.

8. −5 ◯ −9   **9.** +8 ◯ −12   **10.** +21 ◯ −26

Write in order from least to greatest.

11. −4, +11, −11, +4   _____, _____, _____, _____

12. −6, +6, 0, −14   _____, _____, _____, _____

13. +11, −8, +7, −4   _____, _____, _____, _____

14. **Strategy Practice** Which point is farthest to the right on a number line?

A −6   **B** −2   **C** 0   **D** 2

15. **Explain It** In Fenland, U.K., the elevation from sea level is
−4 *m.* In San Diego, U.S., it is +40 ft. The elevations are
given in different units. Explain how to tell which location has
a greater elevation.

_____

_____

_____

Comparing and Ordering Integers

You can compare and order integers.

Karlyn went on a 5-day bike tour. Each day, Karlyn wrote down the elevation she was at when she stopped. What is the order of the elevations from least to greatest?

Step 1: Write the elevations as integers.

+1,250, +750, −500, −250, +250

Day 1	1,250 feet above sea level
Day 2	750 feet above sea level
Day 3	500 feet below sea level
Day 4	250 feet below sea level
Day 5	250 feet above sea level

Step 2: Draw a number line and mark the integers on it.

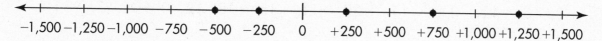

−1,500 −1,250 −1,000 −750 −500 −250 0 +250 +500 +750 +1,000 +1,250 +1,500

Step 3: The values of integers increase as you move to the right on a number line. They decrease as you move to the left.

So, the elevations from least to greatest are:

−500, −250, +250, +750, +1,250

For questions **1–6**, compare. Use <, >, or = for each $\bigcirc$.

1. +4 $\bigcirc$ −1 _____   **2.** −11 $\bigcirc$ +2 _____   **3.** −5 $\bigcirc$ −2 _____

4. +6 $\bigcirc$ +4 _____   **5.** +0 $\bigcirc$ −0 _____   **6.** −10 $\bigcirc$ +10 _____

For questions **7** and **8**, write in order from least to greatest.

7. +3, −1, −4, +2, 0 _____

8. −7, +8, −10, +11, −9 _____

9. Explain It How can you show that +3 is greater than −10?

_____

_____

Comparing and Ordering Integers

For questions **1–3**, compare using >, <, or = .

1. −1 [   ] −3   **2.** +8 [   ] −2   **3.** −10 [   ] 0

For questions **4–12**, order from least to greatest.

4. +9, +6, +12

5. +2, −8, −21

6. −1, −2, −3

_____   _____   _____

7. 0, −10, +10

8. −60, −2, −24

9. +11, −5, 0

_____   _____   _____

10. −9, −6, −12, −3

11. +20, −11, +15, −16   **12.** 0, −1, +7, +34

_____   _____   _____

13. A number *x* is 3 units to the right of negative 21 on the number line. What is the value of *x*? Is *x* greater than or less than negative 21?

_____

14. Jeremiah's mother traveled to four cities in one work trip. In Portland, the temperature was 40°F. In Chicago, it was 15°. In Iowa City, it was −5°, and in Lincoln, it was −21°. List the temperatures in order from least to greatest.

_____

15. **Algebra** Which integer for *x* makes the number sentence below true?

$-2 < x < +4$

A −4   **B** −3   **C** +2   **D** +4

Integers and the Number Line

You can name and plot integers, fractions, and decimals on the same number line.

Lupe cut $\frac{3}{4}$ inch off her hair. Mark's hair grew 0.2 inch. Noor's hair grew $1\frac{2}{5}$ inches. Oliver cut 2 inches off his hair. Plot these numbers on the same number line.

Step 1: Write each measurement as a positive or negative number based on the word descriptions.

$$-\frac{3}{4}, +0.2, +1\frac{2}{5}, -2$$

Step 2: Convert the fractions to equivalent decimal numbers.

$$-\frac{3}{4} = -0.75 \qquad +1\frac{2}{5} = +1\frac{4}{10} = +1.4$$

Step 3: Plot each number on the number line.

For questions 1–3, write the number for each point.

1. $A =$ _____

2. $B =$ _____

3. $C =$ _____

For questions 4–7, write the letter that marks each number.

4. $0.2 =$ _____

5. $-1.45 =$ _____

6. $-0.8 =$ _____

7. $1.75 =$ _____

8. Caleb told Marnie to use the following numbers and the number line to figure out a coded message. What is it?

$0.2, -1, -1, -0.35 \qquad 0.2, -1 \qquad 1.7, -0.35 \qquad -0.35, -1.9, -1$
$0, 1.7, 0.75, -1.2$

Integers and the Number Line

Use the number line below. Write the number for each point.

1. Z _____ 2. Y _____ 3. B _____ 4. W _____ 5. X _____

6. C _____ 7. E _____ 8. V _____ 9. D _____ 10. A _____

Order the numbers in each set from least to greatest.
Show each set of numbers on a number line.

11. –2.5, –3.5, –1

12. 5.5, –3, $2\frac{1}{2}$, 1

_____

_____

13. **Geometry** The perimeter of an equilateral triangle is 10.5 cm. Find the length of each side.

_____

14. Which number makes the number sentence below true?

$-9 > n$

A –13   **B** –8   **C** 0   **D** 10

15. Martin ate $\frac{1}{2}$ a dozen cookies. Esmeralda ate 0.5 of a dozen. Who ate more cookies? How many are left?

_____

Name _____

Adding Integers

You can add two integers together whether they are positive or negative.

Quinn has been keeping track of the water level changes in his family's backyard pond. Monday, Tuesday, and Wednesday were very hot and the pond went down 5 inches. On Thursday it rained, and 2 inches of water fell into the pond. What was the total number of inches of water lost or gained in the pond?

Step 1: Write the integers from the word descriptions and set up your equation.

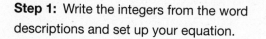

$^-5$ $^+2$

inches lost   inches gained

$^-5 + {}^+2 =$

Step 2: To solve this equation, draw a number line.

$^-5$ 0   5

Step 3: Starting at 0, walk backward the value of the negative integer.

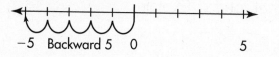

$^-5$ Backward 5   0   5

Step 4: From that point, walk forward the value of the positive integer.

Forward 2

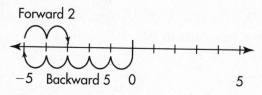

$^-5$ Backward 5   0   5

This point is your sum.

So, $^-5 + {}^+2 = {}^-3$.

For questions **1–6**, find the sum. Use a number line.

1. $^-2 + {}^+1 =$ _____

2. $^+6 + {}^-3 =$ _____

3. $^+4 + {}^-4 =$ _____

4. $^-7 + {}^-3 =$ _____

5. $0 + {}^-5 =$ _____

6. $^+8 + {}^-2 =$ _____

7. Mental Math What is the sum of $^+5 + {}^-3 + {}^-5$? Explain how you found your answer.

_____

_____

Adding Integers

Add. Use a number line.

1. $^+1 + {}^+3 =$ _____

2. $^+4 + {}^-7 =$ _____

3. $^-4 + {}^-2 =$ _____

4. $^-3 + {}^+1 =$ _____

5. $^+6 + {}^-6 =$ _____

6. $^-1 + {}^-4 =$ _____

7. $^+9 + {}^-7 =$ _____

8. $^-6 + {}^+12 =$ _____

9. $^-3 + {}^-8 =$ _____

In a word tile game, you score one positive point for each letter tile that you use and one negative point for each tile that you have left.

10. During one round, Shelley used 14 tiles and could not use 6. What was her score for that round?

_____

11. Pete used 4 tiles, but he could not use 8. What was his score that round?

_____

12. **Reasoning** In the game, if you have 18 tiles and you cannot use 3 of them, what will your score be for that round? Explain how you found the answer.

_____

13. Which is the sum of $^-8 + {}^+5$?

   A $^-13$ **B** $^-3$ **C** $^+3$ **D** $^+13$

14. **Explain It** During a week at camp, Tom started with a zero balance in his account at the camp store. On Monday he deposited $15. He withdrew $6 on Tuesday and $3 on Thursday. What was his account balance after Thursday's withdrawal? Explain.

_____

_____

_____

Name _____

Subtracting Integers

Molly and LaDonna went swimming. Molly swam 4 feet under water. LaDonna swam 6 feet under water. How many feet farther down did LaDonna swim?

Step 1: Write the integers from the word descriptions and set up your equation.

    $^-6$ feet $^-4$ feet

    LaDonna swam   Molly swam

    $^-6 - ^-4 =$

Step 2: Subtracting an integer is the same as adding its opposite. Change the integer you are subtracting to its opposite and add.

    The opposite of $^-4$ is $^+4$.

    So, $^-6 - ^-4 = ^-6 + ^+4$.

Step 3: Draw a number line.

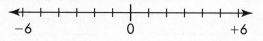

  -6 0 $+6$

Step 4: Starting at 0, walk backward the value of the negative integer.

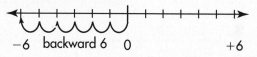

  -6 backward 6 0 $+6$

Step 5: From that point, walk forward the value of the positive integer.

    forward 4

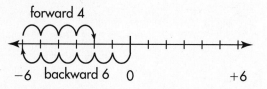

  -6 backward 6 0 $+6$

This point is your sum: $^-6 + ^+4 = ^-2$

So, $^-6 - ^-4 = ^-2$. LaDonna swam 2 feet farther down under water.

For questions **1–6**, rewrite each subtraction problem using addition. Then find the sum. Use a number line to check.

1. $^+10 - ^+4 =$

2. $^-3 - ^-1 =$

3. $^-8 - ^-8 =$

_____   _____   _____

4. $^+6 - ^+2 =$

5. $^+5 - ^-6 =$

6. $^-9 - ^-4 =$

_____   _____   _____

7. Reasoning Pho said that $^-7 - ^+2 = ^-7 + ^+2$. Is this correct?

_____

_____

Subtracting Integers

Rewrite each subtraction using addition. Then find the answer.
Use a number line to check.

1. $^-9 - {}^+1$

_____

2. $^+6 - {}^-3$

_____

3. $^+8 - {}^+4$

_____

4. $^-11 - {}^-16$

_____

5. $^-6 - {}^-1$

_____

6. $^-3 - {}^+4$

_____

	High Temperature	Low Temperature
January 1	$^-1°F$	$^-16°F$
February 1	27°F	18°F
March 1	51°F	42°F

7. How much greater was the high temperature than
   the low temperature on January 1? _____

8. How much less was the low temperature on
   January 1 than the low temperature on February 1? _____

9. How much greater was the high temperature than
   the low temperature on March 1? _____

10. **Number Sense** Which of the following is the same as $^+4 - {}^-9$?

    A $^-4 + {}^-9$ **B** $^+4 + {}^-9$ **C** $^-4 - {}^-9$ **D** $^+4 + {}^+9$

11. **Explain It** Use the information from exercises 7–9. Which
    date had the greatest difference between the high and low
    temperatures? Explain.

    _____

    _____

    _____

Simplifying Expressions

You can evaluate algebraic expressions with integers.

If a football team is penalized for a false start, the team moves backwards 5 yards. The team was on their 30-yard line when they were penalized. What yard line is the team on after the penalty?

Step 1: Find your expression from the word descriptions. Since the team must move backwards 5 yards for the penalty, $p + {}^-5$ = position after the penalty (p = the team's starting position).

Step 2: Solve $p + {}^-5$ for $p = {}^+30$

$p + {}^-5 = {}^+30 + {}^-5$ replace p with its value

$p + {}^-5 = {}^+25$ find the sum

So, the team's new position is on the 25-yard line.

Remember: If you have an expression that has more than one variable, you replace each variable with a number.

For questions 1–4, evaluate each expression for $x = {}^-3$ and $x = {}^+5$.

1. $x + {}^-2 =$ _____

2. ${}^-6 + x =$ _____

3. $x - {}^-4 =$ _____

4. ${}^+3 - x =$ _____

For questions 5–8, evaluate each expression for $a = {}^+1$, $b = {}^-7$, and $c = {}^+6$.

5. $b - {}^+2 =$ _____

6. ${}^+10 + c =$ _____

7. ${}^-3 + a - b =$ _____

8. $a + b + c =$ _____

9. Derek got in an elevator on the ground floor. He rode the elevator up 5 floors and then down 2 floors. Write an expression to show what floor Derek ended up on.

_____

Simplifying Expressions

For questions **1–4**, evaluate each expression for $x = +8$ and $x = -3$.

1. $x - +3$ **2.** $+5 + x$ **3.** $x + -7$ **4.** $+8 + x$

_____   _____   _____   _____

For questions **5–12**, evaluate each expression for $a = -2$, $b = +1$, and $c = -8$.

5. $a + -20$ **6.** $c - +12$ **7.** $b - +1$ **8.** $-25 + a$

_____   _____   _____   _____

9. $c - a$ **10.** $a + b$ **11.** $a + c - b$ **12.** $a - b - c$

_____   _____   _____   _____

13. Reasoning The temperature at the pool was 65°F at 6:00 A.M. Write an expression to name the temperature at 5:00 P.M. after it rose 7 degrees.

_____

14. Which expression names the location of a turtle that started 3 feet under water and climbed up 4 feet onto a log?

    A $3 + 4$ **B** $-3 - 4$ **C** $-3 + -4$ **D** $-3 + +4$

15. The grocery store got a shipment of apples weighing 60 lb. The manager realized the order was short and ordered more for a total of 120 lb. Write an expression to name how many pounds were missing.

_____

16. Explain It Georgia says that if you use the LCD when subtracting fractions, you never have to simplify the answer. Do you agree? Why or why not?

_____

_____

Problem Solving:
Work Backward

Sometimes when you are trying to solve a problem, it is easier to start at the end and work backward.

The Rosewood City train makes its first stop 10 minutes from the main station. The second stop is 20 minutes farther. The third stop is 15 minutes after that, and the fourth stop is 15 minutes after the third stop. The end station is 5 minutes from the fourth stop. The train reaches the end station at 9:00 A.M. What time did the train leave the main station?

To solve this kind of problem, you need to work backward.
Think about if the train were actually going backward.

Since you know it is 5 minutes from the end station back to the fourth stop, subtract 5 from 9:00 a.m Continue subtracting to keep backing the train up until it is back at the main station.

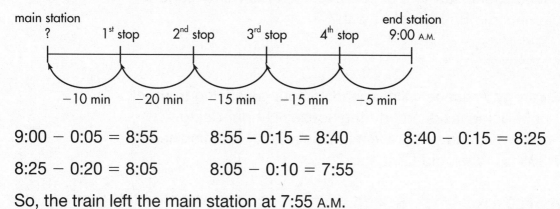

$9:00 - 0:05 = 8:55$ $8:55 - 0:15 = 8:40$ $8:40 - 0:15 = 8:25$

$8:25 - 0:20 = 8:05$ $8:05 - 0:10 = 7:55$

So, the train left the main station at 7:55 A.M.

---

1. Zev has a rosebush in his yard. The first year it grew 3 inches. The second year it grew 12 inches. Zev then cut it back 5 inches. The third year it grew twice as much as the first year. The rose bush is now 42 inches tall. How tall was it when Zev planted it?

_____

2. Jesse went on a bike ride. He rode from his house to the library. Then he rode 2 miles from the library to his friend's house. Then he rode $1\frac{1}{2}$ miles to buy a snack at the store. Finally he rode the 3 miles back to his house. He rode a total of 9 miles. How many miles is it from Jesse's house to the library?

_____

Problem Solving:
Work Backward

Solve each problem by working backward. Write the answers in complete sentences.

Barbara is refilling her bird feeders and squirrel feeders in her yard.

1. After filling her bird feeders, Barbara has $3\frac{1}{2}$ c of mixed birdseed left. The two feeders in the front yard took $4\frac{1}{2}$ c each. The two feeders in the backyard each took $2\frac{3}{4}$ c. The two feeders next to the living room window each took $3\frac{1}{4}$ c. How much mixed birdseed did Barbara have before filling the feeders?

   _____

2. After Barbara fills each of her 4 squirrel feeders with $2\frac{2}{3}$ c of peanuts, she has $1\frac{3}{4}$ c of peanuts left. How many cups of peanuts did Barbara start with?

   _____

3. **Strategy Practice** Clint spends $\frac{1}{4}$ hour practicing trumpet, $\frac{1}{2}$ hour doing tasks around the house, $1\frac{1}{2}$ hour doing homework, and $\frac{3}{4}$ hour cleaning his room. He is finished at 7:30 P.M. When did Clint start?

   A 4:00 P.M.   **B** 4:15 P.M.   **C** 4:30 P.M.   **D** 5:30 P.M.

4. **Write a Problem** Write a real-world problem that you can solve by working backward.

   _____

   _____

Solving Addition and Subtraction Equations

Paige gave 6 peaches to Simon. Paige now has 8 peaches. How many peaches did Paige have to start?

The number of peaches Paige now has equals the number of peaches she had at the start minus the number she gave to Simon.

So, $p - 6 = 8$ p = number of peaches at the start

To solve this equation, you need to get p alone. You can do this by using an inverse operation. Addition and subtraction have an inverse relationship.

To get p alone, add 6 to both sides of the equation.

Tip: If you add or subtract on one side of the equation, you <u>must</u> do the same on the other side.

$p - 6 + 6 = 8 + 6$

$p = 14$ So, Paige started out with 14 peaches.

For questions 1–4, solve each equation.

1. $a + 3 = 5$ _____

2. $y - 14 = 9$ _____

3. $8 + p = 15$ _____

4. $52 = c + 18$ _____

5. Mary's sister is 4 years older than Mary. Her sister is 12. Use the equation $m + 4 = 12$ to find Mary's age.

_____

6. **Explain It** Lyndon solved $x - 18 = 4$. He said the answer was $x = 4$. Explain why this is correct or incorrect.

_____

_____

_____

Solving Addition and Subtraction Equations

Solve and check each equation.

1. $x + 4 = 16$ _____

2. $t - 8 = 15$ _____

3. $m - 9 = 81$ _____

4. $7 + y = 19$ _____

5. $k - 10 = 25$ _____

6. $15 + b = 50$ _____

7. $f + 18 = 20$ _____

8. $w - 99 = 100$ _____

9. $75 + n = 100$ _____

10. $p - 40 = 0$ _____

11. Jennifer has $14. She sold a notebook and pen, and now she has $18. Solve the equation $14 + m = 18$ to find how much money Jennifer received by selling the notebook and pen.

_____

12. Kit Carson was born in 1809. He died in 1868. Use the equation $1{,}809 + x = 1{,}868$ to find how many years Kit Carson lived.

_____

13. **Strategy Practice** Which is the solution for y when $y - 6 = 19$?

A 13 **B** 15 **C** 23 **D** 25

14. **Explain It** Nellie solved $y - 3 = 16$. Is her answer correct? Explain and find the correct answer if she is incorrect.

$$y - 3 = 16$$
$$y = 13$$
$$\text{Subtract 3}$$

_____

_____

_____

_____

Solving Multiplication and Division Equations

Dan's computer prints at the rate of 3 pages per minute. How many pages can he print in 15 minutes?

The number of minutes is equal to the number of pages divided by the rate the pages are printed.

$15 = d \div 3$ d = number of pages

To solve this equation, you can use an inverse operation. Multiplication and division have an inverse relationship.

To get d alone, multiply 3 times both sides of the equation.

Remember: If you multiply or divide one side of an equation, you must do the same to the other side.

$15 \times 3 = d \div 3 \times 3$

$45 = d$

Dan can print 45 pages in 15 minutes.

In **1** through **6**, solve each equation.

1. $12a = 48$ _____

2. $t \div 9 = 7$ _____

3. $250 = 25x$ _____

4. $75 = 3c$ _____

5. $p \div 33 = 3$ _____

6. $4 = y \div 16$ _____

7. Number Sense A carton of eggs is on sale for $0.49. Use the equation $0.49x = $2.45 to find out how many cartons you can purchase for $2.45.

_____

8. Geometry Shanika has a piece of cardboard with an area of 63 square inches; one side is 9 inches long. Write an equation and solve for the value of the other side.

Area = 63 square inches

y

9 inches

_____

Solving Multiplication and Division Equations

Solve each equation.

1. $11y = 55$ _____

2. $\dfrac{c}{9} = 6$ _____

3. $150 = 25p$ _____

4. $16 = \dfrac{w}{4}$ _____

5. $\dfrac{k}{36} = 8$ _____

6. $13d = 39$ _____

7. $30 = 10x$ _____

8. $\dfrac{m}{7} = 13$ _____

9. $81 = 9t$ _____

10. $5b = 30$ _____

11. $20 = 4a$ _____

12. $\dfrac{e}{80} = 2$ _____

13. Reasoning Antoinette divides 54 by 9 to solve an equation for y. One side of the equation is 54. Write the equation.

14. Adam is making a trout dinner for six people. He buys 48 oz of trout. How many ounces of trout will each person get?

15. Which operation would you use to solve the equation $19x = 646$?

A add 19   **B** subtract 17   **C** divide by 19   **D** multiply by 19

16. Explain It How would you use mental math to find m in the equation $63\left(\dfrac{m}{63}\right) = 2$?

Problem Solving:
Use Reasoning

Alayna decorates pages of her notebooks using ink stamps of flowers and butterflies. She has 10 stamps. Half are butterfly stamps. The others are either rose or tulip stamps. She has three more rose stamps than tulip stamps. How many rose stamps does she have?

Use reasoning to make conclusions.

There are 10 stamps of butterflies and flowers.

Flower and Butterfly Stamps

Half are butterfly stamps. The other half are made up of tulip stamps and rose stamps.

Butterfly Stamps   **Rose and Tulip Stamps**

There are three more rose stamps than tulip stamps. *Think: At least three stamps are rose stamps.*

Rose Stamps   **Rose and Tulip Stamps**

There is one tulip stamp. *Think: In the remaining stamps, the numbers of rose stamps and tulip stamps are equal.*

Rose Stamps   **Rose Stamp**   **Tulip Stamp**

There are four rose stamps.

Rose Stamps

Suppose in the problem above Alayna has three fewer rose stamps than tulip stamps.

1. Label the cubes in this step of the solution.

_____
Rose and Tulip Stamps

2. How many rose stamps does Alayna have? _____

Problem Solving:
Use Reasoning

Use reasoning to solve.

1. Joseph has 45 books. One-third of the books are mysteries. Of the books that are left, half are about science, and the rest are about cars. How many books about cars does Joseph have?

_____

2. Mina has visited 20 different countries. One-fifth of the countries were in Europe, and 2 of the countries were in North America. Mina visited twice as many countries in Africa as she did in Europe. How many countries did she visit in Africa?

_____

3. **Geometry** The perimeter of a square table is 100 inches. There is a rectangular table that is 15 in. long and 20 in. wide. Which of the tables has the greater perimeter? Explain.

_____

4. **Number Sense** If $5 + x > 11$, which of the following are possible values of x: 3, 6, 9, or 12?

_____

5. **Reasonableness** Ms. Lee's class had to guess how many jelly beans were in a jar. The clues were that exactly half were red, and that exactly one-third were blue. Based on the information provided, which of the following is **NOT** a reasonable number of jelly beans that can be in the jar?

   A 24   **B** 50   **C** 60   **D** 90

6. **Explain It** Explain how you found your answer for Exercise 5.

_____

_____

Patterns and Equations

You can find a rule for a pattern and use that rule to fill in a table.

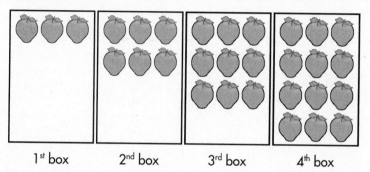

1st box   2nd box   3rd box   4th box

How many apples will be in the 8th box? Which box will have
39 apples?

Step 1: Draw a table to show the information.

Box number (*b*)	Number of apples (*a*)
1	3
2	6
3	9
4	12

Step 2: Find a relationship between the two columns that is the same for each pair. This relationship is the rule for the pattern.

For these two columns the relationship is to multiply the box number by 3.

Step 3: Write an equation to express the rule.

number of apples = 3 times the box number

$a = 3b$

Step 4: Use this equation to find the missing parts of the table.

$a = 3 \times 8$ $39 = 3b$
$a = 24$, 24 apples $39 \div 3 = b$
in the 8th box $13 = b$, 13th box will have
                         39 apples

For questions 1–4, write an equation for each table and solve for the missing values for *x* and *y*.

1.

x	*y*
0	
3	8
	12
10	15

2.

x	*y*
	64
9	36
6	24
4	

3.

x	*y*
6	0
	1
8	2
16	

4.

x	*y*
30	3
40	4
50	
	8

Patterns and Equations

For exercises **1–3**, find a rule for each table. Write an equation for each rule.

1.

x	y
5	15
2	6
11	33
6	18

_____

2.

x	y
18	9
50	25
12	6
34	17

_____

3.

x	y
8	0
12	4
16	8
20	12

_____

4. **Reasoning** Write an equation that will give the answer $y = 5$ when $x = 12$.

_____

5. A farmer sells 200 apples at the market. The next week, he sells 345 apples. How many more apples did he sell the second week?

_____

6. For the equation $y = x - 5$, which value of x would give a negative value for y?

   A 10   **B** 8   **C** 5   **D** 2

7. **Explain It** If you know the rule for a table, how can you add pairs of numbers to the table?

_____

_____

More Patterns and Equations

Claire went to the school carnival. With her admission of
$4.00, she got one raffle ticket. She can buy more raffle tickets
for $0.50 each. How many extra raffle tickets can Claire buy if she
started with $7.00 and she spends all her money?

Step 1: Find the rule and write it down as an
equation.

The cost of admission (including 1 raffle ticket)
plus $0.50 times the number of raffle tickets
purchased equals the total money spent.

$4.00 + 0.50r = m$

Step 2. Make a table and fill in the information
from the rule.

r	m
1	$4.50
2	$5.00
3	$5.50
4	$6.00
5	$6.50
6	$7.00

Claire can buy 6 extra raffle tickets.

For questions **1–3**, complete each table.

1.

x	3x + 2 = y	y
1	3(1) + 2 = y	
	3(2) + 2 = y	8
3		11
4	3(4) + 2 = y	14

2.

x	y = 9x − 18	y
2		0
4	y = 9(4) − 18	18
5	y = 9(5) − 18	
	y = 9(8) − 18	54

3.

x	5x + 4 = y	y
3	5(3) + 4 = y	
7	5(7) + 4 = y	39
	5(11) + 4 = y	59
12		64

4. Does the equation $4x + 6 = y$ describe the
pattern in this table?

_____

x	0	1	2	3	4
y	6	10	14	18	22

More Patterns and Equations

Complete each table.

1.

x	3x + 2 = y	y
0	3(0) + 2 = y	2
1	3(1) + 2 = y	
2	3( ) + 2 = y	
3	3( ) + 2 = y	11

2.

x	y = 5x + 4	y
0	y = 5(0) + 4	4
2	y = 5(2) + 4	
4	y = 5( ) + 4	
6	y = 5( ) + 4	

3.

x	2x + 10 = y	y
0	2(0) + 10 = y	10
2	2(2) + 10 = y	
5	2( ) + 10 = y	
9	2( ) + 10 = y	

4. **Estimation** Admission to the county fair is $2.75 for adults and $1.25 for children. About how much money will it cost John's father if he brings John and John's friend Ruth?

_____

5. Jeremy's class went to the movies. There are eighteen students in the class. How much did each ticket cost if the total cost was $90?

_____

6. Ella bought 4 fine-tip pens and 2 mechanical pencils. Each pencil cost $1.75 and each pen cost $1.25. Which equation can you use to find the total cost?

A $y = 4(3) + 2$

B $y = 2 + 4 (1.25 + 1.75)$

C $y = 1.25(4) + 1.75(2)$

D $y = 3(6)$

7. **Explain It** Jerry's bedroom window gets too much light in the afternoons when he is doing homework. He decides to make a curtain. His window is 3 feet by 4 feet. He purchases 10 square feet of dark green cloth. Does he have enough to block the light?

_____

_____

Problem Solving: Draw a Picture and Write an Equation

Salim collects football cards and baseball cards. He has 38 more baseball cards than football cards. If he has 25 football cards, how many baseball cards does Salim have?

Step 1: Write down what you already know.

Salim has 25 football cards.
He has 38 more baseball cards than football cards.

Step 2: What are you trying to find?

How many baseball cards Salim has.

Step 3: Draw a diagram to show the information. Choose a variable to represent what you are trying to find.

b	
38	25

Step 4: Write an equation and solve.
$b - 38 = 25$
$b = 63$
Salim has 63 baseball cards.

For questions **1–5**, draw a picture or diagram, write an equation, and solve the equation to answer the question.

1. Hallie spent $28 buying two figurines at the flea market. If one figurine costs $11.28, how much did Hallie pay for the other one?

   _____

2. Cody is selling popcorn for his Cub Scout pack. His goal is to sell $350. So far, Cody has sold $284. How much more does Cody need to sell to meet his goal?

   _____

3. In Briana's class there are 5 fewer students than there were last year. There are 21 students in Briana's class. How many students were there last year?

   _____

Problem Solving: Draw a Picture and Write an Equation

Draw a picture, write and solve an equation to answer the question.

1. Suki and Amy made a total of 15 homemade holiday cards. Amy made 7 of them. How many cards did Suki make?

2. Ramon ate 3 more pieces of fruit today than he did yesterday. Today he ate 4 pieces. Write an equation to find out how many pieces of fruit he ate yesterday.

3. **Critical Thinking** A total of 64 children are going on a field trip. If 14 of the children are girls, how many are boys?

_____

_____

4. Naomi's class went to the museum. There are 16 students in her class. If the total cost of admission for the class was $96, what does one admission to the museum cost?

_____

_____

5. Paul is in a 17-kilometer canoe race. He has just reached the 5-kilometer marker. Which of the following equations can you use to find out how many more kilometers he needs to paddle?

   A $k - 5 = 17$ **B** $5 + k = 17$ **C** $5 - k = 17$ **D** $17 + 5 = k$

Understanding Ratios

Coach Sanders has 9 basketballs, 6 footballs, and 5 soccer balls in her equipment bin. What is the ratio of basketballs to footballs? What is the ratio of soccer balls to total balls?

Using ratios, you can compare parts of a whole to the whole, some parts to other parts, or the whole to its parts.

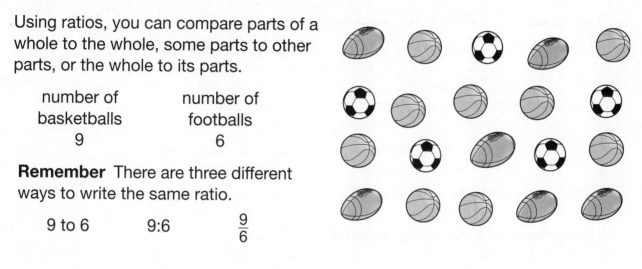

number of basketballs	number of footballs
9	6

Remember There are three different ways to write the same ratio.

9 to 6   9:6 $\frac{9}{6}$

In **1** through **4**, write each ratio. Give each answer in the three different ratio forms.

1. small stars to large stars

_____

2. filled stars to total stars

_____

3. large unfilled stars to small unfilled stars

_____

4. small filled stars to total stars

_____

Understanding Ratios

Use the chart below in **1–4** to write each ratio three ways.

Mr. White's 3rd-Grade Class (24 Students)

Gender:	Male	8	Female	16				
Eye Color:	Blue	6	Brown	4	Hazel	12	Green	2
Hair Color:	Blond	5	Red	1	Brown	15	Black	3

1. male students to female students   _____

2. female students to male students   _____

3. red-haired students to all students   _____

4. all students to green-eyed students   _____

5. **Reasonableness** Is it reasonable to state that the ratio of male students to female students is the same as the ratio of male students to all students? Explain.

   _____

   _____

6. George has 2 sons and 1 daughter. What is the ratio of daughters to sons?

   A   2 to 1   **B**   1 to 2   **C**   3:1   **D** $\frac{2}{1}$

7. **Explain It** The ratio of blue beads to white beads in a necklace is 3:8. Nancy says that for every 11 beads, 3 are blue. Do you agree? Explain.

   _____

   _____

   _____

Name _____

Understanding Percent

A percent is a special kind of ratio that shows the relationship between a number and 100. Percent actually means *per hundred*.

The Hortonville Hoopsters have won 70 games of the last 100 games they have played. What percentage of the games has the team won?

Using a 100-square grid can help.

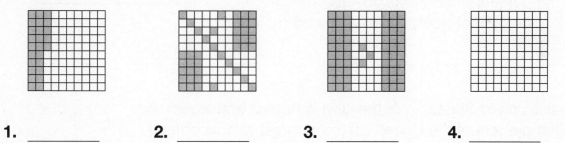

There are 70 squares shaded so the ratio is 70 to 100 or $\frac{70}{100}$.

$\frac{70}{100} = 70\%$.

Remember The % sign is the same thing as saying "out of 100."

In **1** through **4**, write the ratio and percent of the shaded section on each grid.

1. _____   2. _____   3. _____   4. _____

Number Sense

5. What is "eighty-two percent" written as a fraction in simplest

   form? _____

6. Mystery Bookstore has 100 books on its shelves. Forty-one are hardbacks and 59 are paperbacks. What percentage of hardbacks and what percentage of paperbacks are there?

_____

Name _____

Understanding Percent

Write the fraction in lowest terms and the percent that represents
the shaded part of each figure.

1.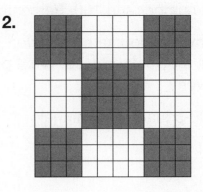

_____

2.

_____

3. Strategy Practice In the square, if part A is
$\frac{1}{4}$ of the square and part C is $\frac{1}{10}$ of the square,
what percent of the square is part B?

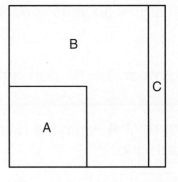

_____

4. In Russia, $\frac{1}{4}$ of the land is covered by forests.
What percent of Russia is covered by forest?
What percent of Russia is not covered by forest?

_____

5. In the United States, $\frac{3}{10}$ of the land is forests and woodland.
What percent of the United States is forest and woodland?

_____

6. If $\frac{2}{5}$ of a figure is shaded, what percent is not shaded?

A 20%   **B** 30%   **C** 50%   **D** 60%

7. Explain It Explain how a decimal is related to a percent.

_____

_____

Percents, Fractions, and Decimals

At Slider Park, 40% of the children playing were boys. What is this percent expressed as a fraction and a decimal?

You can change percents into fractions and decimals just as you can change fractions and decimals into percents.

To change a percent into a fraction, drop the percent sign and place the number over 100. Simplify the fraction if possible.

$$40\% = \frac{40}{100} = \frac{2}{5}$$

To change a fraction to a percent, divide the numerator by the denominator. Make sure your quotient goes to the hundredths place. If your quotient has too few digits, add zeros as placeholders. If your quotient has too many places, round to the hundredths. Then move the decimal point two places to the right and add the percent sign.

$$\frac{2}{5} = 0.40 = 40\%$$

To change a percent to a decimal, drop the percent sign and move the decimal point two places to the left.

$$40\% = 0.40$$

In **1** through **3**, write each percent as a decimal and a fraction in simplest form.

1. 36% _____

2. 13% _____

3. 59% _____

4. Reasonableness Pilar wrote that 3% = 0.30. Is this a reasonable answer?

_____

5. On the Pennyville Pigskins football team, two quarterbacks are competing for the starting job. Jake completes 87% of his passes. Brett only has 13% of his passes fall incomplete. Who is the better quarterback?

_____

Percents, Fractions, and Decimals

For questions **1–3**, write the percent, decimal, and fraction in simplest form represented by the shaded part of each 100-grid.

1.

_____

2.

_____

3.

_____

For questions **4–9**, write each percent as a decimal and a fraction in simplest form.

4. 30% _____

5. 60% _____

6. 32% _____

7. 11% _____

8. 150% _____

9. 100% _____

10. Reasoning If 40% of Jeanne's friends play kickball on weekends, what fraction of her friends don't play kickball?

_____

11. If there are 6 eggs in 50% of an egg crate, how many eggs are in the whole crate?

_____

12. What would you do first to order the following numbers from least to greatest?

30%, $\frac{2}{3}$, 0.67, $\frac{8}{9}$, 0.7

A Order the decimals.

B Convert the decimals to percents.

C Order the fractions.

D Convert all numbers to decimals or fractions.

13. Explain It When writing a percent as a decimal, why do you move the decimal point 2 places?

_____

Finding Percent of a Whole Number

Stefani wants to buy a skirt that costs $28. She received a coupon in the mail for a 20% discount from the store. How much will she save?

To find the percent of a whole number, multiply the whole number by the decimal equivalent of the percent.

$$\begin{array}{r} 28 \\ \times\ 0.20 \\ \hline \$5.60 \end{array}$$ discount

In **1** through **6**, find the percent of each number.

1. 17% of 82 _____

2. 3% of 115 _____

3. 42% of 600 _____

4. 50% of 800 _____

5. 73% of 280 _____

6. 39% of 22 _____

7. In the problem above, Stefani is able to save $6 each week. With the discount, how many weeks will it take for Stefani to save enough to buy the skirt?

_____

8. Geometry Kirk ordered a pizza with 10 slices. How many slices would amount to 30% of the pizza?

_____

9. Jackson High School's band sells programs at the State Fair. They receive 15% of the total amount sold. The band sold $3,500 worth of programs. How much money did they receive?

_____

10. Mental Math Using mental math, find 50% of 500. How did you get your answer?

_____

Finding Percent of a Whole Number

Find each using mental math.

1. 20% of 60 _____   **2.** 30% of 500 _____

3. 25% of 88 _____   **4.** 70% of 30 _____

5. Reasoning Order these numbers from least to greatest.
0.85, $\frac{1}{4}$, 72%, $\frac{5}{8}$, 20%, 0.3

_____

6. What is 40% of 240?

A 48   **B** 96   **C** 128   **D** 960

	Rural	Urban
Bermuda	0%	100%
Cuba	25%	75%
Guatemala	60%	40%

The table shows the percent of the population that live in rural and urban areas of each country. Use the table to answer 7 through 9.

7. Out of every 300 people in Cuba, how
many of them live in a rural area?   _____

8. Out of every 1,000 people in Guatemala,
how many live in urban areas?   _____

9. Explain It If there are 1,241,356 people who live in Bermuda,
how many residents of Bermuda live in urban areas? How
many live in rural areas? Explain your answer.

_____

_____

_____

Problem Solving: Make a Table and Look for a Pattern

Sometimes when you are trying to solve a problem, it can help to make a table and look for a pattern.

Nasser has 5 hours every day between when school ends and when he goes to bed. He spent 3 hours last night studying. If he continues like that every night, what percent of his time will be spent studying?

Step 1. Make a table with the information you already know.

Hours spent studying	3			
Total hours	5			

Step 2. Fill in the table using equal ratios until you get a comparison with 100.

Remember You find equal ratios by multiplying or dividing the top and bottom of the ratio by the same number.

Hours spent studying	3	12	30	48	60
Total hours	5	20	50	80	100

So, Nasser spends 60% of his time studying.

In **1** and **2**, find the percent by completing the table.

1. won 7 out of 10 games _____

Games won	7			
Total games	10	20	50	100

2. ran 13 miles out of 20 _____

Miles run	13			
Total miles	20	10	50	100

3. Denise gets 450 minutes each month to use on her cell phone. Last month, she used 360 minutes. What percent of her minutes did Denise use? _____

Problem Solving: Make a Table and Look for a Pattern

For exercises **1–4**, find each percent by completing each table.

1. 12 out of 40 days were rainy. _____

Rainy days	12			
Total days	40	20	10	

2. 2 out of 8 marbles are blue. _____

Blue	2			
Total marbles	8	16	4	

3. 32 out of 40 days were windy. _____

Windy days	32			
Total days	40	5	20	

4. 16 out of 40 pets on Jack's street are dogs. _____

Dogs	16			
Total pets	40	80	10	

5. **Write a Problem** Write a real-world problem that you can solve using a table to find a percent.

_____

_____

6. Emmy plans to hike 32 miles this weekend. On Saturday, she hiked 24 miles. What percent of her goal has Emmy hiked?

_____

7. **Explain It** Dave estimated 45% of 87 by finding 50% of 90. Will his estimate be greater than or less than the exact answer?

_____

Ordered Pairs

You can locate points on a grid using ordered pairs.

Draw a point on the grid for (+1, −3).

On a grid, the axis that goes across is called the *x*-axis. The axis that goes up and down is called the *y*-axis. The point where the *x*-axis and the *y*-axis cross is called the origin.

To locate a point on a grid using an ordered pair, start at the origin.

The first number in the ordered pair is called the *x*-coordinate. It tells how far to move to the right (if positive) or to the left (if negative). Since +1 is positive, move 1 unit to the right.

The second number in the ordered pair is the *y*-coordinate. It tells how far to move up (if positive) or down (if negative). Since −3 is negative, move 3 units down to the point (+1, −3).

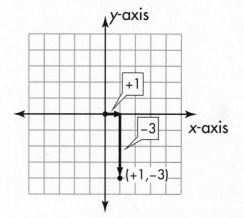

Write the ordered pair for each point.

1. *B* _____   **2.** *D* _____

Name the point for each ordered pair.

3. (+3, +4) _____   **4.** (−2, +2) _____

5. What is the ordered pair for the origin?

_____

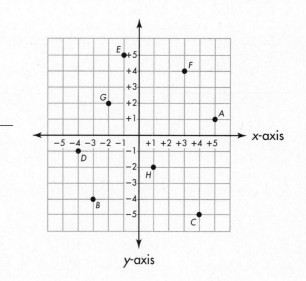

The Coordinate Plane

Write the ordered pair for each point.

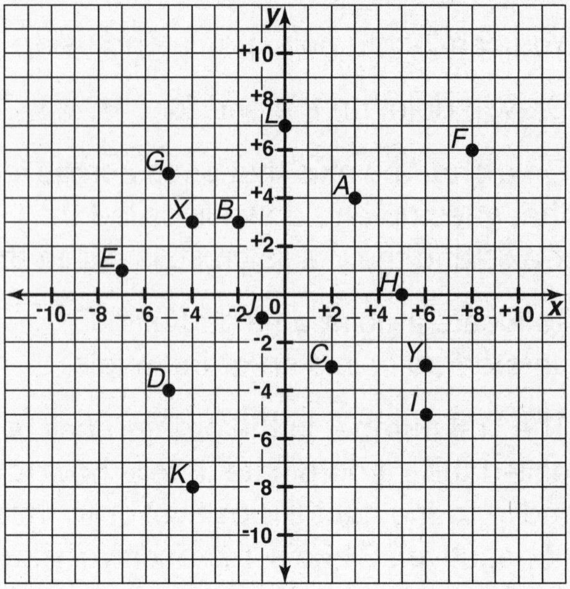

1. *A* _____

2. *B* _____

3. *C* _____

4. *D* _____

5. *E* _____

6. *F* _____

Name the point for each ordered pair.

7. ($^+$5, 0) _____   **8.** ($^-$1, $^-$1) _____   **9.** (0, $^+$7) _____

10. ($^+$6, $^-$5) _____   **11.** ($^-$4, $^-$8) _____   **12.** ($^-$5, $^+$5) _____

13. Strategy Practice If a taxicab were to start at the point (0, 0) and drive 6 units left, 3 units down, 1 unit right, and 9 units up, what ordered pair would name the point the cab would finish at?   _____

14. Use the coordinate graph above. Which is the *y*-coordinate for point *X*?

   A $^+$6   **B** $^+$3   **C** $^-$3   **D** $^-$6

15. Explain It Explain how to graph the ordered pair ($^-$2, $^+$3).

_____

_____

_____

_____

Line Graphs

How to make a line graph

Step 1
Put the data into a table so that each set of data has two values.

Step 2
Choose what to plot on the horizontal axis and what to plot on the vertical axis.

Choose the starting point and ending point for each axis. (The starting and ending points must include the smallest and largest data values.)

Choose an interval for each axis. Label and number the axes.

Step 3
Graph the data by using the coordinates for each set of data as a point. Draw lines to connect the points.

Step 4
Title your graph.

STEP 1

Months passed	Weight lifted (pounds)
1	70
2	100
3	100
4	120
5	140

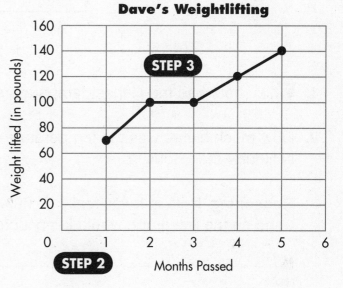

Dave's Weightlifting

STEP 3

STEP 2

Make a line graph of the data.

Since the data for the x-axis are from 1 to 5, the scale can go from 0 to _____.

Since the data for the y-axis are from 20 to 45, the scale can go from 0 to _____.

Blood Drive	
Week	Number of donors
1	20
2	20
3	30
4	35
5	45

Line Graphs

Display the data in the table below on the line graph.

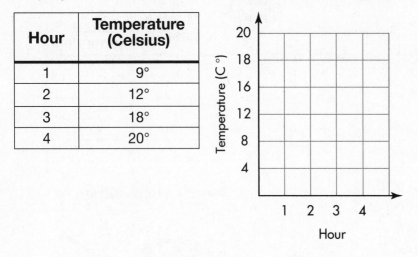

Hour	Temperature (Celsius)
1	9°
2	12°
3	18°
4	20°

1. Which hour had the highest temperature? _____

2. How much higher was the temperature
   in Hour 4 than Hour 1? _____

3. **Reasoning** If Hour 1 was really 10:00 A.M., do you think the
   trend on the line graph would keep increasing? Explain.

   _____

   _____

4. **Think About the Process** Look at the line
   graph at the right. What do you know about
   the trend of the housing prices?

   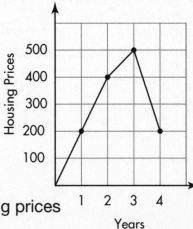

   A Housing prices increased.

   B Housing prices decreased.

   C Housing prices increased, then decreased.

   D Housing prices decreased, then increased.

5. **Writing to Explain** In the example above, if housing prices
   had stayed the same for all four years, what would
   the line graph look like? Explain.

   _____

   _____

Graphing Equations

You can graph an equation on a coordinate grid.

Graph $y = x + {}^+3$.

Step 1. Solve the equation for y using several different values for x. Make a table to show the values.

x	y
0	+3
−2	+1
+2	+5
−5	−2

Step 2. Using these x and y values as ordered pairs, plot the points on the coordinate plane. Connect the points with a solid line.

(0, +3)

(−2, +1)

(+2, +5)

(−5, −2)

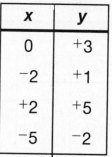

1. Give the rule for the table.

x	−4	+2	0	+1
y	+4	−2	0	−1

Number Sense

2. Does the ordered pair (+2, −5) belong on the graph of the equation $y = x - {}^+6$?

_____

Name _____

Graphing Equations

Complete each table.

1. $y = x + {}^+2$

x	y
+3	
+2	
0	
−3	

2. $y = x - {}^+4$

x	y
+4	
0	
−4	
−6	

In **3** and **4**, write an equation to describe the relationship between x and y.

3.

x	+5	+2	0	−3
y	3	0	−2	−5

_____

4.

x	+2	+1	0	−2
y	+5	+4	+3	+1

_____

5. Reasoning If the points $({}^+3, {}^+7)$, $({}^+2, {}^+7)$, $(0, {}^+7)$ and $(-4, {}^+7)$ were graphed, they would form a horizontal line. Do you think the equation for this line would be $x = {}^+7$ or $y = {}^+7$? Explain.

_____

_____

6. If you are wading in a fountain on an autumn day, the temperature of the water near your feet may be 15.6°C, but the air near your head in the chilly wind may be 2.9°C colder. What would be the temperature near your head?

_____

_____

7. Which ordered pair is on the graph of $y = x + {}^+11$?

A $({}^+3, -14)$　　　**B** $({}^+4, 16)$　　　**C** $(-8, 3)$　　　**D** $(3, 8)$

8. Writing to Explain John's graph included the points $({}^+5, {}^+2)$, $({}^+2, -1)$ and $(-2, -5)$. Jenny's graph included the points $({}^+8, {}^+5)$, $({}^+2, -1)$ and $(-3, -6)$. Would all six points be included on the same graph? Why or why not?

_____

_____

Problem Solving:
Work Backward

The movement of point A on a coordinate grid is described in the chart. What are the coordinates of A's starting location?

Time	Starting		1		2		Ending
Position	(x, y)		(9, 7)		(9, 5)		(6, 5)
Units/Direction		4 →		2 ↓		3 ←	

Read and Understand

What do you know?

The movements of point A and its final location

What are you trying to find?

A's starting location

Plan and Solve

Think: *Running the clock back in time from A's final location will place A back at its starting location.*

Since the clock is running in reverse, all directions will be reversed.

Solve the problem.

Time	Ending		2		1		Starting
Position	(6, 5)		(9, 5)		(9, 7)		(5, 7)
Units/Direction		3 →		2 ↑		4 ←	
Change		(6 **+ 3**, 5)		(9, **5 + 2**)		(9 **− 4**, 7)	

Write the answer in a complete sentence.   A's starting location is (5, 7).

Look Back and Check

Is your answer correct?

Yes, (**5** + 4 − 3, **7** − 2) is (6, 5).

Write the reverse for each of the following location changes.

1. 3 ↑ _____   **2.** 6 → _____   **3.** 4 ← _____   **4.** 2 ↓ _____

Write the new location for each of the following starting points and location changes.

5. (4, 3), 2 ↑ _____   **6.** (5, 3), 6 → _____   **7.** (8, 5), 3 ↓ _____

Problem Solving:
Work Backward

Work backward to find each starting position.

1. **Starting** (x, y). _____
   4 units ➔ (14, 20)
   2 units ↑ (14, 22)
   5 units ⬅ (9, 20) **Ending**

2. **Starting** (x, y). _____
   2 units ↓ (5, 6)
   3 units ➔ (8, 6)
   1 units ↑ (8, 7) **Ending**

3. **Starting** (x, y). _____
   8 units ↑ (5, 13)
   4 units ➔ (9, 13)
   6 units ➔ (15, 13) **Ending**

4. **Reasoning** Martha must finish her math quiz in 35 minutes. She knows
   that there are 10 multiple-choice questions and 5 word problems.
   If each word problem takes her exactly 3 minutes to complete, how
   much time can she spend on each multiple-choice question?

   _____

5. Kori arrived at school on time, at exactly 8:30 A.M. If it took him 15 minutes
   to walk to school, 10 minutes to eat breakfast, and 18 minutes to get ready,
   what time did he wake up this morning?

   A 7:37 A.M.   **C** 7:57 A.M.

   B 7:47 A.M.   **D** 8:07 A.M.

6. **Writing to Explain** Jerry used his $100 gift certificate to go shopping. He
   bought pants for $25, a shirt for $15, and socks for $3. Then he bought
   a pair of shoes. Jerry still has $27 left. How much were the shoes that he
   bought? Explain how you know.

   _____

   _____

Name _____

Bar Graphs and Picture Graphs

A bar graph uses rectangles to show data. A picture graph uses symbols to show data.

How to display data as a bar graph or picture graph

Look at the information about the varsity teams in the frequency table at right. Display this information as a bar graph.

Conference Basketball Championships		
High School	**Varsity**	**Freshman**
Smith	4	5
Phillips	2	6
Dominican	3	4

1. Decide on a scale and its intervals. Draw the graph. Label the axes.

2. Graph the data by drawing bars of the correct height.

3. Title the graph.

Look again at the frequency table above. Display the information about the freshman teams as a picture graph.

1. Decide on a symbol and its value. Draw the graph. Label the axes.

2. Graph the data by showing the correct number of symbols.

3. Title the graph.

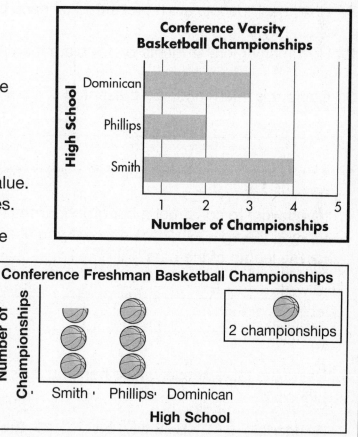

1. Complete the picture graph for Dominican High School.

2. How many varsity championships does the bar graph show? _____

3. How many freshman championships does the picture graph show? _____

Bar Graphs and Picture Graphs

Answer the questions about the picture graph shown below.

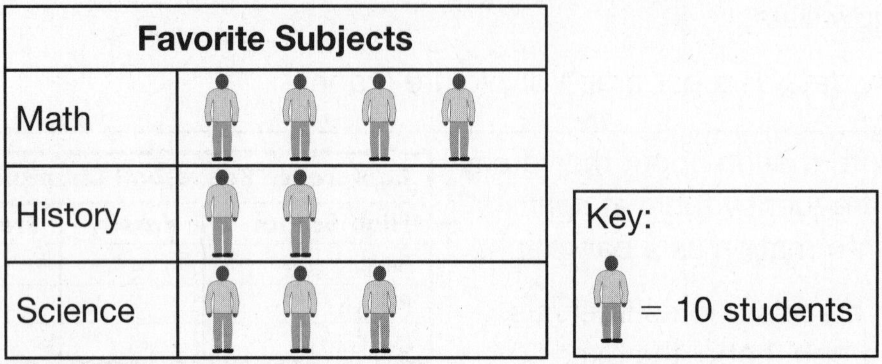

Favorite Subjects	
Math	👤 👤 👤 👤
History	👤 👤
Science	👤 👤 👤

Key:

👤 = 10 students

1. How many people are represented by each picture? _____

2. How many more students prefer math than prefer history? _____

3. Could this information be presented in a bar graph? Explain.

_____

_____

Top 5 names in Hills City, 2006

Jacob	26
Emily	15
Michael	15
Madison	21
Ethan	8

4. If you were to construct a bar graph for the table at the right, what scale would you use for the length of the bars?

_____

_____

5. Using the table above, which bar would be the highest?

   A Jacob   **B** Emily   **C** Ethan   **D** Madison

6. **Explain It** Do picture graphs and bar graphs show you patterns over time? Explain.

_____

_____

_____

Histograms

A histogram is a type of bar graph that shows frequency of data with equal intervals. The equal intervals are shown on the horizontal axis.

Mr. Sato asked each student in his class which month they were born in. He put the data into a table. Make a histogram to determine the two most common birthday months.

Month	Jan.	Feb.	Mar.	Apr.	May	Jun.	Jul.	Aug.	Sept.	Oct.	Nov.	Dec.
Frequency	3	2	1	2	4	1	3	2	5	0	1	2

Step 1. You want to divide the data by month, so lay out the months along the horizontal axis.

Step 2. The number of students born in each month is the frequency data, which goes on the vertical axis.

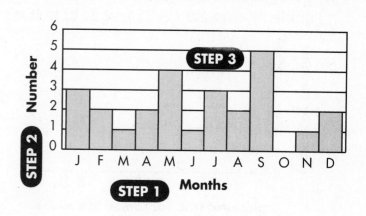

Step 3. Use the data from the table to fill in the histogram.

September and May are the most common birthday months.

1. How many people ages 0–18 and 39–58 combined attended the tournament?

_____

2. What is the total number of people who attended the tournament?

_____

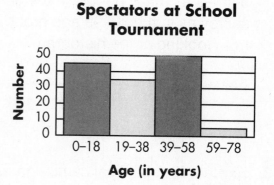

Spectators at School Tournament

Histograms

This table shows the results of a class survey to find
out how many pieces of fruit each student ate that week.

Amount of Fruit	Frequency
0–7	12
8–14	8
15–21	5

1. Complete the histogram below to find the percentage of
   students who ate 15–21 pieces of fruit that week.

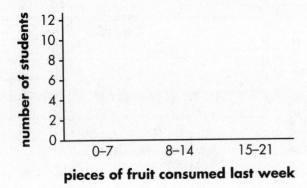

_____

2. **Reasoning** Mary says a histogram shows that about
   3 times as many people in the 60–79 age group answered a
   survey as in the 80–99 age group. How does she know this
   from looking at the histogram?

_____

_____

3. **Explain It** A political campaign recorded the ages of
   100 callers. In a histogram, which data would go on the
   horizontal axis and which on the vertical?

_____

_____

Circle Graphs

A circle graph shows 100% of a data set. Each wedge in the circle represents part of the whole amount.

One hundred people were asked if they owned a pet and if they did, what kind of pet. The table at the right shows the data.

From this table, you can create a circle graph.

Pet	
Dog	50
Cat	25
Bird	10
Other	10
No pet	5

Each category is part of the whole. You can find out how big a wedge to use for each category by changing the ratios into fractions.

50 people out of 100 had a dog.

$\frac{50}{100}$ is $\frac{1}{2}$.

So, the wedge for dog will be $\frac{1}{2}$ of the circle.

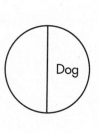

To finish the graph, do the same with the rest of the table.

cat $= \frac{25}{100} = \frac{1}{4}$, bird $= \frac{10}{100} = \frac{1}{10}$

other $= \frac{10}{100} = \frac{1}{10}$, no pet $= \frac{5}{100}$
$= \frac{1}{20}$

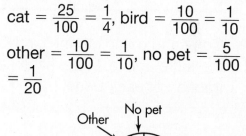

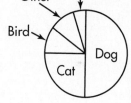

---

1. The table below shows what kind of books people said they had checked out at the library. Using the data, create a circle graph and label each section with the correct type of book and a fraction in simplest form.

Type of book	
Fiction	60
Magazine	20
Nonfiction	20
DVD	20

2. How many total people were asked about their book choice?

Circle Graphs

1. A bagel shop offers a variety of bagels. One morning, the following choices were made by the first 20 customers of the day: plain, 10; poppy seed, 5; sesame seed, 3; multigrain, 2. Complete the table below.

	Fraction	Percent
Plain		
Poppy Seed		
Sesame Seed		
Multigrain		

2. Copy and complete the circle graph below with the data in the table above. Label each section with the percent and fraction of each bagel.

3. **Number Sense** A circle graph is divided into four sections. One section equals 40%. The other three sections are equal in size. What percent does each of the other three sections represent?

_____

4. **Reasoning** If 10 out of 30 students in a survey chose ice skating as their favorite sport, what fraction of the circle should be shaded to represent the students who chose ice skating? How many degrees will that segment of the circle include?

_____

Problem Solving: Make a Graph

Choosing which graph to use depends on what kind of data set you are looking at.

Bar graphs and **circle graphs** are good graphs to use when you are comparing data that can be counted. **Line graphs** are good at showing changes in the data over time. **Histograms** divide the data into intervals and record how many data items fall within each interval.

There are three ferries that run from Port Shoals to Tiger Island. 187 people were on the 12:30 P.M. ferry, 122 people were on the 3:00 P.M. ferry, and 58 people were on the 5:30 P.M. ferry. Make a graph for this data set and analyze the data.

This data set is comparing data that can be counted, so a bar graph or a circle graph would be a good graph choice. Make a bar graph of the data.

What can you say about the data from this graph?

The 12:30 P.M. ferry was the most popular.

The 5:30 P.M. ferry was the least popular.

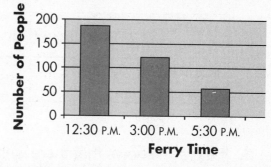

1. Each month, Martina measures the height of a tree she planted. Make a line graph to show the tree's growth.

Month	Height (in.)
April	36
May	42
June	60
July	75
August	84

Name ______________________________

Practice
19-4

Problem Solving: Make a Graph

1. In a survey, 100 students from around the country were asked what news source they preferred. Which news source is most popular? Make a circle graph to solve the problem.

News Source	Number of Votes
Television	50
Internet	25
Newspaper	15
Radio	10

2. In a survey, 32 students from around the country were asked how they traveled to and from school. Make a circle graph to show the data.

Type of Transportation	Subway	Bus	Bike	On Foot	Taxi
Number of Students	8	16	4	4	0

3. If a graph shows that there were 10 people who watched between 7 and 12 movies, what kind of graph could you be looking at?

A Circle **B** Bar **C** Histogram **D** Line

4. Explain It Would a line graph be an appropriate graph in Exercise 3? Why or why not?

____

____

____

____

____

Name _____

Reteaching
19-5

Mean

The mean is the sum of all the values in a set divided by the number of items in the set. The mean is also called the average.

How to find the mean of a set of data:

Eduardo surveyed 7 of his friends to find out how many books they read during the month. The frequency table shows the data. What is the average number of books read by Eduardo's friends?

Book Reading	
Friend	**Number of books read**
Jean	2
Raul	3
Sally	8
Jonathan	5
Haley	6
Kristen	3
Owen	1

1. Add the number of books read by each friend.

2. Divide the sum by the number of friends.

3. Use the average to answer the question.

$2 + 3 + 8 + 5 + 6 + 3 + 1 = 28$

$\frac{28}{7} = 4$

Eduardo's friends read an average of 4 books during the month.

---

1. Find the mean of this set of data: 241, 563, 829, 755. _____

2. This frequency table shows the number of silver medals won by American athletes in Summer Olympic Games between 1972 and 2000. What is the mean of this set of data?

   _____

3. **Estimation** What is the approximate average of these three numbers: 9, 18, and 31? _____

4. Explain how you would find the mean of this set of data: 4, 3, 5.

US Silver Medals Summer Olympics Games	
Year	**Medals**
2000	24
1996	32
1992	38
1988	31
1984	61
1976	35
1972	31

_____

_____

Mean

Find the mean of each set of data.

1. 2, 5, 9, 4

_____

2. 44, 73, 63

_____

3. 11, 38, 65, 4, 67

_____

4. 3, 6, 3, 7, 8

_____

5. 120, 450, 630

_____

6. 4.2, 5.3, 7.1, 4.0, 11.9

_____

Gene's scores on a math game were as follows: 8, 4, 10, 5, 3, 6.

7. What was his average score?

_____

8. If Gene gets two more scores of 10,
   what is his new average?

_____

9. **Reasoning** Krishan wants his quiz average to be at least
   90 so that he can get an A in the class. His current quiz
   scores are: 80, 100, 85. What does he have to get on his
   next quiz to have an average of 90?

   A 85   **B** 90   **C** 92   **D** 95

10. **Explain It** Suppose Krishan's teacher says that he can
    drop one of his test scores. Using his test scores of 80,
    100, and 85, which one should he drop, and why? What is
    his new average?

    _____

    _____

Median, Mode, and Range

The median, mode, and range are each numbers that describe a set of data.

How to find the median, mode, and range of a set of data:

Here is Eduardo's survey of how many books his friends read last month.

What are the median, mode, and range of Eduardo's survey?

Book Reading	
Friend	**Number of books read**
Jean	2
Raul	3
Sally	8
Jonathan	5
Haley	6
Kristen	3
Owen	1

Median: The median is the middle number in a set of data. To find it:

1. Arrange the data in order from least to greatest.

2. Locate the middle number.   1, 2, 3, 3, 5, 6, 8

↑ middle number = 3

The median number of books read is 3.

Mode: The mode is the data value that occurs most often. To find it:

1. List the data.   1, 2, 3, 3, 5, 6, 8

2. Find the number that occurs most.   3

The mode of the books read by Eduardo's friends is 3 books.

Range: The range is the difference between the greatest and least values. To find it:

1. Identify the greatest and least values.   8 and 1

2. Subtract the least from the greatest value. $8 - 1 = 7$

The range of the books read by Eduardo's friends is 7 books.

---

1. Find the median of this data set: 12, 18, 25, 32, 67.   _____

2. Find the mode of this data set: 123, 345, 654, 123, 452, 185.   _____

3. Find the range of this data set: 24, 32, 38, 31, 61, 35, 31.   _____

Median, Mode, and Range

1. Find the range of this data set: 225 342 288 552 263. _____

2. Find the median of this data set: 476 234 355 765 470. _____

3. Find the mode of this data set:
   16 7 8 5 16 7 8 4 7 8 16 7. _____

4. Find the range of this data set:
   64 76 46 88 88 43 99 50 55. _____

5. **Reasoning** Would the mode change if a 76 were added
   to the data in Exercise 4?

   _____

   _____

The table gives the math test scores for Mrs. Jung's
fifth-grade class.

76	54	92	88	76	88
75	93	92	68	88	76
76	88	80	70	88	72
Test Scores					

6. Find the mean of the data. _____

7. Find the mode of the data. _____

8. Find the median of the data. _____

9. What is the range of the data set? _____

10. Find the range of this data set: 247, 366, 785, 998.

    A 998 **B** 781 **C** 751 **D** 538

11. **Explain It** Will a set of data always have a mode?
    Explain your answer.

    _____

    _____

Outcomes

Almond, Keisha, and Mona are running for student
council president. Barry, Andy, and Maurice are running
for vice-president. Each student has an equal chance
of being elected.

You can use a tree diagram to find all the
possible outcomes. The set of all possible
outcomes is called the sample space.

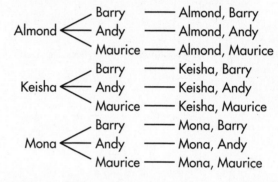

There are 9 possible outcomes in the
sample space.

1. Complete the tree diagram to show the possible outcomes
   when Spinner A and Spinner B are spun.

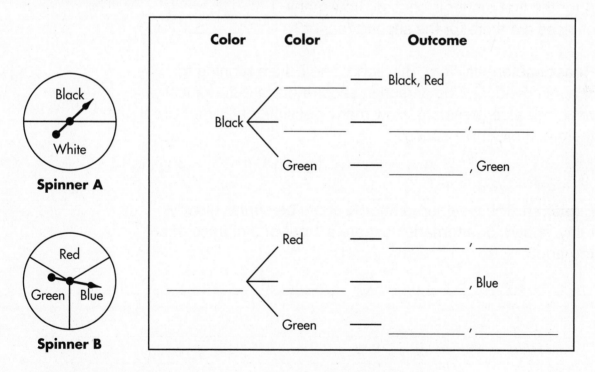

Spinner A

Spinner B

2. How many times does the outcome black/green occur
   in the tree diagram? _____

Name _____

Outcomes

The coach is trying to decide in what order Jane, Pete, and Lou will run a relay race.

1. Complete the tree diagram below to show the sample space.

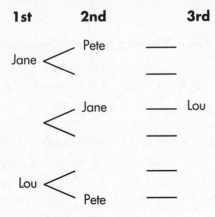

| 1st | 2nd | 3rd |

2. How many possible outcomes are there in the sample space? _____

3. After the first runner is chosen, how many choices are there for the second runner? _____

4. **Reasonableness** Tom, Bill, John, and Ed are running for school president. The person in second place automatically becomes vice-president. How many possible outcomes are there in the sample space?

   A 6 **B** 9 **C** 10 **D** 12

5. **Explain It** The weather tomorrow could be sunny, cloudy, rainy, snowy, or a tornado. Is there a 1 out of 5 chance of a tornado?

   _____

   _____

Name _____

Writing Probability as a Fraction

The probability of an event is a number that describes the chance that an event will occur. Probability can be expressed as a fraction.

Probability of an event $= \dfrac{\text{number of favorable outcomes}}{\text{number of possible outcomes}}$

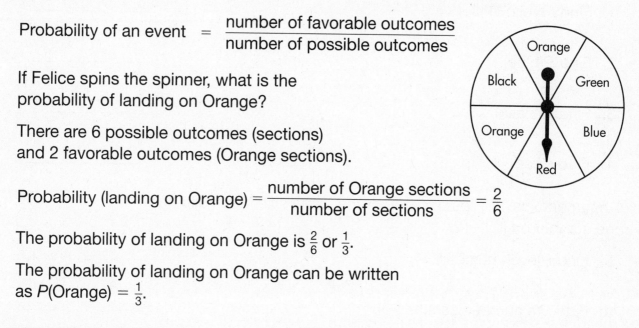

If Felice spins the spinner, what is the probability of landing on Orange?

There are 6 possible outcomes (sections) and 2 favorable outcomes (Orange sections).

Probability (landing on Orange) $= \dfrac{\text{number of Orange sections}}{\text{number of sections}} = \dfrac{2}{6}$

The probability of landing on Orange is $\frac{2}{6}$ or $\frac{1}{3}$.

The probability of landing on Orange can be written as $P(\text{Orange}) = \frac{1}{3}$.

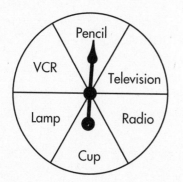

1. Find $P(\text{object that does not use electricity})$ _____

2. Find $P(\text{object that uses electricity})$ _____

3. Find $P(\text{object used for writing})$ _____

4. What does $P(\text{radio})$ mean?

_____

Writing Probability as a Fraction

Tom put 4 yellow marbles, 2 blue marbles, 6 red marbles, and 5 black marbles in a bag.

1. Find *P*(yellow).   _____

2. Find *P*(blue).   _____

3. Find *P*(black).   _____

4. Find *P*(red).   _____

A bag contains 12 slips of paper of the same size. Each slip has one number on it, 1–12.

5. Find *P*(even number).   _____

6. Find *P*(a number less than 6).   _____

7. Find *P*(an odd number).   _____

8. Find *P*(a number greater than 8).   _____

9. Describe an impossible event.

_____

10. A cube has 6 sides and is numbered 1 through 6. If the cube is tossed, what is the probability that a 3 will be tossed?

    A $\frac{1}{6}$ **B** $\frac{2}{6}$ **C** $\frac{3}{6}$ **D** $\frac{6}{6}$

11. **Explain It** Explain the probability of tossing a prime number when you toss the cube with numbers 1 through 6.

    _____

    _____

Problem Solving:
Solve a Simpler Problem

A farmer has 4 garden plots in a row. He wants to build paths connecting each pair of plots. He also doesn't want the paths to cross. How many paths must he build?

Read and Understand

What do you know?

There are four plots in a row.

Each pair of plots must be connected by a path.

The paths cannot cross.

What are you trying to find?

The total number of paths

Plan and Solve

Solve a simpler problem.

1. Construct a picture of two garden plots as shown below.

2. Then draw another picture of three plots. Look for a pattern for the design and number of paths.

3. Construct a diagram of the four plots.

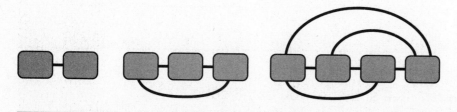

A farmer has four garden plots arranged in a square. Look at the following diagrams. Use them to help answer this question. Can the four garden plots be connected by six paths that do not cross? _____

Problem Solving:
Solve a Simpler Problem

Solve the simpler problems. Use the solutions to
help you solve the original problem.

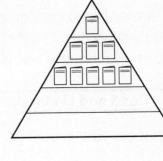

1. Reggie is designing a triangular magazine rack with
   5 shelves. The top shelf will hold 1 magazine. The
   second shelf will hold 3 magazines, and the third
   shelf will hold 5 magazines. This pattern continues
   to the bottom shelf. How many magazines will the
   magazine rack hold altogether?

   Simpler Problem What is the pattern?

   _____

   _____

   How many magazines will the fourth shelf hold? _____

   How many magazines will the bottom shelf hold? _____

   Solution:

   _____

   _____

2. At the deli, you receive 1 free sub after you buy 8 subs.
   How many free subs will you receive from the deli if you
   buy 24 subs?

   _____

3. The chef has 5 different kinds of pasta and 3 different flavors
   of sauce. How many different meals is she able to make?

   _____

   _____

Constructing Angles

You can construct congruent angles using a compass and straightedge.

Construct ∠H congruent ∠A.

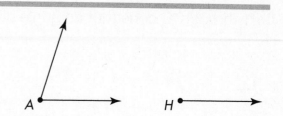

Step 1: Using endpoint *A* from the original angle as the center, take your compass and draw an arc across ∠A that intersects both rays of the angle. These are points *B* and *C*.

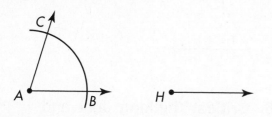

Step 2: Without changing your compass opening, make an identical arc on the new ray using endpoint *H* as the center. The point where the arc and the ray intersect is point *I*.

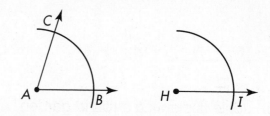

Step 3: Open your compass to the distance between points *B* and *C* on the original angle. Using that distance and point *I* as the center, draw an arc that intersects the first arc. Where the two arcs intersect is point *J*.

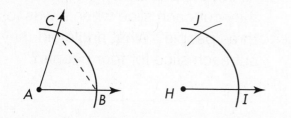

Step 4: Using the straightedge, draw a ray beginning at endpoint *H* going through point *J*.

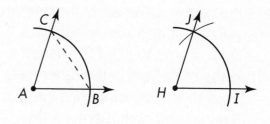

In **1** through **4**, trace each angle on a sheet of paper.
Then construct an angle congruent to each given angle.

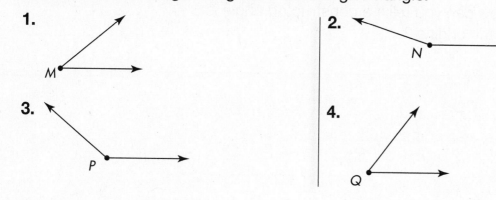

1.

2.

3.

4.

Constructing Angles

In **1** through **4**, construct an angle congruent to each given angle.

1.
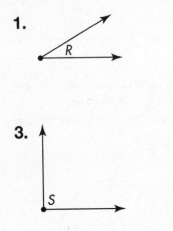

2.
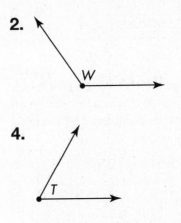

3.

4.

5. Josie is planting a round garden with her grandmother. On a piece of paper, they draw a circle with a diameter, or a line segment through the center. One half of the garden will be planted with vegetables. Josie wants to plant 3 different kinds of flowers in the other half. They divide the other half into 3 equal and congruent angles. How many degrees of the circle will each kind of flower take up?

_____

6. **Critical Thinking** June and 2 friends are sharing a pizza. The three of them share half the pizza. Then another friend comes over. The four of them divide the other half of the pizza. What angle did they cut each slice when it was for three people? What angle did they cut each slice for four people?

_____

_____

7. **Explain It** How can you tell if a constructed angle is congruent to the original?

_____

Constructing Lines

Construct a line perpendicular to $\overleftrightarrow{CD}$.

Step 1: Open your compass so that it is more than half the distance between C and D. With the compass point on C, draw an arc that goes both above and below the line.

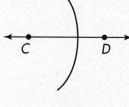

Step 2: Without changing your compass width, place the point on D and make another arc that goes above and below the line. Make sure this arc intersects the first arc above and below the line. The points where the arcs intersect each other are E and F.

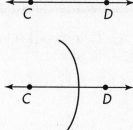

Step 3: Using a straightedge, draw a line through points E and F that crosses $\overleftrightarrow{CD}$. This new line $\overleftrightarrow{EF}$ is perpendicular to $\overleftrightarrow{CD}$.

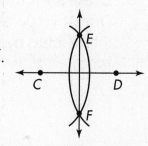

1. Construct a line perpendicular to $\overleftrightarrow{PQ}$.

P ———————————————— Q

2. **Explain It** Cisco's teacher asked him to name an object that has both parallel and perpendicular lines. Cisco said a ladder. Is this correct?

_____

_____

Constructing Lines

In **1** through **4**, copy the figures on a separate sheet of paper and follow the directions.

1. Construct a line that is parallel to line $\overleftrightarrow{EF}$.

2. Construct a line that intersects line $\overleftrightarrow{AB}$ that is not perpendicular.

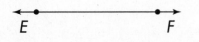

E   F

3. Construct a line segment that is congruent to line segment $\overline{CD}$.

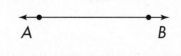

A   B

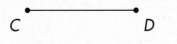

C   D

4. Construct a line that is perpendicular to line $\overleftrightarrow{RS}$.

5. Draw a Picture/Diagram
Draw two parallel roads being intersected by a perpendicular road.

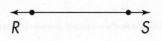

R   S

6. A city park wants to build a mini railroad for children to tour the park. It costs $110 to lay down 1 mile of tracks. If the park has mapped a 6-mile route where the tracks could go, how much will it cost?

_____

7. Study the diagram. Which statement below is true?

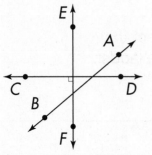

8. Explain It Explain how perpendicular lines are similar to intersecting lines.

_____

_____

_____

A $\overleftrightarrow{AB}$ intersects $\overrightarrow{CD}$

B $\overleftrightarrow{EF}$ is parallel to $\overrightarrow{AB}$

C $\overleftrightarrow{AB}$ is perpendicular to $\overleftrightarrow{CD}$

D $\overleftrightarrow{EF}$ is parallel to $\overleftrightarrow{CD}$

_____

Congruent Shapes

You can construct congruent shapes by using congruent angles and lines.

Construct a triangle that is congruent to △RST.

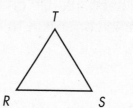

Step 1: Construct ∠A congruent to ∠R.

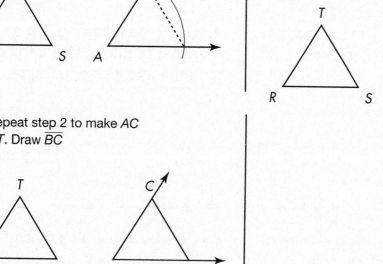

Step 2: Open your compass to the measurement of RS. Without changing the compass width, place the point on A. Label the point at the other end of the compass width B. AB is now equal to RS.

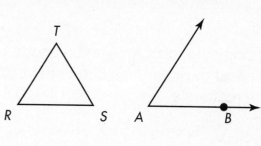

Step 3: Repeat step 2 to make AC equal to RT. Draw $\overline{BC}$

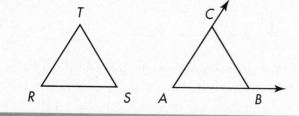

In **1** through **3**, copy each shape and construct a congruent shape.

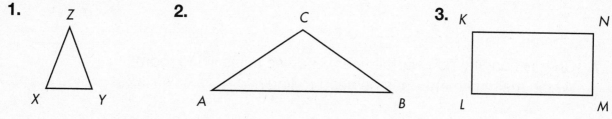

1.   **2.**   **3.**

Constructing Shapes

In **1** and **2**, copy each triangle on another sheet of paper. Then construct a triangle congruent to it.

1.

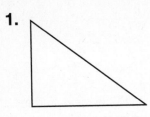

2.

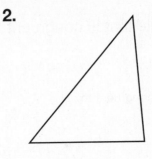

3. Copy the following line on another sheet of paper. Use it to construct a rectangle.

4. Copy the following line on another sheet of paper. Use it to construct a triangle with equal sides.

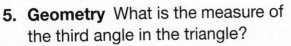

5. Geometry What is the measure of the third angle in the triangle?

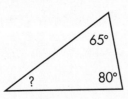

65°

80°

?

6. Jeremy is hanging a painting for his aunt. She wants it centered on a wall that measures 14 ft. Where should Jeremy hammer in the nail?

_____

7. Greg is hanging new curtains for windows in his living room. Which measurement does he need to find?

A perimeter   **B** area   **C** volume   **D** circumference

8. Explain It How can you be sure that the triangles you construct are congruent to the original?

_____

Problem Solving: Use Objects

A tetramino is an arrangement of four identical squares in a plane. The squares are attached to each other edge to edge. A tetramino is a unique arrangement. It cannot be matched to another by rotating (turning) or reflecting (flipping). Use square tiles to show if the two figures are unique.

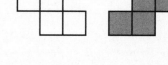

1. Construct the two figures using tiles.

2. Construct a rotation of the first figure.

3. Check for a match. *Think: If figures match, they are not unique. If figures do not match, figures may be unique.*

4. Construct a reflection of the first figure.

5. Repeat Step 3.

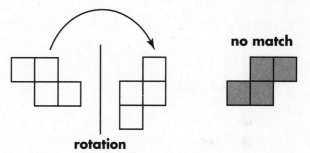

no match

rotation

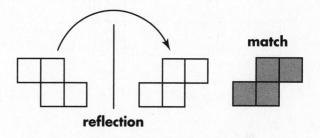

match

reflection

6. Write your answer in a complete sentence.

The two figures are not unique, because they match by reflection.

---

1. Show if these two figures are unique tetraminoes. Explain your answer.

_____

_____

_____

Problem Solving: Use Objects

1. Is the following a pentomino? Explain.

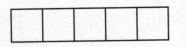

_____

_____

Tell whether the pentominoes in each pair are related by
a reflection or a rotation.

2.

_____

3.

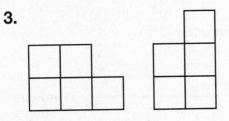

_____

4. How many possible different pentominoes can be formed?

   A 3   **B** 7   **C** 10   **D** 12

5. **Explain It** Use objects to build pentominoes with 1 square in
   each row. How many of these kinds of pentominoes can be
   built? Explain.

   _____

   _____

   _____

Step Up to Grade 6

Comparing and Ordering Rational Numbers

1. Plot and label $1\frac{4}{5}$ and $-1\frac{4}{5}$ on the number line below. Notice how the negatives are mirror images of the positives. So $-1\frac{4}{5}$ is opposite $1\frac{4}{5}$.

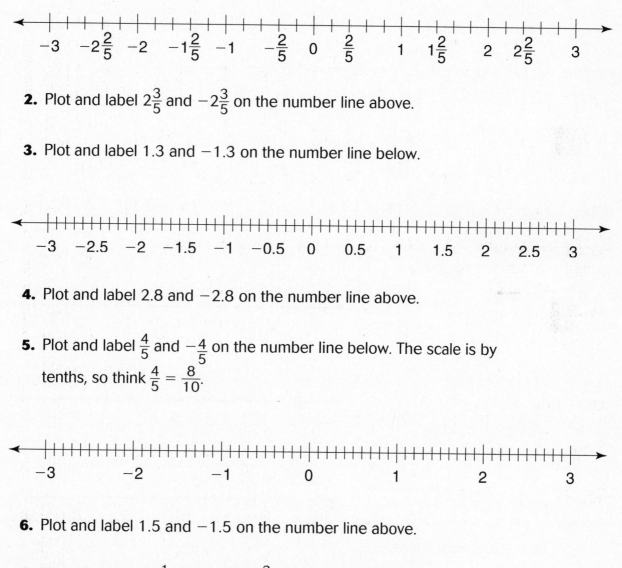

2. Plot and label $2\frac{3}{5}$ and $-2\frac{3}{5}$ on the number line above.

3. Plot and label 1.3 and -1.3 on the number line below.

4. Plot and label 2.8 and -2.8 on the number line above.

5. Plot and label $\frac{4}{5}$ and $-\frac{4}{5}$ on the number line below. The scale is by tenths, so think $\frac{4}{5} = \frac{8}{10}$.

6. Plot and label 1.5 and -1.5 on the number line above.

7. Plot and label $-2\frac{1}{2}$, -0.3, and $2\frac{3}{5}$ on the number line above.

For negatives, think about the opposite.

Name _____

Comparing and Ordering Rational Numbers (continued)

On the number line, numbers increase in value from left to right.

So, $-\frac{4}{5} < -0.3$.

8. Use the number line on the previous page to write $\frac{4}{5}$, $-\frac{4}{5}$, 1.5,

-1.5, $-2\frac{1}{2}$, -0.3, and $2\frac{3}{5}$ in order from least to greatest.

Use the number line to compare numbers. Fill in each circle with > or <.

9. 2.3 $\bigcirc$ -1.4 **10.** $-2\frac{3}{5}$ $\bigcirc$ -1.3 **11.** 1.6 $\bigcirc$ $1\frac{4}{5}$

12. -2.7 $\bigcirc$ -2.3 **13.** -1.75 $\bigcirc$ $-1\frac{4}{5}$ **14.** -0.25 $\bigcirc$ -0.5

Place each set of numbers on the number line. Then write the numbers in order from least to greatest.

15. 2, -1.5, $-2\frac{1}{4}$, 1.75, -1

_____

16. -1.8, $-\frac{4}{5}$, $-\frac{1}{5}$, -1, 1.3

_____

17. $-1\frac{1}{3}$, $2\frac{5}{6}$, 1, $-2\frac{1}{6}$, $1\frac{2}{3}$

_____

18. Reasoning How can you easily tell that 5.7 is greater than -8.6?

Multiplying and Dividing Integers

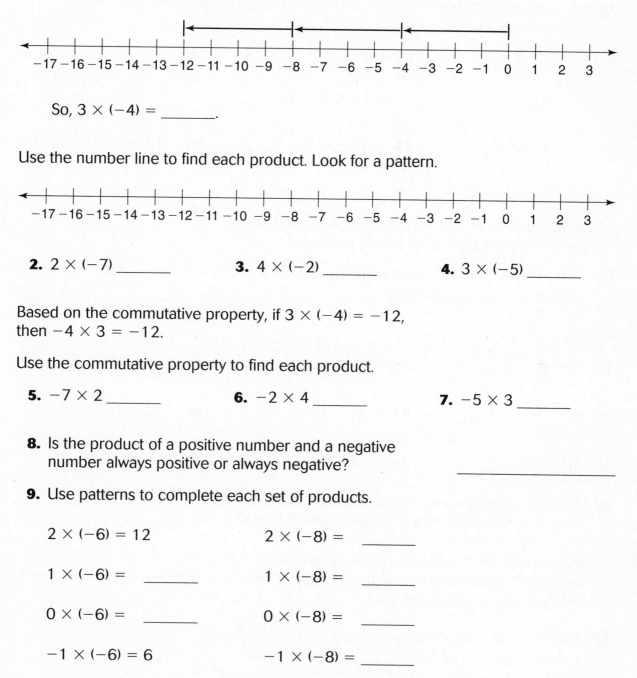

1. To find $3 \times (-4)$ on a number line, move backward 4 spaces,
3 times.

So, $3 \times (-4) =$ _____.

Use the number line to find each product. Look for a pattern.

2. $2 \times (-7)$ _____

3. $4 \times (-2)$ _____

4. $3 \times (-5)$ _____

Based on the commutative property, if $3 \times (-4) = -12$,
then $-4 \times 3 = -12$.

Use the commutative property to find each product.

5. -7×2 _____

6. -2×4 _____

7. -5×3 _____

8. Is the product of a positive number and a negative
number always positive or always negative?

_____

9. Use patterns to complete each set of products.

$2 \times (-6) = 12$ $2 \times (-8) =$ _____

$1 \times (-6) =$ _____ $1 \times (-8) =$ _____

$0 \times (-6) =$ _____ $0 \times (-8) =$ _____

$-1 \times (-6) = 6$ $-1 \times (-8) =$ _____

$-2 \times (-6) =$ _____ $-2 \times (-8) =$ _____

Multiplying and Dividing Integers (continued)

10. Is the product of two negative numbers always
positive or always negative?   _____

Use the relationship between multiplication and division to find each
quotient. Look for patterns.

11. 6 × _____ = −24   **12.** 9 × _____ = −18   **13.** −8 × _____ = 24

−24 ÷ 6 _____   −18 ÷ 9 _____   24 ÷ (−8) _____

14. −35 ÷ (−7) _____   **15.** −40 ÷ (−5) _____   **16.** −18 ÷ (−3) _____

−7 × _____ = −35   −5 × _____ = −40   −3 × _____ = −18

17. Is the quotient of a positive number and a negative
number always positive or always negative?   _____

18. Is the quotient of two negative numbers always
positive or always negative?   _____

Multiply or Divide

19. −3 × 2 _____   **20.** −10 × (−7) _____   **21.** 8 × (−9) _____

22. 5 × (−24) _____   **23.** −31 × (−7) _____   **24.** −49 ÷ (−7) _____

25. 36 ÷ (−4) _____   **26.** −42 ÷ 3 _____   **27.** 90 ÷ (−15) _____

28. The temperature starts at 0 degrees and falls 2 degrees
every hour. What is the temperature after 5 hours?   _____

29. Reasoning What is the sign of the answer if you
multiply 2 negative numbers and then divide the
product by a negative number?   _____

30. During a week, Mike's daily balances in his checking
account were $40, $12, −$15, −$23, and −$44.
What was his average daily balance during that week?   _____

Properties of Operations

1. Fill in the blanks to complete the table and summarize the properties of addition and multiplication.

Property	Example	Generalization for Any Numbers *a, b,* and *c*
Commutative Property of Addition	$12 + 4 = 4 + $ _____	$a + b = b + $ _____
Associative Property of Addition	$(7 + 3) + 8 = 7 + (3 + $ _____ $)$ _____ $+ 8 = 7 + $ _____	$(a + b) + c = $ $a + (b + $ _____ $)$
Identity Property of Addition	$5 + 0 = $ _____ $0 + 71 = $ _____	$a + 0 = $ _____ and $0 + a = $ _____
Commutative Property of Multiplication	$5 \times 8 = 8 \times $ _____	$a \times b = b \times $ _____
Associative Property of Multiplication	$(6 \times 2) \times 4 = 6 \times ($ _____ $\times 4)$ _____ $\times 4 = 6 \times $ _____	$(a \times b) \times c = $ $a \times (b \times $ _____ $)$
Identity Property of Multiplication	$17 \times 1 = $ _____ $1 \times 6 = $ _____	$a \times 1 = $ _____ and $1 \times a = $ _____
Zero Property of Multiplication	$34 \times 0 = $ _____ $0 \times 98 = $ _____	$a \times 0 = $ _____ and $0 \times a = $ _____

2. Tell which property is used.

   $(5 \times 7) \times 20 = (7 \times 5) \times 20$

   _____ Property of _____

   $(7 \times 5) \times 20 = 7 \times (5 \times 20)$

   _____ Property of _____

Name _____

Properties of Operations (continued)

Find each *n*. Name the property that you used.

3. $3 \times 6 = 6 \times n$

_____

_____

4. $n \times 5 = 0$

_____

_____

5. $365 \times n = 365$

_____

_____

6. $(3 \times 2) \times n = 3 \times (2 \times 10)$

_____

_____

7. $5 \times 6 \times 4 \times 0 = n$

_____

_____

8. $n + 45 = 45$

_____

_____

9. $17 + 62 = 62 + n$

_____

_____

10. $21 + (n + 14) = (21 + 50) + 14$

_____

_____

11. $3 \times (14 - 14) = n$

_____

_____

12. $6 + (9 - n) = 6$

_____

_____

13. Reasoning Katie says she is thinking of two numbers whose
product is 0. John claims that he knows one number for certain.
Is he right? How does he know?

Use the Properties of Operations to Complete.

14. $10 + $ _____ $ = 10$

15. $(10 \times 6) \times 2 = $ _____ $ \times (6 \times 2)$

16. $(8 + 2) + 6 = (2 + $ _____ $) + 6$

17. $14 + 16 = $ _____ $ + 14$

18. $c \times d = d \times $ _____

19. $(q \times r) \times s = q \times ($ _____ $ \times s)$

Writing Multiplication and Division Equations

Earthquakes occur along faults. The San Andreas Fault in California moves about 25 millimeters a year. Answer the questions below to find how many years it would take the San Andreas Fault to move 150 millimeters.

1. What are you trying to find?

Let y equal what you are trying to find.

2. Describe the problem and translate words to symbols.

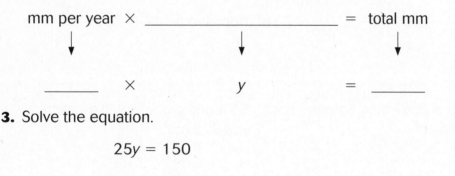

mm per year $\times$ _____ = total mm

_____ $\times$ y = _____

3. Solve the equation.

$$25y = 150$$

$$\frac{25y}{\boxed{}} = \frac{150}{\boxed{}}$$

$$y = \underline{}$$

4. How many years would it take the San Andreas fault to move 150 mm?

_____

A geologist divided the total number of acres she needs to map in 5 days by 5. She found she needs to map 635 acres each day. Answer the questions below to find how many total acres she needs to map.

5. What are you trying to find?

Let a equal what you are trying to find.

Writing Multiplication and Division Equations (continued)

6. Describe the problem and translate words to symbols.

_____ ÷ Number of days = _____

↓   ↓   ↓

_____   ÷   _____   =   _____

7. Solve the equation in 6 above.

8. How many total acres does the geologist need to map? _____

Write an equation for each sentence.

9. 8 times k is 144.

10. x divided by 14 is 322.

_____

_____

11. d dollars shared equally by 4 friends equals 8 dollars each.

12. 5 friends giving d dollars each equals $75.

_____

_____

Write an equation and solve each problem.

13. The North Anatolian Fault in Turkey moves about 24 millimeters a year. The total 8-year movement, m, along the fault divided by 8 equals 24. How far does the fault move in 8 years?

14. A classroom has 5 rows of desks, and each row has the same number of desks. There are 35 desks altogether. How many desks, d, are in each row?

Solving Equations with Integers

Materials two color counters, 20 per student or pair; sheets of paper
cut in half, 6 half-sheets per student or pair

Let red (gray) represent negatives and yellow (white) represent positives.

1. Show $-3 + n = 5$ with counters and papers as shown below.

2. Since $-3 + 3 = 0$, solve the equation by adding 3 to each side as
shown below.

3. A red counter and a yellow counter together
makes a zero pair, since $-1 + 1 = 0$.
Remove all zero pairs. What is left? $n =$ _____

4. Fill in the blanks to show what you did.

$$-3 + n = 5$$

$$-3 + n + \text{_____} = 5 + \text{_____}$$

$$n = \text{_____}$$

5. Show $-6 + k = -2$ with counters and pieces of paper.

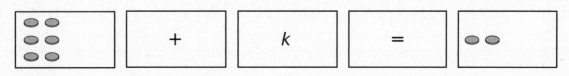

6. Add 6 yellow counters to each side.
Remember $-6 + 6 + k = -2 + 6$
Remove zero pairs. What is left? $k =$ _____

Solving Equations with Integers (continued)

7. Fill in the blanks to show what you did.

$$k - 6 = -2$$

$$k - 6 + \underline{\hspace{1.5cm}} = -2 + \underline{\hspace{1.5cm}}$$

$$k = \underline{\hspace{1.5cm}}$$

8. Show $3y = -9$ with counters and pieces of paper.

  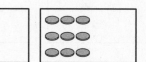

9. Divide each side into three equal parts and
remove all but one part. What is left? $y = \underline{\hspace{1.5cm}}$

10. Fill in the blanks to show what you did.

$$3y = -9$$

$$3y \div \underline{\hspace{1.5cm}} = -9 \div \underline{\hspace{1.5cm}}$$

$$y = \underline{\hspace{1.5cm}}$$

Solve each equation.

11. $n - 4 = -5$ **12.** $17p = -51$ **13.** $x - 12 = 13$ **14.** $k - 51 = -13$

_____   _____   _____   _____

15. $\dfrac{k}{-10} = 13$ **16.** $-8d = -80$ **17.** $6r = -132$ **18.** $\dfrac{n}{12} = 5$

_____   _____   _____   _____

19. $3x = -33$ **20.** $r + 17 = 10$ **21.** $\dfrac{p}{-31} = 2$ **22.** $r + 1 = -2$

_____   _____   _____   _____

23. One day in winter it felt like it was $-11°F$ outside because the
wind was blowing. However, this was actually $17°F$ less than
the actual temperature. Use the equation $a - 17 = -11$ to
find the actual temperature. _____

Reasoning Without solving, tell whether each variable is positive or negative.

24. $\dfrac{n}{-13} = -273$ **25.** $17k = -85$ **26.** $-3x = 111$

_____   _____   _____

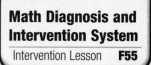

Solving Equations with More Than One Operation

1. Explain how to solve $x - 2 = 19$.

2. Explain how to solve $7x = 21$.

To solve an equation like $7x - 2 = 19$, combine the two steps in 1 and 2 above. Do the opposite of the order of operations. Undo addition and subtraction before undoing multiplication and division.

3. Fill in the blanks to solve the equation.

$$7x - 2 = 19$$

$$7x - 2 + \underline{\hspace{1cm}} = 19 + \underline{\hspace{1cm}}$$ Add 2 to both sides.

$$7x = \underline{\hspace{1cm}}$$

$$7x \div \underline{\hspace{1cm}} = \underline{\hspace{1cm}} \div \underline{\hspace{1cm}}$$ Divide both sides by 7.

$$x = \underline{\hspace{1cm}}$$

To solve an equation like $21 - 5x = 31$, use properties of integers to change it to $21 + (-5x) = 31$.

4. Fill in the blanks to solve the equation.

$$21 - 5x = 31$$

$$21 + (-5x) = 31$$

$$21 + (-5x) - \underline{\hspace{1cm}} = 31 - \underline{\hspace{1cm}}$$ Subtract 21 from both sides.

$$-5x = \underline{\hspace{1cm}}$$

$$-5x \div (-5) = \underline{\hspace{1cm}} \div \underline{\hspace{1cm}}$$ Divide both sides by -5.

$$x = \underline{\hspace{1cm}}$$

Solving Equations with More Than One Operation (continued)

5. Fill in the blanks to solve the equation.

$$\frac{n}{8} + 3 = 7$$

$$\frac{n}{8} + 3 - \underline{\hspace{1cm}} = 7 - \underline{\hspace{1cm}}$$ Subtract 3 from both sides.

$$\frac{n}{8} = \underline{\hspace{1cm}}$$

$$\underline{\hspace{1cm}} \times \frac{n}{8} = 8 \times \underline{\hspace{1cm}}$$ Multiply both sides by 4.

$$n = \underline{\hspace{1cm}}$$

Solve each equation. Check your answer.

6. $3x + 11 = 8$ **7.** $\frac{m}{7} - 3 = 0$ **8.** $5h + 13 = 13$ **9.** $1 - 2t = 3$

_____   _____   _____   _____

10. $40 = 8 - 16k$ **11.** $50x - 2 = 48$ **12.** $6 = 10h + 36$ **13.** $33x - 33 = 33$

_____   _____   _____   _____

14. $51 - 3t = 111$ **15.** $12 = \frac{r}{3} + 16$ **16.** $181 + 3m = 1$ **17.** $\frac{k}{4} - 1 = 9$

_____   _____   _____   _____

18. Sally paid $94 for 4 concert tickets. This price included a $10 transaction fee. Solve the equation $4p + 10 = 94$ to find the price, p, of one concert ticket.

19. Reasoning Amanda has a slow leak in the front tire of her motorcycle. She knows the tire pressure is 41 pounds, and that it is leaking at 2 pounds per minute. She must stop driving on the tire if the pressure hits 17 pounds. Solve the equation $41 - 2t = 17$ to find out how long Amanda can drive on the tire.

Dividing Greater Numbers

The Camara family wants to travel the same distance each of
6 days. They need to travel 1,716 miles in all. Answer 1 to 15 to
find how far they should travel each day.

Find 1,716 ÷ 6.

1. Are there enough thousands to put one in each of 6 groups?   _____

2. Regroup the thousand into hundreds and add the other 7 hundreds.

   1 thousand + 7 hundreds = _____ hundreds

3. How many hundreds can go into each of 6 groups?   _____
   Record the 2 in the hundreds place of the quotient, below.

4. How many hundreds were used?

   6 × 2 hundreds = _____ hundreds
   Record the hundreds used below the 17 in 1,716, below.

5. How many hundreds are leftover?

   17 hundreds − 12 hundreds

   = _____ hundreds
   Record the 5 under the 12.

6. Regroup the hundreds into tens and
   add the other 1 ten.

   5 hundreds + 1 ten = _____ tens
   Bring down the 1 ten next to the 5 to show how many tens in all.

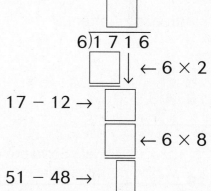

$6\overline{)1\ 7\ 1\ 6}$

← 6 × 2

17 − 12 →

← 6 × 8

51 − 48 →

7. How many tens can go into each of 6 groups? _____
   Record the 8 in the tens place of the quotient.

8. How many tens were used? 6 × 8 tens = _____ tens
   Record 48 below the 51.

9. How many tens are leftover? _____
   Record the tens left below the 48 and the line.

Dividing Greater Numbers (continued)

10. Regroup the tens into ones and add
the other 6 ones. Bring down the 6
to show the total ones.

3 tens + 6 ones = _____ ones

11. How many ones can go into each of
6 groups?   _____
Record the 6 in the ones place of the quotient.

12. How many ones were used?

6 × 6 ones = _____ ones
Record the 36 below the regrouped 36.

13. How many ones are leftover? 36 − 36 = _____
Record the ones left below the 36 and the line.

14. What is 1,716 ÷ 6? _____

15. How far should the Camara family travel each day? _____ miles

Find each quotient.

16. $4\overline{)3,560}$ **17.** $6\overline{)1,836}$ **18.** $4\overline{)4,112}$

19. $2\overline{)2,246}$ **20.** $8\overline{)832}$ **21.** $7\overline{)6,510}$

22. Reasoning How can you use estimation to find out
if the answer of 286 is reasonable for 1,716 ÷ 6?

Estimating Sums and Differences of Mixed Numbers

Last week, Dwayne spent $4\frac{1}{3}$ hours playing basketball and $1\frac{2}{3}$ hours playing soccer. Answer 1 to 9 to estimate how much time Dwayne spent in all playing these two sports.

Estimate $4\frac{1}{3} + 1\frac{2}{3}$.

1. What two whole numbers is $4\frac{1}{3}$ between? _____ and _____

2. Use the number line.
   Is $4\frac{1}{3}$ closer to 4 or 5? _____

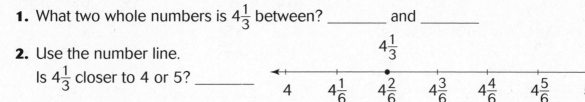

3. What is the number halfway between 4 and 5? _____

4. Compare. Write >, <, or =. $\frac{1}{3} \bigcirc \frac{1}{2}$

By comparing $\frac{1}{3}$ and $\frac{1}{2}$, you can tell that $4\frac{1}{3}$ is closer to 4 than 5, without using a number line. So, $4\frac{1}{3}$ rounded to the nearest whole number is 4.

5. What two whole numbers is $1\frac{2}{3}$ between? _____ and _____

6. Compare. Write >, <, or =. $\frac{2}{3} \bigcirc \frac{1}{2}$

7. What is $1\frac{2}{3}$ rounded to the nearest whole number? _____

$$4\frac{1}{3} \longrightarrow 4$$
$$+ 1\frac{2}{3} \longrightarrow + 2$$

8. Use the rounded numbers to estimate $4\frac{1}{3} + 1\frac{2}{3}$.

9. About how much time did Dwayne spend playing basketball and soccer? _____

About how much more time did Dwayne spend playing basketball than soccer?

$$4\frac{1}{3} \longrightarrow 4$$
$$- 1\frac{2}{3} \longrightarrow - 2$$

10. Estimate $4\frac{1}{3} - 1\frac{2}{3}$ at the right.

11. About how much more time did Dwayne spend playing basketball than soccer? _____

Name _____

Estimating Sums and Differences of Mixed Numbers (continued)

Estimate each sum or difference.

12. $2\frac{2}{3}$
$-1\frac{1}{3}$
_____

13. $2\frac{9}{10}$
$-1\frac{5}{10}$
_____

14. 5
$+4\frac{2}{4}$
_____

15. $6\frac{4}{6}$
$+1\frac{5}{6}$
_____

16. $6\frac{7}{8}$
$-5\frac{3}{8}$
_____

17. 6
$-3\frac{3}{9}$
_____

18. $4\frac{9}{14}$
$+2\frac{11}{14}$
_____

19. 6
$+4\frac{2}{16}$
_____

20. $2\frac{3}{4}-1$
_____

21. $7\frac{2}{6}+6\frac{5}{6}$
_____

22. $3\frac{2}{5}+1\frac{2}{5}$
_____

23. $6\frac{1}{8}-1\frac{5}{8}$
_____

24. $7-2\frac{3}{7}$
_____

25. $3\frac{4}{8}+1\frac{7}{8}$
_____

26. Yolanda walked $2\frac{3}{5}$ miles on Monday, $1\frac{1}{5}$ miles on Tuesday, and $3\frac{4}{5}$ miles on Wednesday. Estimate her total distance walked.

_____

27. Chris was going to add $2\frac{1}{4}$ cups of a chemical to the swimming pool until he found out that Richard already added $1\frac{1}{8}$ cups of the chemical. Estimate how much more Chris should add so that the total is his original amount.

_____

28. Reasoning Is $3\frac{1}{2}$ closer to 3 or 4? Explain.

Estimating Products and Quotients of Mixed Numbers

Karina's recipe for tacos uses $1\frac{3}{4}$ pounds of beef. She needs to make $3\frac{1}{3}$ times the recipe for a party. About how many pounds of beef does she need?

Estimate $3\frac{1}{3} \times 1\frac{3}{4}$ by answering 1 to 9.

1. What two whole numbers is $3\frac{1}{3}$ between? _____ and _____

2. Use the number line below. Is $3\frac{1}{3}$ closer to 3 or 4? _____

3. What number is halfway between 3 and 4? _____

4. Compare. Write >, <, or =. $\frac{1}{3}$ ◯ $\frac{1}{2}$

By comparing $\frac{1}{3}$ and $\frac{1}{2}$, you can tell that $3\frac{1}{3}$ is closer to 3 than 4, without using a number line.

$3\frac{1}{3}$ rounded to the nearest whole number is 3.

5. What two whole numbers is $1\frac{3}{4}$ between? _____ and _____

6. Compare. Write >, <, or =. $\frac{3}{4}$ ◯ $\frac{1}{2}$

7. What is $1\frac{3}{4}$ rounded to the nearest whole number? _____

8. Use the rounded numbers to estimate.

$3\frac{1}{3} \times 1\frac{3}{4}$ is about _____ × _____ _____

9. About how many pounds of beef does Karina need?   About _____

Marco is making $12\frac{2}{3}$ pounds of lasagna. Each pan can hold $2\frac{3}{4}$ pounds. About how many pans does he need?

Estimate $12\frac{2}{3} \div 2\frac{3}{4}$ by answering 10 to 13.

10. What is $12\frac{2}{3}$ rounded to the nearest whole number? _____

Name _____

Estimating Products and Quotients of Mixed Numbers (continued)

11. What is $2\frac{3}{4}$ rounded to the nearest whole number? _____

12. Since $13 \div 3$ is not easy to divide, use compatible numbers.
What numbers are close to $12\frac{2}{3} \div 2\frac{3}{4}$ and easy to divide?

$12\frac{2}{3} \div 2\frac{3}{4}$ is about _____ ÷ _____ = _____.

13. About how many pans does Marco need?   About _____

Estimate.

14. $2\frac{7}{8} \times 7\frac{3}{5}$ **15.** $6\frac{1}{5} \times 8\frac{3}{4}$ **16.** $5\frac{7}{12} \div 1\frac{1}{5}$

_____   _____   _____

17. $5\frac{2}{7} \times 9\frac{4}{5}$ **18.** $8\frac{5}{7} \div 2\frac{2}{3}$ **19.** $7\frac{5}{7} \div 1\frac{9}{10}$

_____   _____   _____

20. $3\frac{5}{12} \times 1\frac{3}{5}$ **21.** $1\frac{5}{9} \times 7\frac{1}{2}$ **22.** $1\frac{1}{3} \times 5\frac{2}{9}$

_____   _____   _____

23. $4\frac{3}{12} \times 7$ **24.** $25 \div 4\frac{7}{9}$ **25.** $9\frac{1}{10} \div 3\frac{1}{12}$

_____   _____   _____

26. The Hummingbird Trail at Camp Redlands is $1\frac{7}{8}$ miles long.
Surinder, a camp counselor, hikes the trail $2\frac{1}{4}$ times a day.
About how far does he hike each day?   About _____

27. Tammy needs to hike $15\frac{1}{4}$ miles to win an award. About how
many times does she need to hike a trail that is $2\frac{7}{8}$ miles long? About _____

28. Reasoning Explain how to use compatible numbers to find
$17\frac{2}{3} \div 5\frac{9}{10}$.

Distance, Rate, and Time

The formula $d = r \times t$ relates distance, d, rate, r, and time, t. Rate in this formula means average speed.

The table shows the results of practice races run by some members of a track team. Rates written as 6 meters/second are read 6 meters per second.

Complete the table by answering 1 to 13.

Name	Distance	Rate	Time
Hannah	600 meters	6 meters/second	
Mya	800 meters		160 seconds
Adrienne		5 meters/second	120 seconds

1. What is the formula that relates distance, rate, and time?   _____

2. For Hannah, what is the value of d ?   _____

3. For Hannah, what is the value of r ?   _____

4. For Hannah, which variable is unknown?   _____

5. Substitute Hannah's values for d and r in the formula.

$$d \ = \ r \ \times \ t$$

$$\text{_____} = \text{_____} \times \ t$$

6. Solve $600 = 6t$. Show your work.

$t = \text{_____}$

7. How fast did Hannah run the race?
Write this amount in the table.   _____ seconds

8. Substitute Mya's values for d and t in the formula.

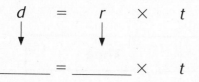

$$\text{_____} = \ r \ \times \text{_____}$$

Distance, Rate, and Time (continued)

9. Solve the equation $800 = 160r$.

$r =$ _____

10. How fast did Mya run the race?
Write this amount in the table.   _____ meters/second

11. Substitute Adrienne's values for r and t in the formula.

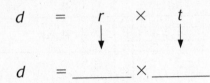

$$d \quad = \quad \_\_\_\_ \times \_\_\_\_$$

12. What is the value of d?   _____

13. How far did Adrienne run?
Write this amount in the table.   _____

Solve the equation for the missing variable.

14. $d = 55$ miles/hour $\times$ 7 hours

15. 300 feet = 15 feet/second $\times t$

$d =$ _____ $t =$ _____

Complete the table.

	Distance	Rate	Time
16.	200 meters	2 meters/second	
17.	10 miles		4 hours
18.		8 yards/minute	10 minutes

19. **Reasoning** If two people run the same distance but one person takes less time than the other, how do their rates compare?

Name _____

Percents Greater than 100 or Less Than 1

Shea bought a pair of shoes at a discount store. She found the same shoes at a department store where the price was 120% the price at the discount store. Use the diagram and answer 1 to 7 to write a decimal and a fraction to represent 120%.

1. To change a percent to a fraction, remove the percent sign and write the number over a denominator of 100. What is 120% in fraction form? _____

2. Is the fraction that represents 120% proper or improper? _____

3. What is 120% written as an improper fraction in simplest form? _____

4. Since 120% is greater than 100%, should a decimal that represents 120% be greater than or less than 1? _____

5. To change a percent to a decimal, remove the percent sign and move the decimal point two places to the left. What is 120% in decimal form? _____

6. Is the decimal you wrote for 120% greater than 1? _____

7. Is 120% written as an improper fraction greater than 1? _____

A report states that a company's revenue increased $\frac{1}{4}$% during the prior year. Use the diagram to write a decimal and a fraction to represent $\frac{1}{4}$%.

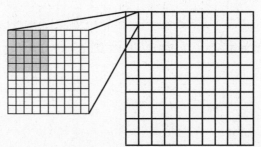

Percents Greater than 100 or Less than 1 (continued)

8. What is the decimal equivalent of $\frac{1}{4}$?   _____

9. Write $\frac{1}{4}$% as a decimal percent.   _____

10. To change a percent to a decimal, remove the percent
sign and move the decimal point two places to the left.
What is 0.25% in decimal form?   _____

11. What is 0.25% = 0.0025 as a fraction?   _____

12. What is the fraction in simplest form?   _____

Express each shaded part as a decimal, a percent and a fraction in
simplest form.

13.

14.

Write each percent as a fraction and a decimal. Write fractions in
simplest form.

15. 150%   **16.** $\frac{3}{4}$%   **17.** 240%

_____   _____   _____

18. 0.3%   **19.** 310%   **20.** 115%

_____   _____

21. Reasoning When is the fraction equivalent to a percent an improper
fraction? Explain.

Computing Discounts

A clothing store has all its merchandise on sale at a 15% discount.
If Pilar chooses a shirt that regularly costs $18.50, how much is
the sale price?

Find the discount and sale price by answering 1 to 5.

1. What is 15% written in decimal form? _____

2. To find 15% of $18.50, multiply the decimal form by 18.5.
Write an expression that can be used to find 15% of 18.5. _____

3. What is 0.15×18.5? _____

4. Round the discount to the nearest cent.
What is the amount of discount? $_____

5. Sale price = Regular price − Discount
What is the sale price? $_____

Teachers get a 30% discount on books at a local book store. A teacher
buys a book regularly priced at $24.49. What is the teacher's price?

Find the teacher's price by answering 6 to 12.

6. What is 30% written in decimal form? _____

7. To find 30% of $24.49, multiply the decimal form by 24.49.
Write an expression that can be used to find 30% of 24.49. _____

8. What is 0.3×24.49? _____

9. Round the discount to the nearest cent.
What is the amount of discount? $_____

10. Sale price = Regular price − Discount
What is the sale price? $_____

11. The teacher pays 100% − 30% = 70%.
Find 70% of $24.49, rounded to the nearest cent. $_____

12. **Reasoning** Is 70% of $24.49 to the nearest cent the same
as the sale price you found by subtracting the discount? _____

Computing Discounts (continued)

Find the discount and the sale price.

13. regular price: $35
rate of discount: 10%

_____

14. regular price: $24.50
rate of discount: 15%

_____

15. regular price: $72
rate of discount: 25%

_____

16. regular price: $60
rate of discount: 30%

_____

17. regular price: $90
rate of discount: 40%

_____

18. regular price: $46.80
rate of discount: 50%

_____

19. William bought two CDs on sale at a 15% discount. One CD cost
$15.99 and the other CD cost $14.99. How much did he pay for
both CDs after the discount?   _____

Use the following for Exercises 20–23.

Mary bought a new television for $250. The television was on sale at a
10% discount. The sales tax rate was 6%.

20. What was the discount?   _____

21. What was the sale price?   _____

22. What is the amount of tax?   _____

23. What is the total cost of the television?   _____

24. Reasoning If an item has a discount of 20%, what percent of the
original price will the customer pay? How can this be used to find
the discounted price?

Converting Between Measurement Systems

The table shows the relationships between customary and metric unts. Only the equivalent for inches and centimeters is exact. All other equivalents are approximate. The symbol ≈ means "approximately equal to."

A standard CD has a diameter of 4.75 inches. How many centimeters is the diameter of the CD?

Convert 4.75 inches to centimeters by answering 1 to 4.

1. How many centimeters equal one inch?   _____

To change larger units to smaller units multiply. To change smaller units to larger units, divide.

Customary and Metric Unit Equivalent
Length
1 in. = 2.54 cm
1 m ≈ 39.97 in.
1 mi ≈ 1.61 km
Weight and Mass
1 oz ≈ 28.35 g
1 kg ≈ 2.2 lb
1 metric ton (t) ≈ 1.102 tons (T)
Capacity
1 L ≈ 1.06 qt
1 gal ≈ 3.79 L

2. Do you need to multiply or divide to change from inches to centimeters?   _____

3. What is 4.75 × 2.54 to the nearest tenth?   _____

4. How many centimeters is the diameter of the CD?   _____ cm

The average golden retriever weighs 65 pounds. What is the approximate mass in kilograms of an average golden retriever?

Convert 65 pounds to kilograms by answering 5 to 8.

5. According to the table, how many pounds equal about one kilogram?   _____

6. Do you need to multiply or divide to change from pounds to kilograms?   _____

7. What is 65 ÷ 2.2 rounded to the nearest tenth?   _____

8. What is the approximate mass in kilograms of an average golden retriever?   _____ kg

Converting Between Measurement Systems (continued)

Complete. Round to the nearest tenth, if necessary.

9. 3.8 m ≈ ▨ in.   **10.** 50 g ≈ ▨ oz   **11.** 3 L ≈ ▨ gal

_____   _____   _____

12. 44 in. ≈ ▨ cm   **13.** 2.5 t ≈ ▨ T   **14.** $3\frac{1}{2}$ kg ≈ ▨ lb

_____   _____   _____

15. $5\frac{1}{4}$ qt ≈ ▨ L   **16.** 100 km ≈ ▨ mi   **17.** 10 cm ≈ ▨ in.

_____   _____   _____

18. 2 cm ≈ ▨ in.   **19.** 2.4 t ≈ ▨ T   **20.** $8\frac{2}{3}$ m ≈ ▨ yd

_____   _____   _____

21. $3\frac{1}{2}$ yd ≈ ▨ m   **22.** 500 lb ≈ ▨ kg   **23.** 11 in. ≈ ▨ m

_____   _____   _____

24. Rewrite the materials list at the right using meters for
fabric, inches for thread, and kilograms for stuffing.
Write your conversions to the nearest tenth below:

Materials List
$1\frac{1}{2}$ yd fabric
65 cm thread
$1\frac{3}{4}$ lb stuffing

   fabric: _____ m   thread: _____ in.   stuffing: _____ kg.

25. Reasoning A necklace measures $16\frac{1}{2}$ inches.

   About how many centimeters is this to the nearest tenth?   _____

Comparing Volume and Surface Area

Materials 24 unit cubes for each student

Kira's dad is making her a toy box in the shape of a rectangular prism. The volume of the toy box is 24 cubic feet. He wants to know how much outside area of the box he will need to paint.

The area which needs to be painted is the surface area of the box. Find the surface area of a rectangular prism with a volume of 24 cubic feet by answering 1 to 5.

1. Use 24 cubes to make a rectangular prism like the one shown at the right. If each cube represents a cubic foot, what is the volume of the prism?

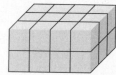

_____

2. You can find the surface area of a figure by finding the sum of the areas of each face of the figure. Complete the first row of the table for the prism you made.

Length	Width	Height	Area of Front and Back	Area of Sides	Area of Top and Bottom	Surface Area
4	3	2				
	2	2				

3. If Kira's dad makes the toy box 4 feet by 3 feet by 2 feet, how much outside area of the box will he need to paint?

_____ ft²

4. Use the cubes to make a different rectangular prism with a volume of 24, a width of 2, and a height of 2. Use this prism to complete the second row of the table.

5 If Kira's dad makes the toy box 6 feet by 2 feet by 2 feet, how much outside area of the box will he need to paint?

_____ ft²

The area Kira's dad needs to paint depends on the dimensions he uses.

6. Reasoning Why is the volume of the toy box given in cubic feet and the surface area given in square feet?

Comparing Volume and Surface Area (continued)

Find the surface area and volume of each figure.

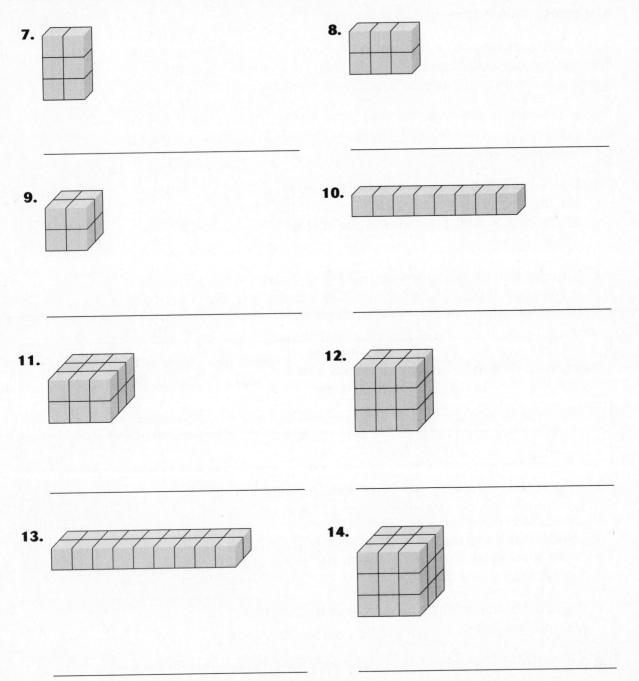

7.

8.

9.

10.

11.

12.

13.

14.

15. Reasoning Janet needs to determine how much wrapping paper
she needs to wrap three presents of the same size. Will she need
to determine the surface area or volume of the present? Explain.

Name _____

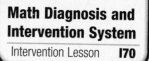
Double Bar Graphs

Materials colored pencils

A **double bar graph** uses two different-colored or shaded bars to compare sets of data that can be counted.

Make a double bar graph for the data in the table by answering 1 to 6.

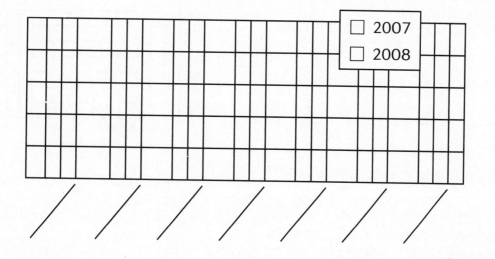

1. List the days of the week in each blank along the horizontal axis in the order in which they appear in the table.

2. What is the greatest number in the table? _____

3. Label the scale along the vertical axis. Choose numbers so that each interval is the same and the scale reaches to at least 9.

4. Label the horizontal axis "Days," the vertical axis "Attendance (in thousands)," and title the graph.

State Fair Attendance
(in thousands)

Day	2007	2008
Friday	5.5	6.5
Saturday	6.5	9
Sunday	8	9
Monday	5	6
Tuesday	2	5
Wednesday	2.5	5.5
Thursday	3	6

5. Use a yellow pencil to color in the square in the key that is labeled 2007. Color the first bar for each day yellow. Make the height of each bar according to the values in the 2007 column of the table.

6. Use a red pencil to color in the square in the key that is labeled 2008. Color the second bar for each day red. Make the height of each bar according to the values in the 2008 column of the table.

Name _____

Double Bar Graphs (continued)

Use the double bar graph you created on the previous page for Exercises 7 and 8.

7. Was attendance generally higher in 2007 or 2008? _____

8. Which two days of the week had higher attendance than the other days, both years?

_____ and _____

Use the graph at the right to answer Exercises 9 to 13.

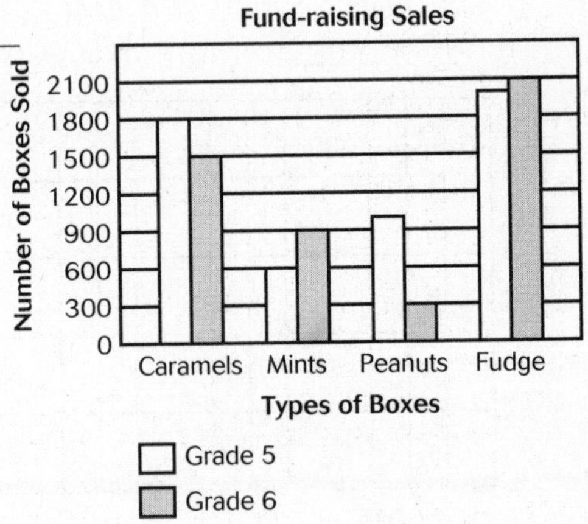

9. What does each pair of bars represent?

_____

_____

10. For which item were the most boxes sold?

_____

11. How many more caramels did 5th graders sell as compared to 6th graders?

12. Which type of box had the most sales for 5th graders? _____

13. Which type of box had the most sales for 6th graders? _____

Fund-raising Sales

Number of Boxes Sold: 2100, 1800, 1500, 1200, 900, 600, 300, 0

Types of Boxes: Caramels, Mints, Peanuts, Fudge

☐ Grade 5
▨ Grade 6

Use the graph at the right to answer Exercises 14 to 18.

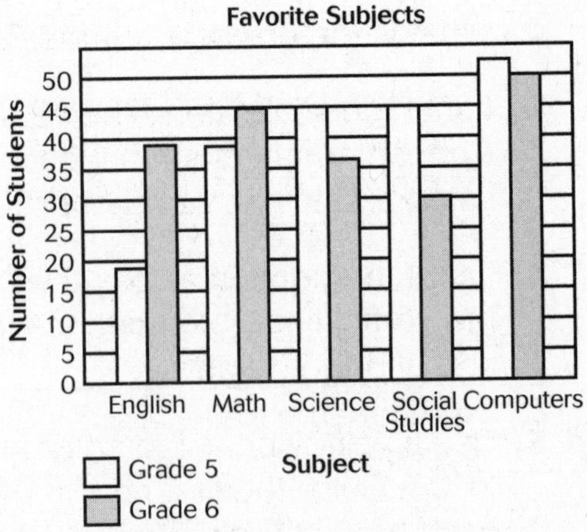

14. Reasoning For which subject is the difference in choice the greatest?

_____

15. Which subject was chosen as favorite the most?

_____

16. What was the total number of students who chose Math as their favorite subject?

_____

17. Which subject was least popular with 5th graders? _____

18. Which subject was least popular with 6th graders? _____

Favorite Subjects

Number of Students: 50, 45, 40, 35, 30, 25, 20, 15, 10, 5, 0

Subject: English, Math, Science, Social Studies, Computers

☐ Grade 5
▨ Grade 6

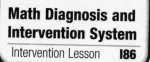

Experimental Probability and Predictions

Materials 8 yellow, 7 red, and 5 blue color tiles in a small paper bag,
for each student or pair

Do not look in the bag of tiles Use it
to help answer 1 to 12.

1. Do the following experiment. Pull
out one tile from the bag without
looking, and record the color in
the tally chart. Place the tile back
into the bag. Repeat this process
40 times.

Tile Experiment		
Color	**Tally**	**Number**
Yellow		
Red		
Blue		

Experimental probability is based on
the results of an experiment.

2. How many times did you get a yellow tile?

3. How many trials were there, that is, how many times did you pull a tile? _____

4. Complete to find the experimental probability that the next tile
pulled from the bag will be yellow.

$$P = \frac{\text{Number of Yellow Tiles Pulled}}{\text{Total Number of Trials}} = \frac{\boxed{}}{40}$$

5. Complete to find the experimental probability that the next tile
pulled from the bag will be red.

$$P = \frac{\text{Number of Red Tiles Pulled}}{\text{Total of Number of Trials}} = \frac{\boxed{}}{40}$$

6. Complete to find the experimental probability that the next tile
pulled from the bag will be blue.

$$P = \frac{\text{Number of Blue Tiles Pulled}}{\text{Total of Number of Trials}} = \frac{\boxed{}}{40}$$

7. Find the sum of the experimental probability of randomly selecting
a yellow tile, a red tile, or a blue tile.

_____ + _____ + _____ = _____

The probability of an event can be any number from 0 to 1. So the sum
of each event occurring in an experiment should equal 1.

8. Does the sum of the probabilities equal 1? _____

© Pearson Education, Inc.

Experimental Probability and Predictions (continued)

You can use the experimental probability of an event to make predictions.

9. There are 20 tiles in the bag. Use the results of your experiment to predict how many tiles of each color are in the bag.

_____ yellow, _____ red, and _____ blue

10. Look in the bag. Were your predictions close to the actual number of each color of tiles in the bag?   _____

11. Predict how many tiles would be yellow, if a tile was pulled from the bag 200 times.

Multiply the experimental probability from item 4 by 200.   _____

12. Predict how many tiles would be red, if a tile was pulled from the bag 200 times.   _____

The table at the right shows the number of times Jeffrey's school bus has been early, on time, and late to pick him up over the past 10 days. Use the table to answer Exercises 13 to 17.

Jeffrey's Bus		
Early	On Time	Late
2	5	3

13. What is the experimental probability that the bus will be early the next time Jeffrey rides it?   _____

14. How many times can Jeffrey expect the bus to be early over the next 20 school days?   _____

15. What is the experimental probability that the bus will be late the next time Jeffrey rides it?   _____

16. How many times can Jeffrey expect the bus to be late over the next 20 school days?   _____

17. What is the sum of the experimental probabilities of the bus being early, the bus being on time, and the bus being late?   _____

18. A manufacturer sampled 100 screws and found that 5% were defective. Predict how many screws, out of 500, you would expect to be defective,   _____

19. **Reasoning** A craft store recorded the colors of yarn they sold. After 50 packages were sold, they found there was a 20% chance that a shopper buying yarn would buy a red color. How many of the 50 packages sold were red?   _____

Adding Probabilities

Materials index card, scissors, and a small bag for each student or group

Cut an index card into 12 pieces and label each with a number 1 to 12. Place the card pieces into a bag. Draw one card at random from the bag. Answer 1 to 9 to determine the probability that the number drawn is a prime number or a 6.

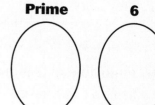

Prime   **6**

1. Write the prime numbers from 1 to 12 in the circle at the right labeled Prime. Write the number 6 in the circle labeled 6.

   Are any of the numbers in both circles?

Mutually exclusive events are events that cannot happen at the same time.

2. Can you randomly draw a card that is both a prime number and the number 6?

   _____

3. So, are the events "drawing a prime number or a 6" mutually exclusive?

   _____

If events are mutually exclusive you can add their probabilities to find the probability of either event happening.

4. How many favorable outcomes are there for randomly drawing a prime number?

   _____

5. What is the probability of drawing a prime number?

   _____

6. How many favorable outcomes are there for randomly drawing a 6?

   _____

7. What is the probability of drawing a 6?

   _____

8. Find the sum of the two probabilities.

   $P(\text{prime number}) + P(6) = P(\text{prime or } 6)$

   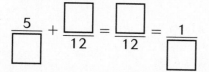

9. So, what is the probability of choosing a prime number or a 6?

   _____

© Pearson Education, Inc.

Adding Probabilities (continued)

You have a bag containing tiles with numbers labeled 1 to 20. Tell
whether the events are mutually exclusive. Write Yes or No.

10. P(odd or 13)

11. P(odd or 14)

12. P(even or odd)

_____

_____

_____

13. P(even or prime)

14. P(2 or less than 12)

15. P(14 or greater than 18)

_____

_____

_____

16. P(multiple of 3 or multiple of 5)

17. P(divisible by 2 or 7)

_____

_____

You toss two number cubes each labeled with the numbers 1–6. Tell
whether the events are mutually exclusive. Then, find the probability.

18. P(3 or 4)

_____

19. P(1 or number less than 3)

_____

20. P(even or 3)

_____

21. P(number less than 3 or number greater than 3)

_____

22. Reasoning The probability that it will rain today is 25%. The
probability that it will rain tomorrow is 75%. Mark concludes that
the probability it will rain in the next 2 days is 100%. Is he right?
Why or why not.

Make an Organized List

Carrie and Susi are playing a game. They spin the two spinners shown. If the spinners land on the same color, Carrie gets a point. Otherwise, Susi gets a point. How many combinations of two spins are possible? Is the game fair?

Solve by answering 1 to 8.

Answer 1 and 2 to **understand** the problem.

1. What do you know from reading the problem?

Carrie gets a point if _____

_____.

Susi gets a point if _____

_____.

2. What do you need to find?

Answer 3 to 7 to **plan and solve** the problem.

You can solve the problem by making an organized list.

3. Use R for red, B for blue, Y for yellow, and G for green. Complete the list at the right.

4. How many combinations of spins are possible?

_____

RR	BR	YR
RB		
____	____	____
____	____	____

Each combination is equally likely as any other.

5. For how many of the combinations does Carrie get a point?   _____

6. For how many of the combinations does Susi get a point?   _____

7. Is the game fair?   _____

Make an Organized List (continued)

Answer 8 to **look back** at how you solved the problem.

8. Reasoning Did you answer the right questions? Explain.

Solve each problem.

9. At a jewelry store, you can have your purchase gift-wrapped in silver, gold, or red paper with a white, pink, or blue ribbon. You can choose one color of paper and one color of ribbon. How many gift-wrap combinations are available?

_____

10. Mr. Johnson is making sandwiches. He has wheat bread and rye bread. He has ham and salami. He also has colby and cheddar cheese. Each sandwich will have one kind of bread, one kind of meat, and one kind of cheese. How many different kinds of sandwiches can he make?

_____

11. Leslie has a penny, a nickel, and a dime in her pocket. If she picks out 2 coins, what amounts of money could she get?

_____

12. Each child at Heather's party has chosen a sandwich and a drink. If there are 7 children at the party, can they each have a different lunch?

Sandwiches	Drinks
Turkey	Milk
Ham	Juice
Tuna	
Peanut butter	

_____

Name _____

Make a Table and Look for a Pattern

Ann and Jane began reading the same book on the same day. If Ann reads 8 pages each day and Jane reads 5 pages each day, what page will Jane read on the day that Ann reads page 40?

Solve by answering 1 to 6.

Answer 1 and 2 to **understand** the problem.

1. What do you know from reading the problem?

Ann reads _____ pages each day.

Jane reads _____ pages each day.

They started the same day.

2. What do you need to find?

Answer 3 to 5 to **plan and solve** the problem.

You can solve the problem by making a table and looking for a pattern.

3. Use patterns to complete the table below.

Day	1	2	3	4	5	6
Ann's Page	8	16				
Jane's Page	5					

4. What day will Ann read page 40? _____

5. What page will Jane read on the day Ann reads page 40? _____

Name _____

Make a Table and Look for a Pattern (continued)

Answer 6 to **look back** at your solution.

6. Did you answer the right question? _____

Use patterns to complete each table. Solve each problem.

7. Rebecca must put 4 eggs in each basket. There are
8 baskets. How many eggs does she need?   _____

Number of Baskets	1	2	3	4	5	6	7	8
Number of Eggs	4	8						

8. Martin needs to water each tree with 3 gallons of water.
How many gallons of water will he need for 7 trees?

Number of trees	1	2	3	4	5	6	7
Gallons of water							

_____

9. Diego recorded the height of a bean plant. The first week, the
plant was 2 inches high. The second, third, and fourth week, it
was 4 inches, 6 inches, and 8 inches high. At this rate, when
will the bean plant be 12 inches high?

Week	1	2	3	4	5	6	7
Height							

_____

10. Each quilt square has 2 red sections and 3 blue sections. If
18 blue sections are used, how many red sections are needed?

squares						
red sections						
blue sections						

_____

Make a Graph

Will's family has two dogs. The tables below show how each of the two dogs grew as puppies in their first 5 months. How does the growth of the two puppies compare?

Socks' Growth	
Month	**Weight (pounds)**
1	2
2	5
3	10
4	8
5	15

Buddy's Growth	
Month	**Weight (pounds)**
1	2
2	6
3	9
4	15
5	20

You can solve by making and interpreting two line graphs. Answer 1 to 6.

1. Make a line graph of each set of data.

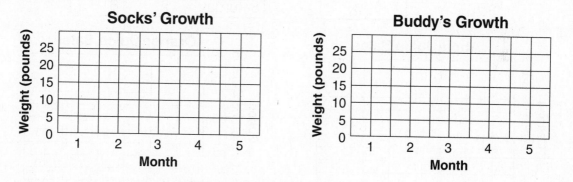

2. Which puppy had the most steady weight gain? _____

3. Which puppy had the greatest weight gain in one month? _____

4. Which puppy lost weight one month? _____

5. Reasoning Which full grown dog probably weighs the most? Why?

Make a Graph (continued)

Answer 6 to **look back at and extend** the problem.

6. Reasoning How did the line graphs help you compare the growth of the two puppies?

7. The data in the two tables below show the gallons of apple and orange juice sold by a company each day for a week. Make a bar graph of each set of data.

Apple Juice Sales	
Day	**Gallons**
Sunday	4
Monday	8
Tuesday	10
Wednesday	14
Thursday	18
Friday	7
Saturday	9

Orange Juice Sales	
Day	**Gallons**
Sunday	6
Monday	8
Tuesday	10
Wednesday	12
Thursday	14
Friday	16
Saturday	18

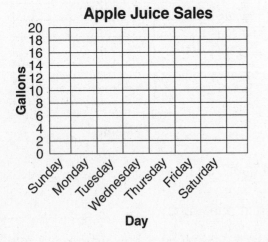
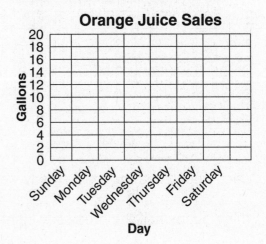

Use the bar graphs above for Exercises 8 to 10.

8. Which type of juice had a steady increase in sales? _____

9. Between which two days did the sales of apple juice decrease? _____

10. On which two days did the company sell a lot more orange juice than apple juice? _____